Acting and Living
in Discovery

Acting and Living
in Discovery

Carol Rosenfeld

Focus Publishing
Newburyport, Massachusetts

Acting and Living in Discovery
© 2014 Carol Rosenfeld

Focus Publishing/R. Pullins Company
PO Box 369
Newburyport, MA 01950
www.pullins.com

Cover painting: **Rebirth** by Michael Massee. Michael Massee is a former set and costume designer who is now a full time painter. He is also honored to be married to Carol Rosenfeld.

ISBN: 978-1-58510-703-2

Library of Congress Cataloging-in-Publication Data

Rosenfeld, Carol.

 Living in discovery : a workbook for the actor / by Carol Rosenfeld.

    pages cm

 Includes index.

 ISBN 978-1-58510-703-2

 1. Acting--Handbooks, manuals, etc. I. Title.

 PN2061.R64 2013

 792.02'8--dc23

                          2013022785

Printed in the United States of America.

10 9 8 7 6 5 4 3 2 1

0813V

Table of Contents

Foreword by Janine Pearson — xiii

Preface — xv

Discovering a Transcendental Art — xvii

How to Use the Workbook — xxiii

Chapter 1: The Play and Its World — 1

Chapter 2: Meeting Yourself, Meeting Your Partner — 37

Chapter 3: Time, Place and Stuff — 71

Chapter 4: Wanting, Needing, Obstacle and Doing — 115

Chapter 5: Creating Relationships: Complicating Life — 187

Chapter 6: Character, Who Am I? Stepping Into a New Pair of Shoes — 231

Afterword — 311

Appendix A: Places and Locations — 315

Appendix B: Occupations and Professions — 317

Appendix C: Clothing — 321

Appendix D: Naming Your Relationships — 323

Endnotes — 325

Acknowledgments — 327

Bibliography — 331

Detailed Table of Contents

Foreword by Janine Pearson — xiii

Preface — xv

Discovering a Transcendental Art — xvii

How to Use the Workbook — xxiii

   Guidelines — xxv

Chapter 1: The Play and its World — 1

      Get Going | Read the Play Like an Actor | Read the Play, the Whole Play | — 3
      Cherish Losing Your Virginity—It Only Happens Once | Hear the Play |
      Reread Your Play—Always With Intention, Discover | Identify: Story,
      Happenings, Themes, Spine | Sidestep the Traps—Stage directions,
      Adverbs/Adjectives, Pause, Punctuation and Ellipses | Mine the Text |
      First Discover: What am I saying? | Particularize | Conduct Hands-On
      Research | Use What You Know

   Write Your Life Story (Not Your Character's) — 19

   The Events or Happenings in Your Life — 20

   The Themes in Your Life — 21

   The Spine of Your Life — 23

   The Cast of Characters Who Fill Your Life — 24

   On Reading — 25

   First Impressions — 26

   The Story of the Play — 28

   The Events or Happenings in the Play — 29

   The Themes in the Play — 30

   The Spine of the Play — 31

   Mining the Text — 32

   Prioritizing — 33

   The Real Deal — 34

   Particularizing — 35

Chapter 2: Meeting Yourself, Meeting Your Partner — 37

   Meeting Yourself — 38

      Learn Your Instrument | Mindfulness: An Essential Tool | Your Four Selves |
      Show Up | Commit

   Meeting Your Partner — 45

      Collaborate | Meet in the Work | Work with Integrity | Discard Attitude
      and Judgment

   My Training History — 52

   Staying in Tune — 53

   My Future — 54

   My Class Goals and Achievements — 55

   Motivation and Commitment — 56

   Reflection upon Completion — 57

   Realities and Excuses — 59

   My Track Record: Working with Others — 61

Communicate Honestly: Your Scene Partner's Vitals	65
Frequently Used Words and Phrases:	66
Common Mistakes	68
Charting Your Rehearsals	69
My Critique Checklist	70
Chapter 3: Time, Place and Stuff	71
Read for Time and Place	72
Time	73
Place	75
Build Your Rehearsal Environment	
Stuff	78
Gather Your Stuff | Endow Objects	
Your Current Circumstances	84
Events Leading to My Now	85
Current Trends Affecting My Life	87
The Stuff in My Life	88
Awakening Your Senses and Emotions	90
More on Stuff	92
Discovering Hot Objects	93
Factual Notes on Time	94
The World of the Play	95
Rehearsal Preparation	96
Given Circumstances	97
Your Secondary Activities and Your Time Line	98
Time Specifics and Influences	99
Craft Your Preparation	100
History of Events	101
"Your" Age	102
The Description of the Set	103
Facts on Place Gathered from the Text	104
Rehearsal Set-up	105
Planning Ahead	106
Scouting Locations	109
The Rest of the Apartment or House	110
Objects for Your Early Rehearsals	111
Hot Objects	112
Making Objects and Activities Your Own	113
Chapter 4: Wanting, Needing, Obstacle and Doing	115
Live with the Play	116
The Objective	117
Wonder—What Makes People Tick? | Think Person, Human Being | Choose Uncomplicated, Simply Stated Wants | Keep the Change in Your Pocket | Create Stakes—The Courage to Go All the Way | Intuit, Sense: The Actor's Way of Knowing	
The Obstacle	123
Conflict and Obstacle: Unforeseen, Unexpected | Allow Yourself to Be Vulnerable; Value Discomfort | Learn from Obstacles	

Action   128

> Think Action | Leave No Room for Second-guessing | Send with Expectation |
> Find Your First Action | Action Your Scene—A Way to Begin | Talk with
> Purpose, Intention | The Actor's Way

A Self-Assessment   138

Your Needs, Wishes, Dreams & Desires   140

Where Your Wants Come From   142

My Objectives   143

Your Goals in Acting Class   146

Your Artistic Aspirations   147

What Do I Have to Lose?   148

The Obstacles in My Life: Obstacles from Within   149

Stress, Tension and Nerves   157

The Obstacles in My Life: Obstacles from Without   159

More on Obstacles in My Life   163

Tough Calls   165

Selecting Actions   167

Your Additions   168

You and Your Actions   169

"My" Objectives   171

What is at Stake?   172

"My" Objectives and Possible Obstacles   173

"My" Needs   174

Sending and Receiving   175

Identifying Obstacles   176

Playing Actions   177

Possible Actions   178

Verbs/Actions/Doings   179

Sending with Expectation   182

That First Beat   183

Rehearsal Notes/Class Notes   185

Chapter 5: Creating Relationships: Complicating Life   187

The Tangled Web of Relationships   189

> Excavate What Matters | Read for Relationships | Know Where You Stand:
> Status/Class, Culture, Control, Trust and Sex | Investigate the Past and
> Background of Your Relationship | Accept—Work off of Your Fellow Actors |
> Play Your Best Game | Endowment – the Magic "As If" | Transference and
> Your Imagination | Respect the Tools of Your Craft | Test in Rehearsal |
> Respect Limits | Protect Your Secrets

The People In My Life   208

Risks I Take in Committing to Relationships   210

Where You Stand   211

Family   212

Your Aversions and Attractions   214

My Closest Relationship   215

People Whom You Have Endowed In Your Life   216

My Scene Partner   217
"My" Relationship To The Other Characters In The Play   218
What "I" Say About The Other Characters In The Play   219
Rehearsal Relationship Discoveries   220
You and Other Characters in the Play   223
Endowing Your Partner   224
Using Your Imagination   225
"My" Relationship With The Other Character In The Scene   227
Transference   229
Rehearsal Notes/Class Notes   230
Chapter 6: Character: Who Am I? Stepping Into a New Pair of Shoes   231
     Search the Attic   233
Five Conduits to Find the New You   233
     #1: Be Subjective: The First Person Singular | #2: Know Your Past, Your
     Background | #3: Find New Points Of View | #4: Get to Work—Your
     Profession, Your Job | #5: Get Dressed—Clothing (Not Costume)
Stepping Into New Shoes…and Stepping Out   242
     Learn Your Boundaries —Safety and Your Mental Health
Under No Circumstances!   243
     Don't Settle, Keep Seeking
My Background   247
What I Say About Myself & How Others See Me   252
My 'Who Am I' List   253
My Physicality   254
What Matters to Me   255
My Big Stones   256
On Temperament   258
My Knee-Jerks   260
My Relationships to…   261
My Essence   272
What I Want out of Life   273
My Skills and Work History   274
My Sense of Humor   276
My Favorite…   278
Shocking Friends and Family   279
My Beliefs   280
My Prejudices   283
Difference and Eccentricity   284
Unchallenged Beliefs that Limit   285
Expanding My Beliefs   286
My Wardrobe   287
Dressing Up   290
Hair, Hands and Makeup   291
My Fashion Expertise   292
"My" Background   294
"My" Family; "My" Ancestors   295

What "I" Say about Myself/What Others Say about "Me" 296

Who Am "I"? 297

Me, the Actor and "Me," the Character 298

What "I" Want out of Life—"My" Life Drive 299

What "I" Do For A Living 300

"My" Sense of Humor 301

"My" Favorites 302

Research is Exciting! 303

Planning What to Wear: Female Roles 304

Planning What to Wear: Male Roles 305

"My" Physicality 306

"My" Point of View 307

What "I" Say and Feel: More Points of View 308

What the Other Characters Say about "Me" 309

Afterword 311

Appendix A: Places and Locations 315

Appendix B: Occupations and Professions 317

Appendix C: Types of Clothing 321

Appendix D: Naming Your Relationships 323

Endnotes 325

Acknowledgments 327

Bibliography 331

For my soul mate, Michael Massee,
who knows what is needed and does it without fanfare —
theatre, whether he likes it or not, is in his DNA.
And now paint away!

Foreword

This book is valuable for both the student and professional actor alike, for the work it holds brings a depth and honesty to the ongoing process of the actor's craft. The exercises do not constitute any particular method: rather, they embrace a lifetime of study and work.

I was first introduced to Ms. Rosenfeld at the National Theatre School of Canada, where she arrived every September to teach contemporary scene study to the actors in their second year of study. Unknowingly, she struck fear into the hearts of these emerging artists as the work she shared caused them to struggle and to doubt, but above all to learn.

Acting, and the study of acting, is not for the faint of heart. The constant examination of your art, your craft and your life can be joyous, painful, and most importantly, never ending. If you want to graduate, or if you believe that there is a limit to what you can discover, then this book is not for you.

I coordinate a team of specialist coaches who act as a support to the actors' and directors' work at North America's largest repertory company, The Stratford Festival. Every day I witness the work of actors from 20 to 80 years of age and observe that regardless of experience, their desire and ability to hold themselves to the challenges of the work is relentless.

Learning often begins with a seemingly irrational desire to reach or seek for something that we initially perceive is outside of ourselves. But for the actor who has been properly taught, the acquisition of technique is something that sets them free. True technique holds the gift and supports the artist in expressing their gift. The best of technique will give the artist the feeling of returning home – to something that they have innately always known or understood.

If you are a student beginning your journey you will be fortunate to find this book and be guided by a master teacher who has agreed to share the most intimate parts of her own learning. If you are a professional and you are picking up this book, it means that you continue to thirst to know more and to grow; or perhaps you are tired and wounded from the challenges of the artist's life and questioning your creativity and your path. If so, then read this book, for here you will be mentored by an artist who shares her craft and her personal journey towards acquiring this expression we call "acting".

Janine Pearson, Head of Coaching
Stratford Festival — Stratford, Ontario, Canada
2013

Preface

The HB Studio, in New York City's Greenwich Village, has been my artistic home and sanctuary for many, many years. I, along with countless others, had a truly great teacher, Uta Hagen. Her teachings, her world-famous books on acting (*Respect for Acting* and *A Challenge for the Actor*) and my own continuing discovery of the craft and art of acting are the inspiration behind this workbook. I am deeply indebted to all of my teachers, collaborators, and especially the actors who have studied with me and grappled with the same issues I faced as a young actor.

I dared to begin writing "a book on acting," *The Actors Retreat Workbook*, in 1996. It has gone through hundreds of rewrites—starting as a pamphlet for my workshops, transforming into a book on my technique exercises to prepare students for Uta Hagen's class, growing into 32 chapters on scene study and rehearsal, and now down to these six.

I have tested many titles—always with "*A Workbook*" appended—in an effort to capture the essence of what is inside (and, yes, to capture your attention, respected reader):

The Actor's Retreat: A Workbook about Living and Acting
The Actor's Barre
Moments: A Workbook about Acting and Living
I Am-I Want-I Do
The Actor's Process
The Acting Class
The Actor's Way
The Mystery of Acting
Engaged!
The Actor's Homework Big Book
Deliberate Practice

Remember…

Training is to be digested,
not consumed

---

and now, finally, *Acting and Living in Discovery: A Workbook for the Actor.*

Full disclosure: Do not expect to learn to act from a book. As a performing artist, you learn by doing, and that is what this book is about—doing. My intention has always been to create a workbook with a dual approach, focusing 1) on *you, the actor,* and 2) on *the fundamental work* that makes your craft so compelling. The workbook pages guide you as you practice and hone your craft. They encourage your process of continual self-discovery—a process that is integral to mastering the art of acting.

When you find the courage to really develop and trust your imagination and to embrace doubt and curiosity, you begin to live in a state of discovery—you discover *you, the world around you* and *everything that happens in any play on which you are working.* Most of all you discover possibility! Discovery happens when you are in search of something—stated or not—when you dare to say, "I don't know," or "I wonder what will happen if I do _____." And then you do it, 110%.

Flynn. Doubt can be a bond as powerful and sustaining as certainty. When you are lost, you are not alone.

Doubt –John Patrick Shanley

Acting classes cannot provide all that you require in the development of yourself as an actor and there is no single path in the acquisition of skill. Over time, as you train and learn the tools of your craft, you discover how fundamentals serve you throughout your artistic life. While learning and practicing your craft, prepare to struggle, live in confusion and test your determination and courage. The level of commitment needed is absolute. You must have the need to act, a fire in your belly.

Discovering a Transcendental Art

discover

verb

1

Firemen discovered a body in the debris: find, locate, come across/upon, stumble on, chance on, light on, bring to light, uncover, unearth, turn up; track down.

2

Eventually, I discovered the truth: find out, learn, realize, recognize, fathom, see, ascertain, work out, dig up/out, ferret out, root out; informal figure out, dope out.

3

Scientists discovered a new way of dating fossil crustaceans: hit on, come up with, invent, originate, devise, design, contrive, conceive of, pioneer, develop.[1]

When you are exposed to the non-negotiable demands that theater makes, you learn everything you need to get on in this world. When you take any acting class, or take on any role, you are first and foremost awakening to what it means to be a human being. You begin to see better and hear better—all your senses become sharper as life's human comedy captures your curiosity. Curiosity and imagination go hand in hand.

> **Remember…**
>
> Theater is the most disciplined place in the world.

You discover that you have to be punctual, responsible, imaginative, patient, courageous, present, generous, demanding and empathetic. You have to practice. You have to have a sense of humor. You have to awaken your senses and permit them to soak up all aspects of the world around you. You have to be interested in detail and specifics. You have to accept that, in art, there is no right or wrong, good or bad—but other people will always have their own opinions about you and your work. You have to open yourself to possibility. You have to be willing to admit what you don't know, that you might not even know who you are. You doubt. You face the simple, harsh truths of reality. This is when you begin to live in discovery.

You must have the energy and desire to listen to and trust yourself while working collaboratively with many others. You must have the humility and desire to hear and value what others can teach you. You need to build emotional and physical stamina, and expose your vulnerability as you acknowledge what really matters to you. You will listen to all types of music, sing, dance, look at great art and architecture. You will play and feel the wonders of language and the deliciousness of words.

Thanks to the plays of Shakespeare, Chekhov, Wilder, Williams, the two Wilsons, Odets, Inge, O'Neill, Moliere, Durang, Treadwell, Molnar, LaBute, Greenberg, Baker, Herzog, Beckett, Ives, Kauffman and Hart, Shanley, Albee, Shaw, Coward, Wilde and Ibsen—just to name a few— along with the folk who come to see the plays you are in – lives will be enriched because you want to act.

There are no magic answers or guarantees that will get you where you want to go. There are no short cuts to truly living in discovery. The only things you have are your craft, yourself and your scripts. If you want to act, don't expect instant gratification or a quick-fix; you must have stamina, focus, imagination, patience and a tolerance for frustration. Though acting can be easy at times, growing as an actor is not always easy or fun. It is an obsessive calling.

> **Remember…**
>
> Crossing a finish line takes a second. Getting to the starting line again and again takes years of sacrifice and training. Be as mindful as you can along the way.

You, unlike the violinist and his Stradivarius, are the player *and* the instrument. Your artistry requires more self-knowledge than you might otherwise need if you didn't want to act. This self-knowledge requires that you become conscious of your current behavior, habits and thought processes. Along with your increasing awareness, you must become interested in how you walk, how you move, where you hold your tension, how you speak and what your speech patterns are. You do not make these discoveries overnight.

Your super-objective is to give the play, tell its story, to strangers who make up the audience. The presence of your colleagues in an acting class or the audience in the theater is an integral part of your process. You need your classmates when you present a rehearsed scene in class. Without them, you would not be aware of the areas of your scene that you really haven't filled. And of course, through previews and performance, the audience takes you into an even deeper understanding of what the play is about.

If along the way, you become more mindful, your commitment grows, and you wish to expand your worldview, find teachers or mentors who can guide you, who ask more of you.

As much as you might often like to, you can't change other people, places or things; you can only change yourself. You can change your behavior, your habits, the way you think and the way you perceive the world around you. Expecting this to happen without experiencing pain, set-backs, discomfort or failure is unrealistic. Acting costs.

In the acquisition of any skill, readiness is all. You cannot force this state of readiness and you cannot make yourself learn faster than you do.

Remember…

As an artist you are always deepening your process and exploration of the human experience.

Remember this old joke? Q: "How do you get to Carnegie Hall?" A: "Practice, practice, practice!" The joke may be old—it is true nonetheless. If you continue taking classes, rehearsing, auditioning, reading plays and performing, you will learn just how expansive, fascinating and bottomless this great art is.

Acting is as demanding as a jealous lover who, while often pulling you away from family and friends, wants your undivided attention, who wants you to always be present and who can be confrontational and personally challenging on every level imaginable: spiritual, psychological, intellectual, physical and emotional. Dedicated actors face these challenges continuously. Mightn't actors be the Samurai of the Arts?

Before art, however, you must have craft. Paradoxically, although this workbook will make you think about the craft of acting, your ultimate aim is to perform *without worrying about your acting* at all. As you apply your teachers' critiques or director's requests, continue to rehearse, and use the workbook, you will find *your way* of gently guiding your attention where it will benefit you the most—off of your acting and towards allowing yourself to actually be affected by your fellow actors and the circumstances of the play.

Gwen. Work! Acting isn't anything. What's acting compared to—

Fanny. It's everything. It's work and play and meat and drink. They'll tell you it isn't—your fancy friends—but it's a lie! And they know it's a lie! They'd give their ears to be in your place. Don't make any mistake about that.

The Royal Family

—Edna Ferber and George S. Kaufman

Notice. Allow. Gently guide. Breathe. Open.

These are some of the actions that I hope you will incorporate into your process.

The more you let the play capture your curiosity and imagination, the more you need to tell the story, the greater the satisfaction you will have in your work.

While very basic, *Living in Discovery* is filled with the complexities and contradictions of life and art. It identifies crucial acting fundamentals that you as a performer begin with and return to throughout your life. All successful performers, be they musicians, dancers, actors, leaders, speakers, teachers or athletes, have become one with the core fundamentals of their discipline. The quality of time you spend, the focus of your practice, and the knowledge and experience you amass are important factors in the acquisition of the kind of skill that leads to a thrilling performance. In the hands of a great artist, acting is a transcendental art.

> **Remember…**
>
> The purpose of technique for any artist is not to bind, constipate or inhibit your expression. The purpose of technique is to set you free—to release and channel your energy.

As you live and grow as a person and an artist, return to *Living in Discovery* time and again. It is a home where you center yourself in your craft. Within its pages, you will find the means for recognizing and absorbing the massive wealth of material that plays and life will inevitably bring you.

> **Sooze.** But do you stand for anything? What? What do you stand for?
>
> *SuBurbia* –Eric Bogosian

Life is your teacher. Experience is your teacher. Plays are your teachers. And finally, the audience is your teacher.

Here and Now

Why do you want to act? When did you know you wanted to be an actor? What makes you different from people who don't want to act? How did this book get into your hands? What do you hope to learn from it? What are the actor's tools and materials? What is the homework of an actor? Why do you have to do so much homework? Does the research you do for a play differ from other types of research? If so, how? How and why should you rehearse and practice so much? How do you use your own life in your acting?

> **Remember…**
>
> You rehearse to discover things you don't know.

These are some of the questions that will be addressed as you work with this workbook. They are the questions with which all actors contend. You can learn anything if you learn to ask questions; developing as an artist means *learning what questions you must ask.*

Acting is Acting

Theater is the focus of *Living in Discovery*. When you work on a film or in TV, you use the same essential acting fundamentals that you need to sustain a character's life onstage. Acting is acting.

Acquiring skill takes time and practice. Your process engages full use of your instrument—all of you. The work in this book is only a piece of the whole. It is imperative that you acknowledge that Acting Technique, Voice, Movement, the Alexander Technique, and Speech classes are core to your practice as well. No acting class covers everything you need to be a well-trained actor. You must have more knowledge of your instrument (yourself) because you are a performer. Every part of your being in needed to do your job. Alexander Technique is a means for awakening to your use of self and discovering choices that release and free your body, voice and breath. Voice classes are essential for expanding your vocal range and opening your breathing and channeling sound. Movement classes strengthen and increase your flexibility as you experience your body's capacity to communicate. Speech is fascinating and physical; intelligibility is key for communication. The work in these classes should remain a part of your continued practice as you mature as an artist. Although taught as separate disciplines, they overlap. Do not compartmentalize the instruction you receive by dismissing the teachings in one class when you take another. Acting is physical, and as you continue your practice you come to see how all classes support your craft and your art.

Remember…

Acting is the coordination of many systems coming together in you. Breathe as you call yourself to the fire!

How to Use the Workbook

Use *Living in Discovery* alongside an acting class you are taking, when you are rehearsing for a role, or when you are between roles and have time to begin researching roles you would like to play someday.

Each chapter in *Living in Discovery* delves into fundamental aspects of your craft and focuses your attention on your *homework*—the work that you must do as an actor outside of the classroom and between rehearsals. Revisiting the basic fundamentals of your craft is learning and relearning to ask the questions that lead you into deeper, richer, unexplored territory of the world of your play. The play and your rehearsals will influence your approach to, and the order in which you work with, the questions in a chapter.

Remember…

Living in discovery keeps you vital — not natural.

By its very nature, reading is a linear process. However, you do not have to read this book from cover to cover as you would a play or novel. After reading the first three chapters, feel free to flip to a section that addresses a problem in a scene you are trying to solve. Or open the book randomly to any page and see what grabs your attention. This way you will be using the book to support a dynamic rehearsal process of discovery.

Living in discovery is the way of the actor. *Acting and Living in Discovery* is a workbook centered on the actor's homework; the Workbook Pages guide this homework.

The Workbook Pages

Characters in plays are human beings; actors are lifelong students of human behavior.

All character's lives onstage are controlled and selected—prescribed by the playwright. Your life is real. *Never forgetting the absolute difference between real and imaginary*, the workbook pages help you find bridges between your life's actual circumstances and the imaginary circumstances of the play. These links are the keys to using your imagination and finding the way you uniquely embody the new you. The workbook exercises poke your unconscious, leading you to deeper, truly specific and meaningful choices.

This is a self-directed, hands-on book. I encourage you to write in it and not to censor or worry about what you write. You don't have to answer every question. You will be successful no matter what because even glancing at a page will trigger your imagination and engage your subconscious.

Two types of workbook pages accompany each chapter: **Me, Myself & I** and **The Work.** The **Me Myself and I** pages contain exercises designed to deepen your awareness of yourself, *in your real life*; the exercises in **The Work** pages focus on the essentials you must practice and consider when stepping into a role and *the fictional world of the play*. I use the same vocabulary in both sets of workbook pages. The same words provide a context for both your self-observation and the vast exploration of human behavior that engages the actor when creating a character.

Me, Myself & I

The **Me, Myself and I** pages are all about *you*. To act, you must know more about your*self* than the average person. The exercises confront and challenge you to uncover your potential, your spirit, and to discover what really makes you the original, one-of-a-kind artist that you are.

You carry the mystery of acting in you. You are your instrument—all of you—your body, your voice, your speech, your imagination, your physical, emotional, verbal and mental stamina and flexibility, your unconscious habits, how you think, what you know, what you think you know, what you do not know, what matters to you, your opinions, your point of view about everything, your relationships to people, places and things, your dreams and desires, your wants, needs and your secrets.

The **Me, Myself and I** pages are a way for you to expand your perception of yourself as you find more fearless and honest personal connections which lead you into the world of the play. They cannot and should not be used to take the place of professional therapy; nor is therapy the point of your process. This is a lifelong exploratory journey of learning your instrument, your capabilities.

The Work

The Work pages focus on the specific tools and materials that give you real traction when working on a role. They help organize your work on your character's background, relationships, objectives, and actions.

The Work pages assist you in preparing for rehearsals, suggest ways to consider what occurs during rehearsals, and help you weigh where you are in your process.

Returning to these pages again and again with each role, every new character you play will give you the opportunity to expand your self-perception. Every character asks that you think, feel, fully and spontaneously express and behave in ways that may, at first, feel uncomfortable and unfamiliar. Isn't that why you want to act?

The Elements of Your Process

As you work through the workbook, the ★ symbol will focus your attention when reading. These sections are key *elements of your process*—they set forth craft fundamentals, specific aspects of approach and technique. They are necessary actions to practice and repeat with the development of each new scene or role. With steady use, they become a natural part of your process and manifest in your work.

Guidelines

Be your own guide:

- Approach the exercises in a way that works for you.

- Use the workbook to stimulate and activate your rehearsal process.

- Let the questions remind you of specifics you may or may not have considered.

- Work with the exercises that truly have relevance for you as your work progresses.

- Is there an order that you must follow when you use the workbook? Perhaps, if you are working on a play. No, if you are concentrating on self-observation and reflection.

- Do you have to complete every exercise before you go to the next? No.

- Do you have to begin with the **Me, Myself & I** pages before you approach **The Work** pages? No.

- Do you have to do the pages in Chapter One before you proceed to Chapter Two? No.

- Can you begin with the exercises in Chapter Four? Yes, you can begin with any chapter.

Experiment:

- Feel free to experiment. Approach the book at your own pace in your own way. Bounce back and forth between the chapters and their **Me, Myself & I** and **The Work** exercises, or begin at the beginning and focus on one chapter at a time.

- The discussions and exercises in the chapters alert you to the things you can explore as you rehearse. Use the book for every scene or play you tackle.

Remember…

The journey is the destination

Joan. There is great wisdom in the simplicity of a beast, let me tell you; and sometimes great foolishness is the wisdom of scholars.

Saint Joan

—George Bernard Shaw

- Your mind and spirit must be permitted to roam wherever the play takes you. What research compels you? What preparatory steps will strengthen your immersion in the circumstances of the play?

- Simply reading through the questions will open doors to unconscious personal connections that affect you when you rehearse.

Remember…

Life is messy.

- Use a pencil and a good eraser. As your choices evolve and change, you will be able to adjust your notes.

Rehearse:

- Rehearsal is your way into your body.

- Everything comes together as you explore your choices when you rehearse with your partner. *Discoveries begin to happen when you are on your feet in rehearsal, and are verified or taken to the next level when you have an audience.*

- Theater is a collaborative art form. You are always going to be working with others and should not, therefore, think of this workbook as a do-it-yourself book.

- The homework you do should make it possible to hear your teacher's critique or your director's thoughts.

- Avoid prematurely answering any of the questions with finality until they are tested in rehearsal. Avoid turning the workbook into an intellectual exercise. Your answers may seem logical and possible but they will remain ideas until they are tested on the floor. You don't get a gold star for answering all the questions.

Remember…

…You do not have to make something up when you are working with the pages. No one expects you to fill in the answers. The pages are here to raise your awareness, bit by bit. Notice what ideas, thoughts or images are stirred. It is not a test.

- Proceed patiently as you rehearse and work with the questions. Notice how what you write changes as your experience in rehearsal deepens.

- Homework, when done correctly, will lead the way to productive rehearsals.

- Your personal homework is private and should not be shared with anyone.

- Leave your homework at home!

~~~

Training as an actor is not a joyride, but it is joyful. It is not a free ride; it costs. It is not a safe ride; it is filled with unforeseen hazards. It is not a straight ride; it twists, circles, corkscrews and turns. You will surely get lost, lose your sense of direction and have to wait for the sunrise to find true north—but rest assured, the sun will always rise. The terrain will be harsh and magnificent, truly awesome, a reminder that you are a mere mortal who will not live forever. You will pass through dark forests, get stuck in mud, climb steep mountain roads overlooking scary inclines that terrify and give you vertigo that gives way to wondrous awe—all in the name of imagination!

You who already live the actor's life know that only those who have the heart, the need and the physical and emotional strength take this journey of endurance and grit.

You who are beginning, discover if you have that need. With it, you are unstoppable.

Voice. I can see you have your heart set on being an actress.

Girl. My heart, my soul, my very breath, the bones in my body, the blood in my veins—

Voice. Yes, yes, we've had enough of your medical history. …But what practical experience have you had?

Girl. As what?

Voice. Well, for example, the thing we're discussing. Acting … How much acting experience have you had?

Girl. …You mean on a stage?

Voice. That's as good a place as any.

The Good Doctor –Neil Simon

Chapter 1

The Play and its World

"We Don't Do That Here"

It is noon, November 28, 1964 and it has been pouring all morning. Reading the theater section of *The New York Times* in my cozy brownstone studio apartment on West 109th Street, I come across a photo of a familiar face and name—Diana Muldaur. We had been roommates one summer at the American Theater Wing Training Program at the Cape Playhouse in Dennis, Massachusetts. Absolutely obsessed by the theater, we spent our free time working strike nights and hanging around the shop with the techies. It was a summer of pure, unadulterated bliss.

Now here I am, years later, seeing Diana's picture in the newspaper. She is co-starring on Broadway with famed British actor Donald Pleasance in Jean Anouilh's *Poor Bitos*. It is closing tonight.

I purchase a ticket that evening at the Cort Theater box office. After the show I head backstage. I tentatively climb the iron staircase in search of her dressing room. I am uncertain if she will remember me.

Eventually, still in makeup, an energized Diana emerges. With instant recognition, she embraces me warmly and grandly, pressing my face into her bosom. She is delighted to see me and reminisces about our time together running through the golden fields of youth. (I recall late nights by the company pick-up truck with the master carpenter, the TD and the unforgettable burning sensation of swigging bourbon from the bottle.)

Inspired, I ask Diana if she can recommend an acting teacher.

"Uta."

Uta Hagen! I had just seen her in Edward Albee's *Who's Afraid of Virginia Woolf*. I cannot imagine studying with this great actress. Diana, however, is as forceful as she is beautiful and says, "I want to audition for her, too. We'll prepare an audition together." I don't say no.

I soon head downtown to the HB Studio in Greenwich Village and audit Miss Hagen's class. Incredible. I understand the technique after one single class.

For our audition, we choose the first scene between Gwendolyn and Cecily from *The Importance of Being Earnest* by Oscar Wilde. Diana's boyfriend makes me a lorgnette out of a coat hanger.

The night before our audition we hold one last rehearsal at Diana's apartment on the East Side before heading to her neighborhood bar with a friend. I have my first boilermaker. Or four. I only remember giggling endlessly and getting poured into a taxi.

The next morning I awake with my very first hangover and legs of rubber. Miss Hagen is holding the auditions on the third floor of HB Studio at 120 Bank Street. As we enter, the statuesque, experienced, confident Diana leads the way; five-foot-three, bewildered, ignorant-of-the-"biz"-me trails behind. Miss Hagen asks, "Miss Muldaur, don't I know you?" Diana mentions some folks they both know.

We do our scene. Miss Hagen responds, "Miss Muldaur, I'll take you. Miss Rosenfeld, you are working for a result. We don't do that here." She then asks if I would like recommendations of other teachers at the school, and gives me the names of three: Elizabeth Dillon, Alice Spivak and Herbert Berghof.

The day I audit Alice Spivak's class, my fate is sealed.

You may well ask what this story has to do with the title of this chapter, *The Play and Its World*: absolutely everything. My audition revealed that I did not have technique for joining the world of the play; nor did I have any idea how to read a play. It was my first lesson from Uta Hagen, and it took me years to translate that phrase—"Working for a result."

Hagen was explicitly saying that I had skipped every step in the development of a role; I had leapt to an extremely general, predictable and superficial idea of character and performance. *Carol* was nowhere in the work. She was implying that I had not discovered the circumstances of the scene, nor had I found a genuine relationship with my partner—I was busy acting my *idea*, and certainly not walking or talking like a human being. And what about *research*? Never entered my mind! Who knew? I certainly didn't.

Get Going ★

There's not a minute to waste. You have so much work to do on your own before you meet with your partner. When you really commit and develop solid habits, you will be keeping company with great artists like Meryl Streep and Al Pacino, Lois Smith, Philip Seymour Hoffman, Laurie Metcalf, James Earl Jones and Alfre Woodard.

Take your work seriously. Risk! Prepare—for a scene for class, an audition or a job!

Read the Play Like an Actor ★

> Remember…
>
> The play is everything. It will be your guide for all your work.

Actors read plays differently than Directors, or Scenic, Costume, Lighting and Sound Designers. Every single time you read the script, you must read with specific intention and purpose. Trust that you can be prepared and spontaneous at the same time. *Tools are not rules.*

Read the Play, the Whole Play ★

You are assigned a scene for your acting class, and you are itching to find out what the scene is about and what part you are going to play. But wait!

You will not know all that you need to know for your scene if you do not know what is in the play. Therefore, channel the excitement and anticipation you feel toward doing a scene to studying the whole play.

Cherish Losing Your Virginity—It Only Happens Once ★

Your experience of reading a play for the first time is a virginal experience that happens every time you read a new script. Don't throw this moment away. Give it the consideration that it deserves.

Your first time reading the play is also similar to being an audience member who is seeing a play that they don't know.

> **Sabina.** I don't understand a word of this play.
>
> *The Skin of Our Teeth* —Thornton Wilder

Think about what happens to you when you watch a play. You believe that you know what the characters are thinking or feeling from what the actors say and do during the performance. You are affected by and react to what you see. Engaged in the story, you unconsciously identify with what you see happening to the characters on the stage. You respond. You are part of the communal experience when the theater fills with laughter, rapt silence, sadness or tears.

Similar things happen to you when you first read any play. As the story unfolds line-by-line, page-by-page, you follow the characters' lives and have spontaneous, unconscious responses. You eagerly turn each page because you want to find out what happens next.

Hear the Play ★

Before you can tell the playwright's story as an actor through word and deed, you must first hear the story he or she is telling. Start by working simply, with an open mind and without premature interpretations.

Right or wrong, put your opinions and judgments aside. While some of your initial ideas might serve you, many may be cliché or stereotypical.

Your first reading of the play is the only time when you are innocent. You don't know what is coming next. It is the only time when you have an audience's fresh experience during your rehearsal process. I still recall when I first read *The Years* by Cindy Lou Johnson. Upon finishing Act II, I thought I knew what would happen in Act III. I was very wrong and completely taken by surprise.

As you begin to rehearse, you separate from your experience as audience in order to develop your experience as a character in the story. It is essential that you, the actor, not confuse the two. You are preparing to tell a story in the light onstage. Through your artistry and skill, you affect the *audience,* sitting in the dark. You draw the audience into the world of the play.

Vivian. …It has always been my custom to treat words with respect.

Wit –Margaret Edson

Tips for reading a play for the first time: Consider how very special this time is.

- Forget that you are going to be working on a scene. Let the story of the entire play wash over you.

- Set aside two hours so that you will be able to read the play in one sitting. Give yourself the opportunity to be alone with the play.

- Choose a time when you can concentrate without interruption. Detach yourself from electronics. Turn them *all* off completely. Let nothing disturb this precious experience.

- If you have to leave your home due to uncontrollable distractions, do so. Sit out of doors if the weather is nice. Go to a restaurant where they won't mind you sitting for two hours with a cup of coffee. It may be easier for you to concentrate in a public place. Do whatever you need to do to create an atmosphere that works for you.

- With every play you read, practice clearing your mind so that you can approach the story with curiosity and innocence. You might have to clean your apartment first. You may want to meditate. It may take time to discover what you need to do to quiet your mind so that you are ready to read the play with focus and intention.

- With a dictionary by your side, read the play.

- Sit quietly after the reading. Use **The Work** page "First Impressions" to jot down your initial thoughts and impressions. Revisit and amend this page throughout your rehearsals.

- Develop your own ritual surrounding your first contact with the play.

> Remember...
>
> Reading a play for the first time is an exciting event. It is also a sacred event. Give yourself the chance to experience that event..

Reread Your Play—Always With Intention, Discover ★

As a part of your rehearsal process, include reading your play as often as you need to; *you simply cannot gather, let alone process, the information you need by reading your script one time.*

Every time you come up with a question relating to some aspect of your scene, go back to the play; the answer could leap out at you or a string of new questions could emerge— *true signs that you are in your process.*

The more familiar you are with the play, the more you understand how your scene functions in the play and how it moves the action of the play forward.

Identify: Story, Happenings, Themes, Spine ★

Knowing how to read a play is at the heart of the actor's craft.

What is the play about?

The *second time* you read your script, focus on the story and the themes that run through the play. What holds the play together? How would you describe the *spine* of the play? These elements help you articulate your connection to the play: why you relate to it, why you want to work on it.

> **Isaac.** Something has happened. The way in which people read. Perceive. There used to be silence to life.
>
> *The Substance of Fire* –Jon Robin Baitz

Story

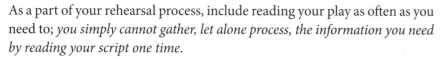

The story, the accounting of an event or series of events either true or fictitious, is the magnet that draws us to watching a play, film or television show. A play's story has already begun before the play begins. It has brought the characters to the first moment when the curtain rises or the lights come up on the stage. It will continue after the curtain comes down and all goes dark.

"We respond to certain stories regardless of how they are told or how often. We find archetypal stories in soap operas and Shakespeare. Stories serve our fundamental human need to make sense of our lives. They create maps for our survival containing genetic imperatives. We are bound to be interested in them. Stories are found in every culture."[2] As you re-read your play, pay attention to the story it is telling—is it a commonly told story? Does it diverge in unexpected ways? Are multiple storylines woven together around a central theme?

The Events or Happenings

When you re-read your play, think in terms of events or happenings. What happens in your play? Identify the events and happenings and track the way the playwright presents them. What occurs in the play that creates a character's struggle or a change in their lives? In what order do the happenings unfold? What is your role in the various events that take place? Identifying each event gives you clues regarding what must happen when you are on your feet playing the scene. Being clear and specific about the actual events that transpire leads you to discover where the play lives.

Theme

Contemplate the themes that run through your play. This is not an academic exercise. A theme is the main idea or underlying meaning of a play. It may be stated outright or implied in the dialogue. The theme makes a statement or expresses an opinion about the play's subject matter.

A *major* theme is an idea the playwright returns to time and again, becoming one of the most important ideas in the story. *Minor* themes are ideas that may appear from time to time. For example, many plays are about family, but the themes, be they major or minor, vary: the havoc of alcoholism, family secrets, denial or abuse within the family constellation, to name a few.

As you wrap your head around your play, some ideas will resonate for you more deeply than others. Some may repel yet fascinate you. Some may frighten you or shut you down. Some may hook you and not let go. Allow yourself to experience these reactions, noticing and acknowledging them without judgment.

Johnny. . . .This is the only chance we have to really come together, I'm convinced of it. People are given one moment to connect.

Frankie and Johnny in the Claire de Lune
—Terrence McNally

Spine

The image of the spine of a book—or even of your own spine—may help as you grasp the concept of the spine of the play.

The spine of the play is *a statement that captures the play's essence or energy.* You may think of the spine of the play as the single distillation of all the actions in the play. It holds the play together.

The spine is not absolute, nor should you arrive at it quickly. Experiment!

Try to articulate it because it will help to succinctly describe the movement of the play. You can do this for the play and for your character. When you articulate your character's spine, it will link you to your journey through the play. It will provide your connection to the spine of the play.

You will want to be aware of the relationship between what you conclude to be the spine of the play and the director's approach. They could be at odds.

To illustrate the idea of the spine of the play, let's consider the very familiar play *Our Town,* by Thornton Wilder. Here are some examples:

- Each day matters.

- Human beings the world over share wants and needs, hopes and dreams.

- Our lives end as stars in the sky.

Possible considerations for the spine of the play *Having Our Say,* by Emily Mann, might be:

- You are not defined by your history. You are defined by what you make of it.

- Honor your history in word and deed.

- Speak out

> **Emily.** It goes so fast. We don't have time to look at one another. I didn't realize. So all that was going on and we never noticed! …Goodbye! Goodbye, world! Goodbye, Grover's Corners — Mama and Papa — Goodbye to clocks ticking — and my butternut tree! And Mama's sunflowers — and food and coffee — and new-ironed dresses and hot baths — and sleeping and waking up! — Oh, earth, you're too wonderful for anyone to realize you! Do any human beings ever realize life while they live it — every, every minute?
>
> **Stage Manager.** No — Saints and poets maybe — they do some.
>
> *Our Town* –Thornton Wilder

Keep seeking to articulate the spine of the play you are working on throughout your rehearsal process. Don't settle on any one solution as definitive or absolute.

Sidestep the Traps—Stage directions, Adverbs/Adjectives, Pause, Punctuation and Ellipses ★

These are common conventions that appear in every script and function as traps for many actors. The words and symbols constituting these conventions influence your acting choices and can limit your rehearsal process when you follow them without questioning them. Begin noticing how these elements affect you during your early readings of your script, even before you get on your feet.

The white pages of your script are covered with black words. Through your rehearsal process you fill the blank white part with life. By discovering a new "you," a living, breathing human being, you supply the details that have not been spelled out by the playwright—the external and inner life of your character. Your collaboration

> **Vivian.** …just the white piece of paper that bears the little black marks.
>
> *Wit* –Margaret Edson

with the other actors, the director, scenographer, costumer, lighting designer and many others breathes life into the story.

All of the information you need to work on the play comes from the date of publication, the cast breakdown, the original cast listing, the description of the set, the time period, occasionally the playwright's notes, and the characters' dialogue.

When reading your script, and later when you are on your feet, notice how you respond to the stage directions, descriptive adjectives and adverbs, punctuation, ellipses and the pause. These elements can stifle your imagination and control your choices.

What you need to use in play

What you should cross out

Stage Directions

Some playwrights include stage directions because they expect their plays to be read as well as seen. But most of the notations you find in your scripts are usually *not* the playwrights'.

The acting version of a script often includes the stage manager's notes taken from the performances of the original production. These stage directions are intended to aid future productions, be they professional or amateur. The following will eliminate some of the natural confusion that arises from these stage directions.

Stage directions can be useful when they reinforce impulses you experience in rehearsal. Some stage directions give you an important sense of the world of the play and offer possibilities of physical actions you might want to use. Of course, if you do, you must provide a true source—an inner motivation—for any action you play.

[*Constance slowly pulls off her toque and drops it into the wastebasket.*]
Good Night Desdemona (Good Morning Juliet)
—Ann-Marie Macdonald

However, most often, stage directions suppress your own imagination. They rid your mind of possibility, of other options for behavior. Controlled by the images the word triggers, you can't think of any other things you might do.

As frightening as it might be, I recommend that you cross out all stage directions. Turn your script upside-down while crossing them out so that you can't read them. Or re-type your scene omitting the directions.

It is natural to want to follow the stage directions, especially if you don't know what else to do. Chapter Three covers the early fundamental stages of your rehearsal process. You begin building the muscles that will free you from the tyranny of stage directions, enabling you to work on a new script or bring your own vision to an iconic role.

Adjectives and Adverbs

Descriptive adjectives and adverbs seem to describe or indicate how a line might be said. For instance, in parentheses, before lines of text you will surely find words such as (shocked), (grimacing like the monster he is), (not too thrilled), (puzzled, laughs), (embarrassed), (confidentially), (glumly) or (crying).

Notice that these words almost always describe an emotion or condition. Descriptive adjectives and adverbs in a script lead you astray when you follow them blindly without questioning them. They lead you to generalizing, pushing emotionally or trying to show a feeling or inner state of being.

Directions such as (laughing), (angrily) or (crying) suggest that you must react accordingly and feel an emotion. When you see this type of notation, can you tell when the action begins, how long it lasts and when it stops? Do you know the source?

Let's take crying. You do not know why the character is crying. (You think he is sad.) You do not know the nature of the crying. Is he sobbing, crying silently, wailing, crying intermittently, hysterically, with moaning or choking sounds? Does he cry and then stop to talk or talk through his crying? How does he stop crying?

Your emotional life is deeper and richer and more important and interesting than a generalized feeling! It is always the consequence of circumstance and how you receive and let yourself be affected by the behavior of your fellow actors. *It is unplanned.* You don't wake up saying, "I am going to laugh when I say good morning to my roommate." When an emotion is triggered, physical sensations and inner objects are released; they manifest in your behavior. I use the term "inner objects" to mean those fleeting thoughts, images, and thought fragments that fly through our minds non-stop. They are not ordered or linear, nor will they necessarily be complete sentences. They are triggered by other people's words, your circumstances and how these things move into your awareness. You will get an even better idea of how your mind is filled with inner objects in Chapter Two.

> **Eugene.** I was the one who should have had to fight with him. Only I didn't know I was so angry. Like there's this part of my head that makes me this nice, likeable, funny kid …and there's the other part, the part that writes, that's an angry, hostile, real son of a bitch.
> **Stan.** You'd better make friends with the son of a bitch, because he's the one who's going to make you a big living.
>
> *Broadway Bound* –Neil Simon

Your emotional life has its own logic. No emotion is experienced as one steady sensation, but rather in different degrees of intensity. Emotions come, go, subside, stop completely and then suddenly well up again. They don't build in any predicable manner.

Adverbial prompts do not suggest what the original actor was *doing*; nor do they give any indication of the specific sources for the emotion or condition.

They can't—the specifics are within the individual actor and no two actors will ever source what appears to be the same behavior the same way! These prompts are a third party's observations noting what it looked like the actor was feeling based on the actor's external behavior.

If you do choose to follow the adjectives or adverbs in your rehearsal process, translate the words into active verbs. Otherwise you will sink into playing an emotional state of being that goes nowhere. Emotions must release into actions that make something happen. *To act is to do.*

The Adverbial Trap

I am in college playing Jennet Jourdemayne in a staged reading of *The Lady's Not for Burning* by Christopher Fry. While rehearsing the play, I think in externals and generalities. I am doing everything I now teach my students not to do! I say my lines out loud, stress a word and listen to how it sounds and then I choose the one I like best. (*she* is my friend. She *is* my friend. She is *my* friend. She is my *friend*. *She is my friend*.)

Things you know

Things you don't know

Things you think you know but don't

Here are some of the notes in my script: "more maturity in voice," "break," "work for more lightness," "don't use hands," "stand still," "extremely light," "sit relaxed," "sit up straight," "still light," "don't lean forward," "light also," "ridicule, no pleading," "strong," "faster," "change," "sarcastic," "laughs," "suddenly," "more real," "sighs," "more speed, intensity," "build," "keep both hands on book!," "be idealistic-ha!," "quicker," "angry," "faster."

I don't know what the play is about, but I am not certain that I even know that. I am not always sure of what I am saying, but it never occurs to me to admit it. Some of my notes also indicate that I am not in control of, let alone aware of, my body.

Jennet is a fantastic part and since I know how to pronounce the words, I pretend that I know what I am saying. Most of the notes come from the director and I don't know how to translate those notes into action. When she tells me to be "stronger" or "lighter" or to "build," I simply nod in agreement and muscle my way through with cliché attitude.

Puritan. …You're going to invite me into the deep place between the notes.

Glenn –David Young

Don't fall into the adverbial trap like I did! When I was in Alice Spivak's class, I began to learn that there were steps I could take to make all the elements in a play specific to myself. I could know *what* I was saying rather than focusing on *how* I was supposed to deliver the lines. This was a transformative

revelation for me! Instead of planning a feeling, I could discover what was
happening in a scene during rehearsal and be surprised by unpredicted
depths of sensation.

The adverbs and adjectives in parentheses you may find in your script
should be crossed out along with the stage directions. Chapter Four handles
replacing adverbs and adjectives with *transitive* verbs.

Know what you are saying rather that how you are going to say it!

Pause

A pause is a moment in time when the actor is not speaking; it is not a time
when the action of the play stops onstage. Does your mind stop working?
Do you stop breathing? Even when it is indicated in the script, a pause must
be motivated and filled, not simply followed as
a stage direction. You will occasionally find the
word "beat" in your script as well.

[*Pauses and blows Corie a kiss and exits*]

Barefoot in the Park –Neil Simon

The pause or beat in a play is analogous to the
space between notes in music. The space is alive as
it affects phrasing and rhythm. It carries a tension, an expectation, between
two notes or phrases.

Similarly, life onstage does not stand still when the dialogue ceases. The
mind and body are alive and fully active even during a pause or beat. No
counts are given to indicate how long a pause should last so its duration will
vary from performance to performance. I daresay—pauses or beats may be
as rapid as a heartbeat.

Another cautionary word: an actor may pause more often and longer than
necessary in an attempt to hold on to a "moment." What might be a precious,
significant moment to you can be deadly for the audience. Kill your darlings.

The Cricket Tape

My husband is working on a production of *The Rhymers of Eldridge*, by
Lanford Wilson. One character has a long speech with cricket sounds
in the background. The cricket tape is timed to last as long as the
speech. As the performances continue, the pauses get longer and
longer...until extra minutes of background crickets have to be added
to cover the duration of the speech.

Talk about self-indulgent acting!

Unnecessary pauses that are not even mentioned
in your script happen when you are *holding onto
your homework*. You will never *experience* the
event in your scene—you will never truly be in the
moment—unless you take out the unnecessary air
surrounding your sending and receiving. There are
several reasons why these pauses occur. You may

Frank. ...What do all these dots mean?

Ira. Hesitations, pauses.

Frank. I don't do hesitations.

Ira. Pinter uses dots.

Frank. Fuck Pinter.

It's Only a Play –Terrence McNally

be artificially controlling how you send and receive rather than playing in the moment; perhaps you are being controlled by—that is, "playing"—the punctuation on the pages of your script; or maybe you are enjoying your own feelings too much. These split-second pauses make for deadly acting and prevent you from getting the scene off the ground. With too much air, you are a beached whale.

Punctuation

There is a vast difference between written language and spoken language. When you have a reason for talking to someone, you know what you want to say and why you want to say it. Your thoughts flow and fly out of your mouth. When talking to another person, you don't know which words you are going to use and you do not think in terms of complete sentences that have a period at the end. The person doesn't know when you are going to stop speaking and often overlaps or cuts you off midstream.

Holding for a dot at the end of a sentence is like a tennis player serving the ball and waiting idly for her opponent to return it. She will be too late if she waits for the ball to come back over the net before she starts running to hit it. It is not the period at the end of your scene partner's sentence that motivates you to speak—you are reacting genuinely to what it is that your partner is saying, and your response is forming while he or she is saying it.

Joyce. Do you think I didn't? /They

Marlene. I still have dreams

Joyce. didn't get to America and drive across it in a fast car. /Bad nights, they had bad nights.

Marlene. America, America, you're jealous. /I had to get out, I knew when I

Joyce. Jealous?

Marlene. was thirteen, …

Top Girls —Caryl Churchill

Perhaps in an attempt to assist actors in finding more spontaneous give and take, playwrights have invented notations to indicate more lively dialogue. You may find a backslash (/) in a speech to indicate the moment that the other character interrupts and overlaps dialogue. These are hard to manage but can really get you on your game, keeping you alert and ready to respond to your partner. Regardless, your words have to be triggered by specifics you are taking off of your partner's words, tone of voice, facial expression or physicality. You and your partner may overlap every now and then, but if you really hear one another and know what you want, the audience will hear everything you both say.

You encounter ellipses (…) whenever the playwright omits words that would finish a sentence. It is the writer's indication of an incomplete thought, a change of thought, or a character's search for a better choice of words or emphasis.

You always need to have a sense of what you were going to say after the ellipses. Always motivate or justify why you don't complete any thought. These shifts happen rapid-fire … they don't drag out. You continue living even if the character is not speaking or hasn't finished the verbal thought.

It's easiest to motivate an incomplete thought when your partner cuts you off. If they don't, however, you may have to justify stopping yourself— perhaps by searching for an exact word, having second thoughts about finishing your sentence or by being distracted by something that interrupts your train of thought.

Now that you know more about the technical elements of your script— elements which may impact or inhibit your reading of the text as well as the choices you make once you start rehearsing—let's return to the early stages of your work grappling with the text.

Mine the Text ★

Astronomers probe the universe and miners mine ore deep under the surface of the earth. You probe and mine a play. Your ore is *meaning*. Your ore is buried in your subconscious and can be dislodged and released through unexpected self- discovery and your imagination.

> Remember…
>
> An unexamined life is not worth living.
>
> —Socrates

Your search for meaning brings you into the most compelling and enriching aspect of the actor's work. Like the miner's or astronomer's quests, your quest will be dirty, dark, murky, dangerous and uncertain. You might also find it sexy as you learn and discover. How great to find a new star or hit upon a rich vein of gold!

As you work on the script, be alert to serendipity and synchronicity appearing in your life. It will feel as if all of a sudden newspaper articles dealing with the issues in your play are prevalent, or that you keep meeting people who can help you understand the play, or you are noticing objects mentioned in the play in shop windows, etc. With no guarantees, continue to probe. Follow the strands of synchronicity. Your discoveries will be surprising and feel accidental. In the end, they may seem obvious in their simplicity. Be ready, aware and steadfast.

First Discover: What am I saying? ★

Mining any text begins with the actual/literal definitions of words, idioms, or colloquialisms used by the playwright. You can't act if you don't know what you are saying—not what you *think* you are saying, but what you are actually saying!

The *third* time you read the play, go through your script with a fine-toothed comb. *Make lists.* Using **The Work** pages, begin listing those words, phrases and references that you cannot pronounce or define. Refrain from glossing over or making quick, arbitrary and often erroneous decisions about their meaning.

> Remember…
>
> When you mispronounce a word, you have given yourself away. So …make friends with your dictionary.

When you really don't understand what the words mean in the context in which they are being used, add them to your list.

Christopher. That's a Jewish store. That would be Nazi rioting, I imagine.

I Am a Camera –John Van Druten

Remember…

Your responsibility to the playwright is to be word perfect. That means no paraphrasing. Find the needs for these sounds and these words and no others.

Your lists will help bring your attention to the script in a more focused, honest manner. Even the slightest doubt qualifies the word, phrase or reference to go on your list.

Begin looking up definitions and researching references as soon as possible.

What is a Matisse? What is a hot water bottle? What does the word *tenacious* mean? How do you pronounce Schiaparelli? Is there a sign that says, "Trenton Makes, The World Takes?"

Idioms

You can't deduce the meaning of an idiom by defining the individual words in the expression. Here are some examples: raining cats and dogs, water under the bridge, blow my stack, see the light, hit the roof, down to the wire, dropping like flies, in the bag, in your face, on the same page, a pig in a poke, an arm and a leg, pipe down, pull the plug, blow off steam.

After you find the meaning of the expressions the playwright uses, start using them in your everyday encounters with friends. Use them until they become yours—until they no longer seem strange, and you stop listening to yourself saying them.

Pronunciation

If you can't or don't know how to pronounce some of the words you come across, ask someone who does know. Record him or her saying the word a few times, leaving space for you to practice saying the word after. Make notations in your script of the proper pronunciation of words with which you are unfamiliar. Check out a Dictionary of English Pronunciation online.

Particularize ★

Celia. Polo, why are you doing this? Why now? We've been together so many nights and you've never been like this –why?

Polo. I'm drunk, that's the prize excuse for anything. I'm drunk and I don't know what I'm saying or doing. I could never say anything if I was sober --…

A Hatful of Rain –Michael V. Gazzo

In your own life, when you speak, your words are triggered by your immediate circumstances: where you are, whom you are with, what is happening, what has happened, your state of mind and being, your wants and/or needs and the challenges that stand in your way. All are specific and loaded with details. These elements converge to produce not only what you say, but your behavior as well. You use words that suit your circumstances and you either behave accordingly or not.

There is a huge difference between your own life and "your" new life in a play. Consequences are real in your own life; in a play, they do not continue for you, the actor, beyond the moment the curtain falls.

In your make-believe life, the writer has given you words and expressions that fit your character. But like an ill-fitting garment, too tight or too large, your dialogue may not fit you. You may have lines that you can't imagine saying; they may sound weird, phony or make you feel foolish, uncomfortable and self-conscious when you say them. No need to dwell in your discomfort. Develop the technique of particularizing.

Particularizing, a process that involves research, your imagination and the discovery of personal parallels, will help make your dialogue inevitable— and *yours.* Particularizing refers to one of the ways you morph a character into a human being. Human beings spontaneously connect thought and deed. How do you connect the inner life of your character to the circumstances of your play? Familiarize yourself with the section on Mindfulness in the following chapter, and begin looking at your own life. Notice the way in which your mind is always filled with images, memories or thoughts that relate to and are triggered by the specifics of your life.

Through particularizing, you flesh out the images and inner objects that the words in your script provoke, fill in details connected to an event you mention, and provide a full landscape of specifics to a relationship or place. All are wired to your point of view and to feelings that then must be released into action.

Particularizing is the process in which everything you say connects you internally to specific and detailed inner objects and/or images. This tool solidifies your faith in your imaginary circumstances and the way you experience them.

You will find some of these particulars through the research you are about to begin.

Remember…

It takes knowledge to know what you don't know.

Conduct Hands-On Research ★

Begin researching the references in your script to subject matter, people, places, and events to see if they exist or existed. Avoid making the assumption that everything mentioned in the play is only a figment of the playwright's imagination. It is quite possible that a reference in your script is to an actual event, place or person. Are there places you can visit? Are there people you can speak to? Is there some new subject you have to know about? Making lists of the areas you need to address will give you a sense of order.

Be very vigilant. As soon as you discover that

Sadie. America has not ever been able to undo the mess created by those Jim Crow laws.

Having Our Say —Emily Mann

the new you has a profession, go to **The Work** page "The Real Deal" at the end of this chapter. Take the necessary steps to find tangible connections to every aspect of your new life. Informants can give you greater insight into the many areas you need to probe when you work on your play. These might include your background, an event, your profession, your physical condition or your class, just to name a few.

One Line, One Police Plaza, Sex Crimes Unit

I have a short scene on the telephone in a play at the Jewish Repertory Theater in New York City. We have been in rehearsal for some time. One line is giving me trouble—it is about my daughter and hints that she has been raped. I am empty—no images, blank. In desperation, I call the NYPD in search of...I know not what. Playing the actor card, I ask if I can talk to someone about the play I am in. They pass me to Public Relations, who set me up with an appointment to talk to the Head of the Sex Crimes Unit.

Simply walking into One Police Plaza gives me chills. Getting a pass, taking the elevator with many men in uniform—it is all intimidating and scary. I am surprised, such is my ignorance, that the Sergeant of the Sex Crimes Unit is a woman.

As she speaks, sitting on the other side of her massive desk, I begin to shake. Images flood my mind and my heart breaks. I have flashes of meeting my daughter in the ER, a police person in attendance, her shame and trauma. The details she has to provide the officer. Seeing her soiled panties when she gets on the examining table to be examined, her tears, the sadness in her eyes.

This triggers all the questions I have to ask myself. Where was I when I got the phone call? What was I doing? Who called? What was the sound of the person's voice like? Or was it my daughter? What did she say? What did I hear in her voice? How did I get dressed, get to my car? What hospital was my daughter taken to? What was the drive to the hospital like? Did I have trouble parking? What was the ER like? Was my daughter there or had she already been taken into an examining room? And on, and on...

Having done my research, when it came to performance, I loved playing that scene—my tank was always full. Make sure your tank is always full as well: work with each event, each person, and each place in detail until you have a *genuine sensory reality* that you can believe in. You will discover how the events, people, and places mentioned in the script really affect your character, how "you" perceive them, and in which ways they further or hinder "your" needs and condition "your" behavior.

Caution: Please bear in mind that, as you conduct your research in the real world, you must *never* do anything that will endanger your life, your safety, or the lives and safety of others. For an example of potentially hazardous research that should be avoided, please turn to the story *Under No Circumstances,* in Chapter Six.

Use What You Know ★

Be aware that it can take time and many rehearsals for the things that happen in a section of a play to have full meaning for you. Some events may not click for you until you are in performance. Also be aware that without realizing it, you are often intuitively connecting to the script.

In addition to conducting research, particularizing sometimes requires drawing personal parallels with your text.

For instance, you are eighteen years old. You are working on a scene from a play in which you talk about your one-year-old daughter. You yourself do not have a child. How are you going to imagine being a new father and falling in love with your baby girl? In an instance like this, *use what you know* to supplement your research. Perhaps you have a nephew, niece or younger sibling to whom you are very attached. Daydream about what you remember – when they were born, how they looked at you or greeted you when they saw you. Remember how you felt when you held the baby. What did the baby's skin feel like? Do you remember the scent of Johnson and Johnson's baby powder? Perhaps you have friends who have just had a baby. Visit them often, if possible. This becomes an important part of your preparation.

Remember…

This is all about you finding *your* way, *your* process.

By conjuring your sense memory in this way, you will have stronger faith in your circumstances within the scene. Be honest with yourself. You stay in your body when you know what you are talking about. You *know/feel*. Our master Fitzmaurice Voice teacher at the HB Studio, Ilse Pfeifer, uses the expression *see/feel* in her class. I love it. It brings the senses into the body immediately. This is not emotional feeling. Instead, it defines the actor's state of mindful receiving. When you see/feel, hear/feel, touch/feel or breathe, you accept the outside world into your body. This process should not slow you down. You don't think it. Mindfulness (see/feel, hear/feel) keeps you alert and present. In this case, I have added to this list know/ feel in hopes of describing the sensations you have when you simply *know* what you are talking about. Receiving is assured when you are breathing. Chapter Two deals with this as well.

Man. *The Guns of Navarone, Where Eagles Dare …Ice Station Zebra?*
Woman. I threw myself a little Alistair MacLean festival.

Fat Pig –Neil LaBute

No one knows what is going on in your mind, so use aspects of your own life that give you a sense of truth. The audience will always believe you if you are telling the truth.

It takes practice to refine your own way of particularizing, but as you do, you will derive greater satisfaction from your work in rehearsals. It is through this process that you personalize a role and make the text your own. To do this quickly and superficially is to impose your will upon the play. While the process of particularizing is providing you with specifics and personal meaning, you do not have license to take liberties with the text and add stories that are not substantiated with the playwright's words.

You will need time to digest and integrate your discoveries. It is an extremely personal, topsy-turvy process. Throughout your rehearsals—and, if you are in a production, sometimes even after the show has opened—you can be continually discovering what the words leaving your mouth mean. Do not expect this to be a conscious, step by step process. Mindfulness, discussed in the following chapter, will help you catch these occurrences.

Tips for mining your script

- If you don't have one, get a dictionary.

- Get a thesaurus as well.

- Go through the play, paying close attention to every word.

- Follow the suggestions on **The Work** page "Mining the Text." List the words, expressions, idioms, subject matter, references and situations in the play that you don't know, don't understand or aren't sure of.

- Use **The Work** page "Prioritizing" for planning and organizing your research.

- Use **The Work** page "Particularizing" to begin brainstorming questions to ask yourself. These questions will trigger within you personal, emotionally charged images that will connect you to the words and circumstances of the play, giving everything you do and say deeper meaning and purpose.

Remember…

All emotion must find release in action.

As you move forward, remember to approach your play with curiosity, wondering what discoveries await you.

Write Your Life Story (Not Your Character's)

This is a huge assignment. Unless you want to stop everything and write your autobiography, do this exercise bit by bit. You don't even have to begin at the beginning, nor do you have to tell your story chronologically. If you are in your seventies, you might want to begin with one decade; give each decade a name that reflects what this time period represents in your life story. If you are in the second decade of your life, you may discover that this assignment takes longer than expected as you find yourself relishing every detail.

Begin with what you remember of your first ten years, then your second ten years, and so on:

0 – 10 years.

10 – 20 years.

20 – 30 years.

30 – 40 years.

40 – 50 years.

50 – 60 years.

60 – 70 years.

70 – 80 years.

80 +

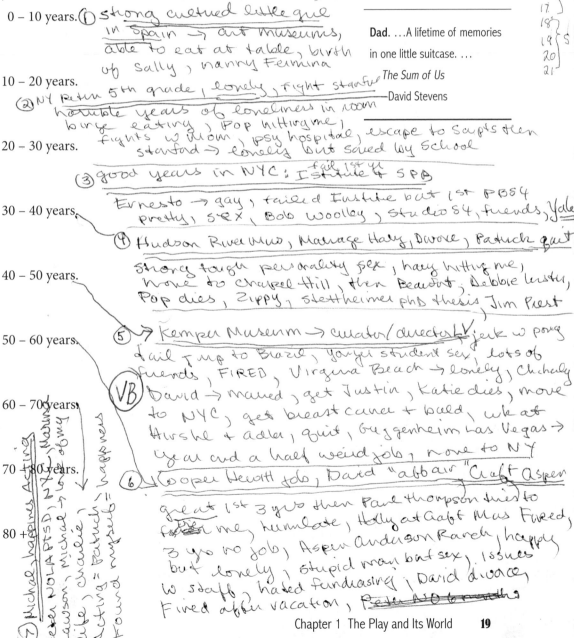

Handwritten annotations:

Top right (triangle): Me / Myself / & I

Right margin list:
1 Spain
2 S
3 S
4 K
5 1
6 2
7 3
8 4
10 5
11 6
12 7
13.8
14
15 } HS
16
17
18
19 } S
20
21

Right side printed quote:
Dad. …A lifetime of memories in one little suitcase. …
The Sum of Us
—David Stevens

Handwritten entries by decade:

① strong cultured little girl in Spain → art museums, able to eat at table, birth of Sally, nanny Fermina

② NY return 5th grade, lonely, fight started horrible years of loneliness in room, binge eating, Pop hitting me, fights w/ Mom, Psy hospital, escape to Scripts then Stanford → lonely but saved by school

③ good years in NYC: Institute & SPB, fail 1st yr, Ernesto → gay, failed Institute but 1st PBS4, pretty, sex, Bob Woolley, Studio 54, friends, Yale

④ Hudson River Mus, Marriage Haly, Divorce, Patrick quit, strong tough personality sex, Haly hitting me, move to Chapel Hill, then Beaufort, Debbie Lusty, Pop dies, Zippy, stettheimer phd thesis, Jim Priest

⑤ → Kemper Museum → curator/director jerk w pony, jail, up to Brazil, younger student sex, lots of friends, FIRED, Virginia Beach → lonely, Chihuly

(VB) David → married, get Justin, Katie dies, move to NYC, get breast cancer + bald, wk at Hirshl + adler, quit, Guggenheim Las Vegas → year and a half weird job, move to NY

⑥ Cooper Hewitt job, David "abb air" Craft Aspen great 1st 3 yrs then Paul Thompson tries to fire me, humilate, Holly at Craft was Fired, 3 yrs no job, Aspen Anderson Ranch, happy but lonely, stupid man bad sex, issues w staff, hated fundraising, David divorce, Fired after vacation,

⑦ Peter NOLA PTSD, NY, Marion Lawson, Michael → wife of my life, Charlie, Acting = Patrick, found myself, Michael happiness Acting, Happiness

The Events or Happenings in Your Life

You may be involved in ongoing issues connected to family members, friends, love interests, work, school, or your career. They could revolve around your living conditions, financial concerns or health matters.

- How many issues do you have going on in your life right now?

6   Bored   Steff Book
②I ear   • weight
control   • NO gym
④ I can't $ w Michael
contol   Reish

- Which issues have been ongoing? How long have they been going on?

  ○ Michael financial situation
        4 years
  ○ Wanting to get married - 1 yr
  ○ Not having enuf to do - 5 yrs
  ○ Not working out - 2 yrs

- What issues have vanished or have been resolved? How?

  ○ No man - true love
        met Michael

  ○ Not having a home
        my NY apt bought

  ○ Not having enuf $ - parent dying

  ○ Not being happy - Michael
        Acting
        Marina

Remember…

Homework is just that. It is to be left at home. It is not something you have to try to remember. Writing as preparation is merely a means to help you focus your attention. You might refer back to things you have writtent or you may never look at them again.

The Themes in Your Life

The *themes* are the various topics that occur or develop in the course of a play—your real life may have themes as well. Use the clouds to list the recurrent themes in your life as they relate to each topic. Also consider:

- How long have these themes been in your life?
- What new themes would you like to become a part of your life?

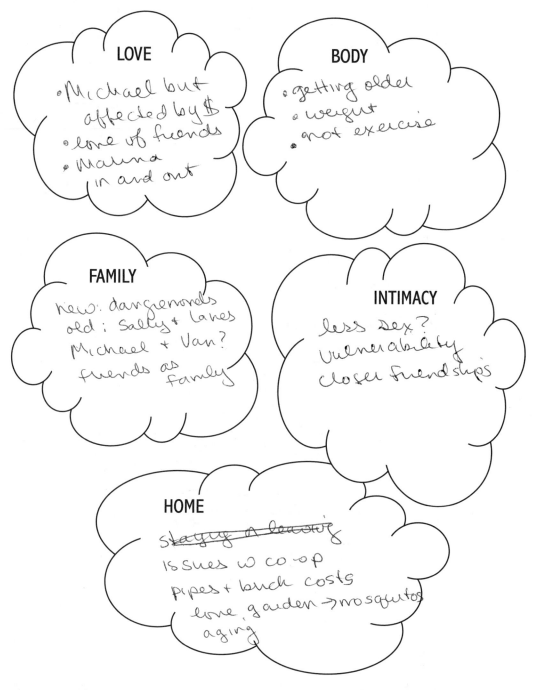

LOVE

- Michael but affected by $
- love of friends
- Malina in and out

BODY

- getting older
- weight
- not exercise

FAMILY

new: dangerousness
old: Sally + Lanes
Michael + Van?
friends as family

INTIMACY

less sex?
vulnerability
closer friendships

HOME

staying ~~+ leaving~~
issues w co-op
pipes + buck costs
love garden → mosquitos
aging

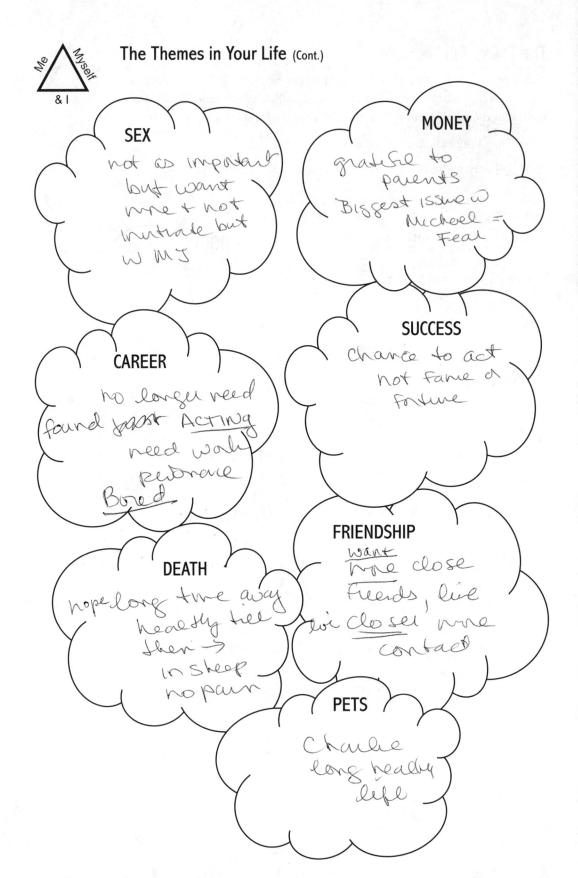

SEX

not as important
but want
more + not
initiate but
w MJ

MONEY

grateful to
parents
Biggest issue w
Michael =
Fear

CAREER

no longer need
found past ACTING
need work
performance
Bored

SUCCESS

Chance to act
not fame or
fortune

DEATH

hope long time away
healthy till
then →
in sleep
no pain

FRIENDSHIP

want
more close
Friends, live
for closer more
contact

PETS

Charlie
long healthy
life

The Spine of Your Life

Take this opportunity to think about the forces that drive you through life. Can you encapsulate what you are about in a simple phrase? Experiment. Try on the expressions that come to you. Don't censor yourself. If something feels right, it is right—at least for now.

For example: *Not be ~~also~~ alone + be loved/love and do something I love that fulfills me*

- To get to the top

- To live in the moment × *less worry about future*

- To be true to myself ×

- To live consciously, honestly, and to share myself as fully and ∧ generously as I am able

- To be loving and compassionate ⤫

- To place no head above my own

- To respect and care for my body ⤫

- To keep the "four agreements" (see *The Four Agreements,* by Don Miguel Ruiz. Amber-Allen Publishing, Inc. 1997)

- To tell the truth ✗

- To judge no one ⤫

- To always do my best ✗

- To take the world as I find it

- Without fame, I am nothing

- Fame won't keep me warm on a bitter cold night

The Cast of Characters Who Fill Your Life

1 Who are the people who have parts in your story?

Michael   Annette   Ariane
Marina   Marjolin   Meredie
Charlie   Ellen

patrick Q

2 Of those, who are the people that help create the themes in your life?

Michael
Marina
Charlie

3 Pick one of your life's plots. List the people who have parts in it.

~~hire~~ → all of those
love   in part 1 except

Patrick

On Reading

Some questions to think about:

- When you are assigned a scene for class, how long does it take you to get a copy of the play?

  a week

- How often do you take scenes or monologues from scene or monologue books? Always, sometimes, never?

  Sometimes — never

- Do you follow up by reading the whole play from which the scene or monologue was taken before you begin rehearsal? Always, sometimes, never?

  Mostly

- Do you have a reading disability? If so, how have you handled it? When you begin to study with a teacher or director, do you tell him or her that you have a reading disability? If so, how come? If not, why not?

  NO

- How many plays have you read? On the average, how many plays do you read a month? What was the last play you read? Why?

  2   Independence — to do it

- Who is your favorite playwright? What draws you to his/her writing? Have you read Chekhov? Ibsen? Shakespeare? Shaw? Arthur Miller? Lillian Hellman? Eugene O'Neill?

  Lilian Hellman

  > **Polonius.** …—What do you read, my lord?
  >
  > **Hamlet.** Words, words, words
  >
  > *Hamlet* —William Shakespeare

- Do you have a favorite play? If so, what is it?

  Lion in Winter

- What do you usually do when you encounter a word you don't know? Do you own a dictionary and thesaurus, or have them as apps on your cell phone or laptop? How often do you use them?

  apps on pc
  rarely → I know most

First Impressions

PLAY: _When Young + Unafraid_

ROLE: _Agnes_

DATE: _____

Make notes about what you experienced when you first read the play. Catch your thoughts, even ones you think you "shouldn't" have had. Write your impressions and opinions of the play and characters.

- What were your impressions and opinions of the play and the characters in the play?

   dated ~ esp. Hannah
   Agnes lesbian? a lonely
   relevant but tough
   realistic diff characters

- What memories did the play trigger for you?

   I'm not a good flirt, not popular
   but followed men
   too sharp + outspoken

- Have you done scenes from the play in other classes?

   yes

- Have you been in productions of the play? When? What part did you play? What do you remember about the play and the production?

- What future projections, if any, did you make as you read the play? Did you imagine yourself doing the scene in class? Did you imagine yourself on opening night?

   Penny gone

- What aspects of the play excited you? Scared you in a challenging way? Made your heart pound?

  how to react w surprize + guy in last act

The Work

- What part of the play has a hold on you and won't let go?

  how to decide intimacy w hannah and aguess

- What are your feelings about the use of language in the play? Does it thrill you, turn you off, feel unnatural? Do you wonder why the play has to be filled with vulgar language?

  Fine / no

- As for the play itself, you love it. You don't like it. Why? You don't understand it nor do you see why people rave about it. Why?

  neutral

- Do you feel that the story must be told? Is the role compelling?

  yes — somewhat

- Does it bore you to tears or do you think the play is the greatest play ever written?

  neither

Return to your notes after you have been rehearsing your scene for a couple of weeks. Have your ideas changed or been affirmed? To move beyond and/or deepen your first impressions, follow the steps in the chapters that follow.

The Story of the Play

PLAY: _____

ROLE: _____

DATE: _____

Tell the story of the play in your own words.

The Events or Happenings in the Play

PLAY: _____

ROLE: _____

DATE: _____

Write everything that happens in each scene in the play.

Act I
   Scene 1:

   Scene 2:

   Scene 3:

Act II
   Scene 1:

   Scene 2:

   Scene 3:

Act III
   Scene 1:

   Scene 2:

   Scene 3:

   etc.

The Work

The Themes in the Play

PLAY: _____

ROLE: _____

DATE: _____

What are the various subjects and ideas raised in the play? Write the themes that you find running through the play. Which themes speak to you?

Echo. I fly with words. Oh, I know it sounds stupid to say, but it's true. Certain words literally lift me up to a ...private altitude.
  Eleemosynary
  —Lee Blessing

The Spine of the Play

PLAY: _____

ROLE: _____

DATE: _____

The spine can be a difficult concept to grasp. It will take time for you to find what you believe the spine of the play to be. Be patient if you don't get it right away or if you don't think you get it at all. You might have to be on your feet and re-read the play many times. Experiment. Don't censor or second-guess yourself as you try to articulate the spine.

- What is the play about?

- What gives the play vitality?

- Try to articulate the spine of your play.

- Modify your ideas throughout your rehearsal process until you feel the phrase in your heart and in your gut.

Epifania. You must learn to take chances in this world. ... What do the unmarried know of this infinitely dangerous heart tearing everchanging life of adventure that we call marriage?

The Millionairess
—George Bernard Shaw

Mining the Text

PLAY: _____

ROLE: _____

DATE: _____

By now you are getting an idea of just how much work goes into creating a role. You can't possibly do all this at once, but it is helpful to have a plan of some kind. The sooner you get to work, the better.

- List the words, expressions, references and situations in the play that you want to make specific to yourself. Your list may be long. Little by little, you will find your way to knowing what you are talking about and what it means to you.

- Include words that you don't know and words that you don't know how to pronounce.

- Include references to other characters.

- Include references to ideas, places, things, people and events, past, present and future.

- Begin with actual definitions. Don't substitute, interpret, guess or assume that you know what something means. If you are not absolutely certain, use your dictionary.

- Begin collecting pictures and articles as they come your way.

Greg. Not to be rude, but I've known you since before we were *freshmen*—where did you ever hear of Clarence Darrow?

reasons to be pretty
—Neil LaBute

Prioritizing

PLAY: _____

ROLE: _____

DATE: _____

The amount of material that you have to absorb in most plays can be overwhelming. You can't do everything at once. Prioritizing the work you want to do is a good way to begin. Start with the easiest and most accessible information available.

- What is the most pressing information you need?

- Go through the lists you have made and put them in the order you want to do your research.

- Make a battle plan and decide when you can set aside time to research information on some of your topics.

- List on-site research or informant consults you need: specific museums, clothing stores, Sotheby's, medical consultation, a trip to Wall Street, a court house, a trial, an ER, a school, a library, etc.

Remember…

This is about time

management.

The Real Deal

PLAY: _____

ROLE: _____

DATE: _____

Whether needing to know about your job or new profession, the topic of the play, a medical condition of a character, the time period of the play, or the setting/s of the play, begin taking actions that will give you sensory reality and that will give you greater faith in your circumstances. If you do not find tangible ways to create your new reality, you run the risk of always being in your head. You want to be in your body, breathing—alive.

For instance:

- Apply for a job in your new profession.

- Spend the day with someone who makes a living doing what your character does.

- If your play is about boxing, go to a boxing match. Spend time hanging around a gym where boxers train.

- If you play a chef, secretary, TV announcer, police officer, lawyer, etc., find someone who will let you trail them or be on site with them for a day or longer.

- Find out how you might be able to borrow a uniform if you wear one.

- If you are playing a mom or dad, go to a playground and sit. Ask a friend who has a baby if you can visit so you can experience holding, feeding and playing with the baby.

- If your play takes place in a bar, go to a bar where you can determine the details of the environment and take note of or ask to borrow objects that they use there. Pay attention to colors, textures, age, odors, light, sound—how the place makes you feel and how it affects your behavior. We will discuss this more completely in Chapter Three.

- If you are pregnant, spend the whole weekend wearing your "baby." Go to the grocery store. Do your laundry. Go to a maternity store to try on clothes. Go shopping for shoes, etc.

- If you play cards (Bridge, Canasta, Gin Rummy, Poker) in a scene, begin playing every day.

Particularizing

PLAY: _____

ROLE: _____

DATE: _____

You will rarely have a literal equivalent in your real life for things that happen or are talked about in any play. I once had some dialogue where my character described the storyline of her favorite soap opera. Having never watched a soap opera, I didn't understand my lines. Not knowing where it would lead, I began watching a few soaps, got hooked and needed to keep up with the lives of the shows' characters. I was able to make sense of my convoluted lines in the play. They became mine.

Spoken and written words naturally trigger images, and often memories, in both the speaker and listener. You reflexively flesh out the things you say, read or hear with your own mental details. The images that come to your mind when you are speaking, reading or listening to someone are uniquely yours. As you continue rehearsing, be ready for even more personally meaningful specifics to emerge and hook you.

As you begin to go more deeply into the text, allow your imagination to guide you. Wonder, and as you do you will begin to create your own memory bank for the new you. Here are examples of the questions that you can ask yourself when you want to particularize an event you mention in a play:

In *A Hatful of Rain*, Polo says, "…. I threw a lemon at a passing car once—and hit the driver in the head."[3] If you were playing Polo, you might ask yourself the following questions:

- Where were you?

- Do you remember where the impulse came from? Was it a dare?

- Where did you get the lemon?

- Had you thrown any others before you hit the target?

- Where were you going? Coming from?

- How many cars were on the road?

- What kind of car? Color? Make? Model?

- What time of year? Summer? Hot? Windows rolled down?

- Were you on the driver's side of the road or the passenger's?

- What happened afterwards?

> **Remember…**
>
> Homework and rehearsal feed what is in many ways an unconscious process.

Chapter 2

Meeting Yourself, Meeting Your Partner

"Oh, fine"

Hal, Barbara and I begin teaching at HB Studio around the same time and are about the same age. Whenever I run into them, they are delightfully warm, upbeat and positive. Smiling and courteous, their greetings always make me feel good because they sound as if they are genuinely happy to see me.

You might say, "So? What's the big deal? That sounds like normal behavior." It is, for them. It isn't for me.

At this time in my life, I am not very mindful. When asked that normal everyday greeting, "How are you?" I respond with a sing-song, "Oh, fine." The message I send with my delivery of these words is that I am not fine at all, and I want everyone to know it. The intention behind my words seems to say, "Feel sorry for me."

One day as I am walking down Bank Street on the way to the Studio, it dawns on me: I am tired of my negative behavior. I want to get to the other side of the street—the sunny side.

With Barbara and Hal as beacons, I begin consciously thinking about

> changing my behavior. This is a crucial moment—until now I had never realized that I could change myself. I don't know how I will do this—but I do know that some of my ways are no longer working for me.
>
> Everything begins with willingness.

This moment of self-realization was the beginning of my journey towards mindfulness—towards unearthing my unconscious motives and behaviors and developing greater awareness of myself, my actions and my effect on others. For an actor, there is no greater tool than being mindful and self-aware. It is absolutely necessary to discover yourself in order to work openly and effectively with others. The first part of this chapter deals with this process of self-discovery, of meeting yourself; the second part will help guide your approach to working with others as it comes time to meet with your partner and start rehearsing.

Remember…

Mindfulness/awakeness is a fluid state. Allow it to be whatever it is in this moment.

Meeting Yourself

Learn Your Instrument ★

As has been mentioned before at the beginning of this book, you, as an actor, unlike the violinist and his Stradivarius, are the player *and* the instrument. You must know your instrument. Therefore, your artistry requires more self-knowledge than you might otherwise need if you didn't want to be an actor. This self-knowledge requires that you become conscious of your current behavior, habits and thought processes. Along with your increasing awareness of your behavioral patterns, you must remain objective as you assess your voluntary and involuntary habits. You will begin to notice how you walk, how you move, where you hold your tension, how you breathe and produce sound and what your speech patterns are.

As the violinist's ability grows and as he sees more in the music, he may crave a finer violin that will produce the quality and resonance of the sounds that he hears in his mind's ear. So too will you demand more from yourself. As you gain greater self-knowledge, you must continue deciding which patterns of behavior are most useful and which inhibit your growth or work against you. As you expand your perception of yourself and assimilate what you learn, you may discover a need to make some changes. At that point, you have to have the willingness and drive to allow those changes to occur. It is easy to talk about changing your ways; it is not that easy to do. Moreover, *it takes time*.

When you act, your engagement with your fellow actors—being acutely alive to what they do—has to be substantively different than the way you engage in everyday life. When you act you are expected to be truly available to your scene partners, open to being affected by what they do. You are also expected to sustain a vital, delving curiosity about the lives of the characters in the play. Your receptivity to being affected by and responsive to others is fundamental in the development of your craft.

To be affected by people, places and things, you need the courage to face yourself, be honest with yourself and, in time, uncover hidden truths. In other words, you need to develop a deeper understanding and acceptance of yourself. This is a life's journey. You need a way to observe yourself, your ways and thoughts, your perceptions and feelings, your needs and wants and the world in which you live. The next section, "Mindfulness: An Essential Tool," starts you on this journey.

Acting requires that you be "present" in your practice and that you become more conscious of your own behavior. As you foster mindfulness, you will inevitably enjoy being more present in your everyday life as well.

Mindfulness: An Essential Tool ★

When participating in an acting class or rehearsing for a performance you are embarking on a highly personal journey within a necessarily interpersonal environment. Your directors and teachers are your colleagues. Their jobs include watching your work objectively, from a distance. Your job is to work subjectively.

Therefore, the deeper your involvement in the circumstances of your play, the more you need a way to assess your experience after you have tested your work. You need to know the elements that created your experience—your inner sensations and the physical actions through which they manifested— so that you can reflect on your work between rehearsals and the reworks of your scenes in class.

You also need to remember that, though critiques from teachers and directors are addressed to you, it is your *work*, and not *you*, that is being discussed; it is imperative that you are able to distinguish between your work and you. Otherwise, depending upon your needs and expectations, you may not be able to truly hear the suggestions offered. You may need time to process your critique. A critique should drive your desire to get back to rehearsal.

Mindfulness, or "awarenessing," is the tool that sharpens your ability to process your experiences in your class, in your life, and in your art. It is the key to being present with yourself and others. It helps you to step outside of and observe your subjective, internal processes. It is synergistically dependent on the life source, the breath. The ancient Buddhist concept of mindfulness is deeply related to the practice of acting. I believe that actors have practiced mindfulness unconsciously and under different names for ages.

Your Four Selves   ★

In his book *Full Catastrophe Living*, Jon Kabat-Zinn talks about the four selves. They are your Thinking Self, your Emotional Self, your Functional Self and your Observing Self.[4]

Since your goal as an actor is to be fully and genuinely present as you live through the imaginary circumstances of the play, it is necessary for you to develop the ability and daring need to engage truthfully in your physical, verbal and emotional life. The idea of your four selves will help you to begin processing and engaging with the world around you in an increasingly conscious, ever-present and mindful way. You will have immediate recognition as you read about the four selves that are part of all human beings. As you gain awareness of your four selves, you will become more honest with yourself. You will see yourself and others more clearly. Truly being present is ultimately less effortful and more satisfying than not being present.

Your Thinking Self ~ Judgments, shoulds, likes

Your Thinking Self is that part of you which fills your mind with non-stop chatter. Rarely quiet, it plays out scenes you anticipate in the near or distant future, and it replays scenarios from your past. Occasionally, it also comments on things happening as they are occurring.

Day and night, in the shower, washing dishes, riding on the bus, making love, cooking, cleaning, reading, conversing…all the while your mind is probably thinking about what you are doing, what you should be doing or what you will be doing. While you are engaged in your normal daily activities, you might also be mentally finishing an argument with your boss, apologizing to a friend, reminding yourself to call someone or planning what you want for dinner. The examples are endless.

Your Thinking Self often has multiple personalities. It encompasses your "judge," your "critic," your "defender," your "squelcher," your "buddy" and your "cheerleader." It is constantly replaying the opinions you have of friends, people at work, family members, people you have met, people you are about to meet and people you would love to meet.

> Remember…
> All creative success requires creative failure.
> *The Artist's Way* –Julia Cameron

Your Thinking Self might be driven by the people-pleasing, guilt-ridden "should," "have to," "ought to," "should have," "if only" or "why didn't I."

Your Thinking Self plans, schemes, obsesses, worries, beats up, chastises, guilt-trips, blames, organizes, regrets, likes, dislikes, loves and hates—and it can do so anywhere, anytime and while engaged in just about any activity.

You may discover how your Thinking Self can disrupt and sap energy from your creativity. It can also energize you. Your Thinking Self will, if you are not careful, talk you out of following your own impulses and lead you to second-guessing your acting choices. That said, your Thinking Self is also a key to your imagination and your emotional life. As you become aware of your thought processes and how your mind is always full, how you always have some kind of *inner occupation flitting rapidly as your consciousness shifts*, you begin to understand one aspect of your work on a role—for if you are creating a whole human being, you fill yourself with "character thoughts" triggered by the play's circumstances.

Your Emotional Self

Your second self, your Emotional Self, consists of your feelings. From childhood, your Emotional Self has responded to people and events in certain ways. You may have developed defenses you don't even know you have. You have probably spent a lot of time justifying your feelings or denying them, being ashamed of them or being embarrassed by them. You may have also learned to squelch many of these feelings—rage, hurt, grief, sorrow, ecstasy, joy, abandon, disgust, playfulness, etc.

Training as an actor, you access a wide range of feelings, even those that you have bottled up or hidden, those that you feel are abhorrent, foolish or shameful. In your work as an actor, you discover the richness of your emotional life and learn how to release it into more expressive and expansive choices. You need to sustain a healthy balance as you explore your emotional palate, cultivate a sense of humor about your own ways.

Your Functional Self – ACTIONS

Your third self is your Functional Self, your "doing" self. It is you—walking, running, jumping, hobbling, sitting, standing, scratching a mosquito bite, carrying your groceries, getting dressed, eating breakfast, making love, playing football, re-potting a plant, waiting for a train, scolding a pet, arguing with a friend, talking, singing, brushing your hair, entertaining company or watching a glorious sunset. It is you going through the actions of your daily routines as well as all the special activities of your life. You are often unaware of the many things you do and how you do them because your Thinking Self is so busy.

Peter. Where's your sense of humor?

James. I never had one. Ever.

It's Only a Play –Terrence McNally

The actions of your Functional Self are always influenced by where you are, what is at stake, what time it is, whom you are with, and what you want. That is to say, your doings are affected by the circumstances in which you find yourself.

Your Observing Self – *what you notice + can describe*

As you work and study, you will find yourself coming into touch with yet another self: your Observing Self.

It is a self that every actor, at first unconsciously and perhaps later consciously, cultivates as part of his or her trade. Mindfulness, or "awarenessing," is the work of your Observing Self.

Your Observing Self is able to describe everything. Your Observing Self focuses your attention. It can attend to and catch a fleeting thought and then recount that thought. It can detail a feeling. It can describe every move you make: how you make the move and the sensations that accompany that move. It can also objectively and subjectively describe people, places and things in as much detail as you wish.

The Observing Self does not have to be right or wrong; it does not have to take sides. It does not have to prove anything. It simply notices and describes—*without interpreting or qualifying*—what it picks up from eavesdropping on your Thinking, Emotional and Functional Selves.

It will take practice to learn how to describe what you notice and see—without judgment, without opinion, without commentary. It will take practice to be able to honor and accept what you see for what it is. Your Observing Self is a self you can and must nurture. Consciously using it will enrich your work and your life. The more you practice, the more your Observing Self becomes a finely tuned personal companion. After I had been studying for a while, I began to feel that I had a constant companion, a kind of "Jiminy Cricket" sitting on my shoulder, pointing out what I was doing at various times during the day.

> **Remember...**
>
> The center of the universe is a very crowded place.

The discoveries I started making about myself I found fascinating. In the middle of a heated argument with my husband, chatting on the phone with a friend, sitting quietly reading—I began to notice my behavior with great interest. It is no wonder I often had to read a sentence ten times or ask my husband to repeat what he just said—in such moments I was more intrigued with myself than I was with "the other."

Your Observing Self can help you to analyze, question, and rethink your opinions and judgments—which, if left unchallenged, can limit your vision and distort what you see. Your Observing Self will also be useful in learning how to embrace uncertainty and doubt—challenges which we all face throughout our development as artists—so that they do not paralyze you.

Your Observing Self will help you do all the things you desire as an actor: engage in the moment; see/feel clearly; touch/feel all the objects of life that surround you; taste and receive the different flavors and textures of everything that passes your lips; listen to and hear/feel the rich symphony of sounds that abound and smell all the scents that the air may carry, be they heavenly or putrid.

As you do your homework you will tap into your Observing Self and you will find yourself becoming more conscious, more aware, more alive to sensory stimuli—more *mindful*, if you will.

All of the four selves I have described are *you;* one never functions without the others. Yet your Thinking Self, your Emotional Self, and your Functional Self often behave like wayward children. The Observing Self is above and beyond the chatter and business of the other three selves. It sits in silent observation, almost outside of you, like a watchful god, or a lifeguard, or an eagle. You are most often unconscious of its presence, because your other selves are loud and preoccupy so much of your mind. Mindfulness, or "awarenessing," is the coming to be conscious of, and tapping into, your Observing Self.

> Helen. …when I lit the candles you were finally going to see all of me.
>
> *The Road to Mecca* —Athol Fugard

So, while you are busy living your "real" life—holding onto your agendas, always wanting to be right or to get it right, struggling to stay in control, trying to get somewhere—invite your Observing Self to join you, because, in the end, there is just hearing, touching, seeing, tasting, smelling, thinking—life itself.

Being truly *present* is to be alive, receptive and responsive to everything.

Rays of Light

When self-knowledge breaks through the shield many of us have created over the years, it can be at once painful and celebratory. Insight into the fact that I really don't know who I am comes very slowly through some very innocuous experiences. Here are some moments which sparked new glimmerings of self-awareness within me that have stayed with me throughout the years:

…It is 1960 and I am stationed in Maiduguri, Nigeria. Inspired by John F. Kennedy's visionary formation of the Peace Corps, my first husband and I apply and are accepted to Nigeria 1, where we train at Harvard and the University College in Ibadan. Extremely immature and naïve, our marriage is doomed from the day of our wedding. Something happens one night in Maiduguri that triggers a final confrontation between us in which I feel that we have to separate. We are in one of the walled gardens of our stucco house. It is 1 a.m. and the moon's rays illuminate the area as I walk from pole to pole…I don't remember one word that I said but I do remember my voice emanating from my whole body—it is a first. I experience powerful sensations that I don't understand but have never forgotten…

…I am getting ready to have a party in my apartment. A friend comes over to help clean and prep. As she begins doing things, I interrupt her with instruction in my way of sweeping, dusting, etc. Not aware of my tendency to give orders, she alerts me to my behavior by commenting, "Once I accepted that I was helping a tyrannical friend, I was fine…"

…I perceive myself as a very passive, quiet person—yet, I recall a relationship with a young man in which I remember walking down the streets of New York City screaming at the top of my lungs…

…It takes my husband's patient, constant reminders to make me aware of how much I grimace, walk around with the ends of my mouth curved downward. I have no idea that my students, thanks to my mask, always think that I am angry at them…

…It takes me years to realize that I unconsciously anticipate people's anger and am afraid of confrontation…

…Alice Spivak assigns me a scene and mentions that the role is on my center. It is the first time that I hear the expression. It sounds dramatic and I make it more so by wondering what my center is—I have no idea. I feel as if I have one hundred "me's" running around inside and wonder about this concept of one's center. Perhaps the character will teach me something about myself…

The journey of the actor is twofold. The journey into himself and the journey into the life of the character.

Show Up ★

Before moving forward let's review the simple non-negotiable facts that all great performers know about training. To explore and develop an approach that gives you a solid foundation when you are working professionally, you need to go to the extra lengths that this book asks of you; you need a means to make your way through the chaos of creativity; you need to know yourself and you need to collaborate.

Remember…

Without your work there will be no class.

Acting classes are not an end but a means. They are the playground, gym or battlefield where you practice. At the beginning of every semester, I ask those students new to acting if any of them play a musical instrument, sing, dance or play a sport. Some students raise their hands. I then ask how many excel at what they do. A few always lower their hands. They are able to assess their level of skill and have a concrete standard against which to measure their accomplishment.

Before the moment they enter class, some students assume that acting demands less expertise than other performing arts or sports; the current climate of Reality TV and YouTube instant celebrity fortifies this assumption. If you have made similar assumptions, let me assure you, here and now: becoming an actor requires *more*, much more.

You must practice, deliberately and with purpose. You must show up, even when you don't feel like it (and you won't always), even when you are discouraged (and you will be) and even when you think you can't act (and some days, perhaps, you can't).

When you do show up, your teachers and colleagues expect you to be present. When your body is in the room, you will learn how to make sure that you are, too.

Vivian. I can recall the time—the very hour of the very day—when I knew words would be my life's work.

Wit –Margaret Edson

You don't achieve performance proficiency or skill by simply wanting it or wishing for it. Think about the road to the Olympics for every athlete competing. Rarely, if ever, does artistry come in the form of immediate gratification or without cost to the artist.

Commit   ★

As you work with this book, you will get a sense of the long range commitment you have to make if you want to master the tools of your craft. You are preparing to meet the demands of a life in the theater. You empower yourself whenever you follow through on even the smallest commitment, especially when the going gets tough. Do the best you can. You will always derive the benefits of any commitment you make—to yourself, your partner, your class and, of course, the play.

Remember...

Only you can create passion and commitment within yourself.

Meeting Your Partner

Collaborate   ★

Imagine the number of people and the variety of personalities and temperaments you will encounter throughout your professional life as an actor. Every time you get a job onstage, in film or in television, you will be working with actors, directors, stage managers, producers, designers, technicians and many others whom you may not know.

Going from audition to audition, job to job, on a regular basis, you will need interpersonal skills in addition to acting ability.

In acting class you develop and practice these interpersonal skills. Scenes for class are usually two-person scenes because it is easier for two people to schedule rehearsals with each other. Preparing your scene for class is a collaborative journey with your partner. Actors each have their own way of working, even when they study with the same teacher. How do you deal with differences of approach, especially since you rehearse without a director guiding you and without a stage manager scheduling or recording your rehearsals?

Rehearsing for an acting class is a skill that you must acquire. Imagine that you and your partner are together in a rowboat, each of you controlling one oar. You have to adapt to each other's approach to rowing—and, you can do this without talking about it, by being aware of what your partner is doing, by accepting what he is doing and adjusting yourself to be in sync with him.

Respect the actors with whom you work and expect the same in return. Be vigilant and grateful when you work with actors who have been acting since before you were born. Be mindful of what you say to your fellow actors. Find ways to handle your personal feelings about them. Be professional: avoid gossip.

> **Remember…**
>
> A goal is not an end in and of itself. Just as a ship adjusts for wind and currents as it sails to its destination, so too must you navigate through tempests and windless seas.

Maintain your equilibrium. When other actors give you suggestions (and they will), learn to say, "Hmmm, that's something to think about." Or, "Thank you for that idea." And then get on with your rehearsal.

Learning how to rehearse without directing yourself or your partner takes time. It feels scary. But it is important that you free yourself of your normal need for reassurance and learn to trust your craft.

Know the work *you* have to do to achieve your goals for your scene—and do it. This is the best way to hold your own. It is also how you fulfill your responsibility in any rehearsal situation.

Meet in the Work ★

You will hear this expression again and again. It is a fabulous mantra. It simply means more doing, less talking. It means working off of one another. It means getting the scene on its feet and delving right into the material without talking about what you are going to do first. Let the idea of meeting in the work suffuse your approach to rehearsals. When you succeed, you will free yourself and clear the way to discover your partner and surprise yourself—and yes, experience some confusion. The following story illustrates how it works.

How Great Was That?

The masterful actor Victor Slezak is teaching a class. He tells a story to illustrate meeting in the work:

He is on location for a film and is scheduled to shoot a scene with Danny Glover, whom he looks forward to meeting. He wonders what that will be like and where the meeting will take place. Victor is asked to sit in the car that will be used for the scene while the lighting is set. All of a sudden, he sees a bum coming towards the car with a squeegee. Victor recognizes Danny Glover. He is about to introduce himself, but instead Glover begins cleaning the windshield. He talks to Victor with the lines from the scene. Victor realizes that, just like a musician, Glover expects him to follow his lead and join in. Victor does. They never say hello or break from what they are there to do. When it comes time to shoot, they are fully prepared. Only after they break from the scene do they say their hellos. Victor and Danny Glover have literally met in the work.

This story should give you an idea of what to aim for when you rehearse— *dive right in!*—and clarify the purpose behind the rehearsal tips that follow. The tips will save you a lot of time as you struggle to find your own way through your scene and will help you have a productive relationship with your partner.

Rehearsal Protocol: Tips for productive rehearsals

When preparing:

- Get your own copy of the same edition of the play as your partner as soon as you know your scene. If the play is in a foreign language, make sure you and your partner get the same translation.

- Be honest with yourself and your partner when discussing your schedule.

- Call or text your partner. Do not wait for him or her to call or text you. Expect a speedy response.

When rehearsing, DO:

- Restrict discussion. Too much talk wastes time and lulls you into a false sense of accomplishment. Work with whatever your partner is doing in rehearsal. Avoid talking about what you are *going* to do in rehearsal, and just *do it*.

- The exception is when physical contact is required in a scene. You must then discuss and respect each other's limits. Negotiate the physicality. Work together. Agree on what will happen and "mark" or map out the physical interaction before you play it fully.

- Treat your rehearsals for class as you would a paying job. Be ten minutes early to your rehearsals and turn off your cell phone before you begin. Apologize if you are late, but don't waste time explaining why.

- If the rehearsal is at your place, be at home and be ready.

- Have a minimum of four two-hour rehearsals before you bring a scene to class.

- When called for, violence must be choreographed. Seek assistance from a qualified Stage Combat professional. Indulging uncontrolled emotional impulse is *intolerable*.

- Let your partner do his or her own work to the best of his or her ability. Allow your partner to be wrong. Don't forget, your partner is in class, too.

- Be patient. Take each step as it comes.

- Schedule another rehearsal when you need or want one, and find the time.

When rehearsing, DON'T:

- Pantomime physical actions.

- Attempt to "block" the scene.

- Ask anyone—classmates, friends or family—to watch your rehearsal.

- Plan or set line-readings. Do not direct yourself.

- Tell your partner what to do, how to do something, how to say a line, where or when to move, etc. Don't direct your partner.

- Be late to rehearsal.

- Talk about your personal problems, or check your phone or text during rehearsal time.

- Use real alcoholic beverages, medications, drugs, weapons or dangerous objects of any kind in any scene EVER!

- Take advantage of your partner's vulnerability when physical contact is called for.

- Throw objects at your partner in the heat of some spontaneous emotion.

- Ask your partner what they think you should be doing or look to your partner for reassurance.

- Tell your partner how good he or she is.

- Discuss how you feel with each other.

- Call attention to something your partner did in rehearsal or class by saying, "I loved it when you did…". The minute you point out something specific to your partner, they will become self-conscious about that moment. They may not have realized what they were doing. By calling attention to the way they said a line or did something, you make them self-conscious of the moment. When they come to it again, they will wonder if they are still doing what you saw, etc.

When reflecting, DO:

- Keep a journal. Track your rehearsals and what you discover in each.

- Make personal notes regarding the sources of the sensations that might surface: thoughts of terror, panic, delight, doubt, sarcasm, excitement, cynicism, pride, etc.

- Be as honest with yourself as possible.

- Keep your personal insights to yourself.

Work with Integrity ★

Unprofessional behavior is not okay and you do not have to tolerate it. Although you will most often be able to get out of an uncomfortable situation in an acting class by dropping the scene, it is unlikely that you will quit a paid acting job even if you are working in a miserable environment with people who are unprofessional. As with any job, this can happen, and you will eventually develop the skills to determine how to navigate the situation and get on with the work.

Here are some situations you may encounter in your acting class:

- Your partner is late for rehearsals.

- Your partner comes to rehearsals unprepared.

- Your partner fails to keep appointments with you.

- Your partner does not return your phone calls, texts or emails promptly.

- Your partner makes excuses for all of these shortcomings.

- Your partner has strong opinions about the character you are playing and the choices you should be making, and does not keep these opinions to him or herself. Your partner tries to direct you or tell you how to say a line or where and when to move.

- Your partner spends rehearsal time talking about his or her personal life.

- Your partner is more experienced than you are and gets impatient with you.

- Your partner wants to rehearse over the phone.

- Your partner only wants to rehearse one time.

- Your partner does not want to use objects or work with a specific floor plan.

- Your partner's work is inconsistent.

- Your partner changes his or her actions so frequently that you can't establish a solid layout for your scene.

- Your partner paraphrases.

- Your partner doesn't learn his or her lines *exactly* as written and thinks that is okay.

- Your partner has an attitude, or is temperamental or moody.

- Your scene requires physical contact with your partner—kissing, being in bed together, or pretending to have sex. If a scene is sexual in nature, your partner may not respect your boundaries. Be sure to speak up and clearly state what is acceptable and what is not for you.

So often we focus on another's failings and *their* role in making a situation unpleasant, but we neglect to look at *our own* contribution to that same situation and work to negotiate mutually beneficial solutions. Some possible things to consider about yourself when conflicts arise are:

- You are the irresponsible party – any of the items on the prior list may apply to you. Too busy blaming, you may not have faced up to your own behavior.

- You are burdened with an attitude and feel entitled to it.

- You are directing yourself and do not realize it.

- You are trying to direct your partner since you believe you know what he or she should be doing.

- You are afraid of or intimidated by your partner.

- You are distracted by your own life situation and may not be fully committing yourself to the class.

- You may think you are working off of your partner, but you are not.

- You are one of many actors who are unrealistically and unproductively hard on themselves.

Discard Attitude and Judgment ★

In some cases, you may have naive expectations about the behavior of other people and find yourself being critical of your colleagues. I once heard an extraordinarily gifted actor criticized because he had demanded a designated on-set coffee runner. Criticism about this kind of thing usually comes from people who have never had the responsibility of carrying a play or film. They have no idea of the kind of pressure such actors are frequently under. Take a moment to consider which is more productive: watching a pro at work, or criticizing them?

Try not to be sidetracked by your negative judgments or adversarial relationships with other actors. If a situation arises, handle it with all the maturity you can muster.

Set your own boundaries for the behavior you will tolerate; depending upon the circumstances, you will probably discover that you can tolerate much more than you ever imagined. But when someone's behavior holds you back or crosses an extremely personal line, you must deal with the individual. Deal directly or seek channels through which you can handle the situation effectively and discreetly.

The **Me, Myself & I** pages that follow give you a chance to look back on your working relationships and also give you some ideas for empowering actions you can take as you continue your training.

Remember...

As you work with the **Me, Myself & I** pages, it's okay not to have answers for the questions or fill-in statements.

My Training History

Training involves attending to your whole instrument. Alexander Technique, Voice, Speech, and Movement classes are an essential part of your training. There is no acting class that will ever address the work you do in these other disciplines. Like acting classes, if you have only taken one class in these other areas, you are certainly not done. Your past experiences influence what you bring to the classes you are presently taking. Take some time to reflect on and write about your past training.

My Skill Level:

Acknowledge your strengths and weaknesses at this moment in time. Notice if you don't know what to say.

- List your strengths as an actor.

- List your weaknesses.

- What do you know you have to work on to improve your acting? Be as specific as possible.

Dierdre. But Andrew — you went to drama school.

Andrew. Only for two years.

Dierdre. But wasn't it wonderful? The great plays

— Ibsen, O'Neill —nothing under four hours. And

Shakespeare — didn't you love it?

Andrew. Sometimes. But I left.

I Hate Hamlet —Paul Rudnick

Staying in Tune

What do you do to stay in shape and *au courant?*

- When I'm not working, I _____ to stay in shape.

Actions I can take to stay in tune

Initiate at least one of the following ideas. Notice how you feel about yourself after you take one action.

- Make a list of roles you want to play and begin working on scenes from those plays in a class.

- As you audition or look for ways to create acting opportunities for yourself, form a support group to whom you are accountable.

- Research and identify theater companies that you could work for. Inquire if you can volunteer in any way, and then volunteer.

- Create a monthly play-reading group. Choose a play a month and assign roles.

- Read five new plays every month.

- Read the theater section of *The New York Times* every day.

- Get together with a friend who has a video camera. Take turns videotaping your monologues. Experiment, and afterwards, articulate what you see.

- Take a class or workshop in a new area: Mask, Clown, Singing, Tap, Shakespeare, etc.

- Develop a repertoire of ten monologues and be ready to use them at any audition.

- Find out how you can become a reader for auditions.

- Attend a playwriting class regularly for the chance to read new scripts on sight.

- Volunteer to usher for theater companies in your area.

> **Remember…**
>
> *Art* begins with *Craft* and there is no *Art* until *Craft* has been mastered.
>
> —Anthony Burgess

My Future

As you continue in the profession, you may discover that you have more to offer than you ever imagined. You might discover that you want to write, that you have leadership qualities or that you have talent in technical areas such as prop construction, puppetry, sound, video, costume design or stage management. Think about the other jobs that put you close to the creative process.

My Limits

Acting is a notoriously difficult profession. The actors in training programs or studying privately flood the job market and far exceed the amount of work available. One worries about the long haul and how to hang in against such incredible odds. The following may help you solidify your determination to be a working actor.

- I will pursue acting for _____ years. If I don't make it by then, I will

- I will/will not sacrifice my life style for my art because

Remember…

Success is different

for each occasion.

- I will/will not change my life style for my art because

My Class Goals and Achievements

It is a good idea to be conscious of your purpose for taking acting classes. Use the first question to state what expectations you have. Use the second question to set goals for the classes you are currently taking. If this is your first acting class, write what you expect from the teacher, from yourself and from the class itself.

- Every time you sign up for a class, think about your aims and current attitude regarding your work and yourself. How long does your class last? A weekend? Six days? Five weeks? Three months? How many times will you be able to work in your class? Articulate the way you want to be during this period: open, relaxed, curious, enthusiastic, willing to risk more, willing to work, reliable, flexible, courteous, honest, daring, etc. State the particular reason you are taking this particular class.

- Write your aims. Be as specific as possible. Look at what you have written. Then check to see if you can accomplish those goals within the specific time frame of your class or workshop. Write your goals again. Consider your own life circumstances and continue writing until you have aims which are specific and feel doable and which will be recognizable when you have achieved them.

> **Remember…**
>
> The acting class is not a place where you are validated as an actor. If that is why you are taking the class, you will miss the entire point of the class!

- How do you want your teacher to be with you?
  ☑ tough ☐ positive ☐ nurturing ☐ strict
  ☐ respectful ☑ honest ☐ gentle
  ☑ other _give advice on how to be better in every class_

- What's your agenda for being in the class or workshop? Do you think you have a hidden agenda for your class or workshop?

  play new roles and learn how to be a better actor in every role/class

Motivation and Commitment

Consider your reasons for acting. You may not know why you want to act. You may know exactly why you do. Why you want to act influences how you approach the acting classes you take. Begin with these questions. Above all, be honest! Tell the truth! Keep the question alive; do not settle for your first few answers.

- Why do you want to act?

- Why do you really want to act?

- Really, why do you want to act?

Your Insecurities

Even though you know how much you want to act, you may be hesitant about giving yourself over to the work as fully as you can. Name your doubts. We all have doubts about ourselves. For a few moments, reflect on these questions.

- If an acting teacher you respected told you that you shouldn't go into the acting profession, what would you do?

- What obstacles do you face because of your desire to act professionally?

  - *age – 65*
  - *TIME – YEARS*
  - *BLinking on camera*
  - *living in NY (fewer theater roles)*
  - *not sure to start own company*

- Name the actors who inspire you. How do their accomplishments motivate you to further your creative exploration? *– age*

  Meryl Streep
  Glenn Close
  Helen Mirren
  Cherry Jones
  Judy Dench

Angela. So you want to be an actor. Why do you want to be an actor?

David. I …It's exciting …it's … everybody watches you …You're doing something and everybody watches you …

Angela. That's a very good reason!

Enter Laughing –Carl Reiner

Reflection upon Completion

Review the overall experience of each class you take. Assess your accomplishments at the end of a course, class, or workshop.

Recommend yourself

- Role-play #1: At the end of a course, pretend that you are the instructor and enlist a friend to play you. Have a conversation where you speak as the teacher about your participation in the course.

- Role-play #2: You have auditioned for a director who is considering casting you in a major role. He does not know a lot about you or your work but he knows that you have studied with a teacher he knows. He calls your instructor to find out what he/she thinks about you and your work. Make notes about what you want the director to know: specifics and details are essential. Find a fellow actor to play the part of the director, you be the instructor. Have that conversation.

Review the journey from beginning to end: When you joined your class or workshop, you began with expectations and encountered unforeseen situations. Track the situations you faced to see how well you did in navigating your way through the class.

- List problems you had choosing a scene.

- What questions arose during your rehearsals? List your questions.

- What didn't you understand about the scene? The play? The character?

- What did you want to say to your partner and felt that you couldn't?

Reflection Upon Completion (Cont.)

- What did you say to your partner that you wish you hadn't?

- What was the most fun thing you did during your rehearsals?

- What did you love about the play you worked on?

- Did you have an underlying objective for taking this class?

- Write about the suggestions you received from your teacher. Were they clear? Contradictory? Confusing? How did you handle the suggestions?

- What was the most frightening thing about being in the class? Most exhilarating? Most inhibiting? Most challenging? Most fun? Worst? Best?

Realities and Excuses

You may have many responsibilities making demands on your time and energy. As I have pointed out numerous times, acting training and the pursuit of a professional career requires a huge commitment. It will be helpful for you to reflect on what life circumstances you have to juggle in order to function optimally in your acting classes and career.

Life distractions — responsibilities

Check those items that apply to you.

I have a hard time committing 100% because:

☐ I have to support myself and pay for basic necessities such as rent, phone, and transportation.

☐ I have other interests.

☐ I am auditioning.

☐ I have a family to support.

☐ I am responsible for caring for an ill relative or friend.

☐ I have a full time class schedule as a college student.

☐ I am depressed.

☐ I have ADD.

☐ Other _____.

Remember...

Learning is a process.

Living is a process.

Creating is a process.

Theater is all process. The process is messy, individual, collaborative, fun, painful, glorious and demanding.

Process produces angst, insecurity, surprise, joy and wonder. Process requires descipline, down time, curiousity, risk, and improvisation.

Realities and Excuses (Cont.)

Psychological baggage that holds you back from making a total commitment

Check those items that strike a chord in your own experience.

I don't make a total commitment because:

☐ My parents think acting should be an avocation.

☐ My father thinks I am wasting my time.

☐ My father thinks I am too old to begin acting professionally.

☐ My mother constantly says that my sister is the actress in the family.

☐ Everyone in my family is a doctor.

☐ My parents are famous actors.

☐ I am pulled in other directions by things I want to do, like

_____.

☐ I don't feel beautiful/thin/tall/handsome/young/good enough.

☐ I think I am stupid if I don't have an answer to a question.

☐ I don't believe people when they praise my work.

☐ I am afraid that I won't "make it" as an actor.

☐ I think I am too old to start acting.

☐ Other _____.

Remember...

Training prepares you but it doesn't ensure success.

Perspective

It might help you to reflect on the following questions at some time in your life. Some thoughts are like heavy weights that drag you down. How you answer these questions may lighten your load. Your answers can free up energy that you can then channel into your work.

- What is the difference between a good actor and a great actor?

- Define success for yourself.

- You feel that you might be able to grow and learn more quickly than you have been. What would make it possible for you to progress faster?

- Is there a difference between achieving celebrity and achieving skill?

My Track Record: Working with Others

Complete these sentences while thinking of your work habits and interactions with your fellow actors. They will give you an indication of how you take responsibility for yourself and how you respect others. Being late and unprepared can get you fired. Not returning phone calls or texts immediately can lose you a job.

- I return phone calls and texts ___✓_____.

- It's not important to _____.

- I expect my partner to ____*retun texts*_____.

- I am really good at ___*dexting, trying to learn lines, rehearsing*___

- I pride myself on ___*method acting*_____.

- My biggest problem is _____*learning lines*_____.

- The last time I told my scene partner how I felt, _____*hard to do reheat from Moscow*_____

- The next time my partner _____, I am going to _____. If that doesn't work, I will _____. But if I do that, I'm afraid _____.

- I want to learn how to ___*be a better actor, be more "natural"*___
  talk less obut
  how "good"
  others are

- I wish I could stand up for _____ instead of _____.

- When I have a problem with someone, I usually _____.

- _____ is/was the most difficult person I ever worked with because _____.

- _____ is/was the best person I ever worked with because _____.

- I will do whatever I can to accommodate my partner if _____.

My Track Record (Cont.)

Rehearsal experiences

Take some time to reflect on some of your past rehearsal experiences.

- Describe your best rehearsal experience. What happened to make it so?

- Describe your worst rehearsal experience. What happened to make it so?

Former colleagues

Review and reflect on your past experiences with other actors before moving forward.

Past scene partners

Use these questions to stir your memory of people you have worked with in class.

- Write about one past scene partner you had, and an experience you shared in or outside of rehearsal. What was the experience? How do you remember it? Is there any one thing that you associate with the experience?

- Was your working relationship satisfactory? If so, why?

- Was your working relationship unsatisfactory? If so, why?

- If you had it to do over again, would you do anything differently? What?

Work experiences

Reflect on some of your past work experiences. Some may be pleasant memories, some may be unresolved, and some still rankle.

- Were you ever fired? What happened?

  yes - Kemper
  yes - Holly Craft Museum

- Write about an unresolved work experience. What was your role in making the experience what it was? What could you do now that would give you some resolution?

  long term - w Kemper - look for another job
  Holly → not leave CHNDM

- How many bridges have you burned as you move forward?

  too many

- Write about a great work experience. What made it so? What was your part in creating that experience?

  early years at CHNDM curating and not pissing off Paul

- Write about actors, directors or writers with whom you have developed life-long friendships. How did those relationships begin?

Being pro-active

There are many empowering actions you can take on your own behalf. Here are just a few.

- List actors in your class with whom you want to work. Approach one of your colleagues and invite him or her to work on a scene that would serve you both.

- List actors and directors with whom you would love to work. See as much of their work as you can.

- With your next scene, determine how you will be when you work with your partner.

- Begin to work on a major role. Do as many scenes from the play as possible.

- Read biographies of actors, directors and writers you admire.

My Track Record (Cont.)

- Interview an actor you admire. Research them to prepare for your interview. What questions will you ask them about their work, their lives, their journey?

- Consult actors who are further along to get advice about networking.

- Gain a reputation as someone who is easy to work with.

- Initiate a project with friends.

- Create a one-person show.

Remember…

We are all visitors to this time, this place we
are just passing through. Our purpose here
is to observe, to learn, to grow, to love …
and then we return home.
—Australian Aboriginal Proverb

Communicate Honestly: Your Scene Partner's Vitals

PLAY: _____

ROLE: _____

DATE: _____

You need to communicate clearly with many people throughout your professional life. Start practicing with your scene partners. Learn their full names. Work with their schedules. Exchange the following information with your partner. You need it to plan your rehearsal schedule. Do this as soon as you know that you will be working together.

- My full name is _____. Here is my cellphone number and email. I can rehearse on _____. I like to have _____ rehearsals before taking my scene to class.

- What is your full name? How do you spell your name? How do you pronounce it?

- What is your work schedule? When are you free to rehearse?

- How often do you like to rehearse before you put a scene up in class?

- What is your home phone number? Work number? Cell number? Email address?

- When is a good time to call you? How early or how late can I call you?

- Do you have space for rehearsal? Will you rehearse at my place? Are you willing to rent rehearsal space?

- Where do you live? What is your address?

- Do you have any pets? Are you allergic to animals?

- When can you get a copy of the script?

- Let's schedule our first rehearsal.

Remember...

There is no perfect way to be, but generous is good.

Frequently Used Words and Phrases:

Their Meaning, Their Usefulness, and Their Power

PLAY: _____

ROLE: _____

DATE: _____

Here are *technical* words we use and hear often. Define them – first without, and then with, a dictionary. Please know that words can be dangerous and using them mindlessly will put you into your head—many of these concepts need to be experienced viscerally and practiced in action before you truly grasp their meaning. Assume that you don't know what they really mean.

Action (Verbal, Physical, Psychological)
Adjustment
Alive
As if
Beat
Behavior
Character
Character action
Circumstances
Conditioning forces
Daydreaming
Destination
Emotional life
Emotional state of being
Endowment
Environment
Event
Expectation
Forward-moving life
Fourth wall/Fourth side
Future
Given circumstances
Happening
Hear/Feel
Imagination
Immediate preceding circumstances
Inner objects
Intention
Knee-jerk
Layout

Life drive
Listen
Meaningful
Moment to moment
Need
Objective
Object
Obstacle
Particularize
Past
Physical life
Physical state of being
Place
Preceding circumstance
Preparation
Present
Receiving
Relationship
Remembered behavior
Score
Secondary life
See/feel
Sending
Sensory life
Situation
Speculation
Spine
Stake
Story /Plot
Subjectivity
Substitution

Surroundings
Theme
⊙ Through line
Time
Transference
Trigger
Truthful behavior
Urgency

Verbal life
⊙ Verbal will
Want
Who am I?
Wish
You, the actor
"You", the character

Words only have genuine meaning when connected to experience. You may know what a word means intellectually and understand the concept on a mental level—but without practically applying the concept and living through its consequences, you lack the body knowledge necessary to truly encompass an understanding of the word. Only through your body will meaning be enriched.

You have already experienced many of these concepts unknowingly in your life. Knowing how to use them in your work takes time and practice. Live in the continued search for deeper experiential meaning. Understanding and knowing only occur with repeated experience.

Common Mistakes

PLAY: _____

ROLE: _____

DATE: _____

In order to distinguish between effective and ineffective work, and to identify places where and reasons why you derail in your work, you will often hear teachers using the following terms. These usually result from an actor's tension or misplaced intentions. Check the terms if your teacher uses them. Then define them. Be specific about the parts of your scene where they were applied:

Anticipating	Pushing
End-gaming	Remembered behavior
Indicating	Second-guess yourself
Illustrating	Showing
Lacks privacy	Talk yourself out of
Lacks spontaneity	Unimaginative
Line driven	Working for an image
Muscling	Working for a result
No preparation	You were not ready to begin
Over-the-top	

If you hear these terms and interpret them as implying that your acting is horrid, you will be in trouble. It is not the end of the world. You need to learn what these terms mean to you in relation to your work. However, don't spend your energy trying to avoid your mistakes, even unconsciously. If you do, avoidance becomes your objective. It takes you out of commission and can reduce you to playing one note or swallowing your words. Instead, continue to make choices and commit to them. Don't second-guess yourself. At some point you may be able to identify and rectify what you do that provokes some of these critiques.

Remember...

A mistake is a creative opportunity.

—Joe Hart

Charting Your Rehearsals

PLAY: _____

ROLE: _____

DATE: _____

The Work

Use this calendar to keep track of your rehearsals and to stay conscious of how much time you have before presenting your scene, your first preview or your opening night.

Your internal clock will help you to pace yourself and keep yourself focused on your work.

Tip: Work backward from your performance date, your presentation date or the day you will do your scene in class. When you are in a class, plan for reworking your scene as well.

Remember…

Practice,

Patience,

Persistence!

Monday	Tuesday	Wednesday	Thursday	Friday	Saturday	Sunday

My Critique Checklist

PLAY: _____

ROLE: _____

DATE: _____

What notes did you receive? What did you accomplish in your scene? What areas can you continue developing?

☐ Place and physical destination

☐ Preparation leading into the first moment of your scene

☐ Your entrance

☐ Your first actions

☐ Relationship

☐ Specifics of time and place

☐ Your scene is line-driven.

☐ You need to work off of your partner and let them affect you.

☐ You are talking too fast. You are not playing your action fully.

☐ Raise your stakes.

☐ Everything is too easy.

☐ Increase your need.

☐ Send with expectation.

☐ You are on the right track.

☐ Strengthen your point of view.

☐ Strengthen your verbal will. I can't hear you.

☐ Particularize.

Remember…

A genuine technique is

not prescriptive.

Chapter 3

Time, Place and Stuff

"What Woods?"

I am playing Hermia in a production of *A Midsummer Night's Dream*. I diligently apply what I am learning in my acting class to my homework for the play. I have been taught the importance of specifying for myself the place and time within which each scene is set. I think I have done my work on place for Acts II – IV: my scenes take place in the woods, of course!

This particular day, I am walking down Fifth Avenue and I am lost in thought about my upcoming rehearsal. No matter what I do while rehearsing these scenes, I have no faith in where I am or what surrounds me.

Standing on the corner of 57th Street waiting for the light to change, I suddenly and quite loudly blurt out, "What woods?"

No one pays any attention to me.

It has occurred to me at this moment that I really haven't done my homework at all. I have not been specific enough about where these scenes take place. I have not selected a place that I know well—

> somewhere familiar that can provide woodland details to ground me in the scene.
>
> It immediately dawns on me that I have a familiar place in my past that I can use to furnish the details I need. Close friends have a cottage on a lake in the woods in the Pine Barrens of New Jersey. As a youngster I would go berry picking, play hide and seek at night and go on chilling snipe hunts with the neighborhood kids. I know what the brush is like and what it feels like crawling around on the uneven, sandy, twig-and-leaf-laden ground. I know what the air smells like. I know the eerie sounds of the leaves rustling when the wind blows through the pine and oak trees. I know the nocturnal creatures' strange noises that come from indistinguishable locations and feel fearfully close.
>
> I don't speak about my discovery with anyone when I get to rehearsal, but I begin to experiment with specifics—and my faith in the experience of being lost in the forest grows. My sensory connection to the woods at the lake puts me into my body. I am able to clearly imagine myself wandering alone through the dark, overgrown forest. I am now able to physically support what is happening in my scenes verbally and emotionally. I am present, open and alive!

Place and *time* are the most necessary elements upon which you build the work that is to follow; *they are the means through which you find your way into your body.* The actor's goals are simple: to walk and talk like a human being. It's easy to walk like a person when you know *where you are* and *why you are moving.* It's easy to talk like a person when you are really *in your body*: "…voice and speech, the soul and the mind, are not separate from the body but originate from it, emanate through it"[5] (Uta Hagen, *A Challenge for the Actor*). This chapter will guide you through the process of establishing environments in which you can be sensorially alive when you step into your character's shoes.

Read for Time and Place ★

Time and *place* are gateways into the world of your play. Through them you enter the realms of history, geography, science, music, literature, art, politics, social systems, religion and business as they exist within the play's world. As you recognize the importance of place and time in your process, you will understand why theater can lay claim to being the great liberal art that it is.

When you read your play for the fourth time, focus on the *time* and *setting*. Does the play take place in one location or many? In what country, state or province, city, locale, building and room does your scene occur? Does it take place outdoors? Does the story unfold over weeks, years or a single day? During what century, year, season and time of day does your scene take place? Does your assigned scene begin the play, end it or sync with the exact moment that ended the first act or scene?

Time

Time rules your life more than anything else, and you and I squander it as if we will live forever.

At any given moment in your life, you are remembering the moment before and speculating on the moments to come. It is impossible to capture, frame, or hold *any* moment. Like the ticking clock, your life is always moving in one direction: forward.

Onstage, you are always in the immediate present. Each present has its own momentum.

As you enter the world created by the playwright and director, the "given" element of time—that is, the information provided in the text regarding the time in which the play takes place—will guide your research and determine much of the following:

What you wear
Your hairstyle
The kind of music you listen to
How you express yourself
Your vocabulary
The books you read
The society and current trends of the period in which you live
Courtship
The dances you do
Current affairs
Your age and your background
Your status
The weather
Elements such as hot, cold, dark, quiet, stuffy, bright, etc.
Your emotional state of being
Your physical state of being
Your relationships

Anne Boleyn in Miami Beach

It is the fall of 1954. I am a junior in high school and doing anything and everything I can to be involved in theater. I learn that Sam Hirsch,[6] a professor at the University of Miami, is establishing a professional summer theater at one of the hotels on Miami Beach. I beg my father, who is pediatrician to Hirsch's two children, to ask him if I can be a part of the venture.

So begins my summer of privilege—mending costumes, ushering, getting coffee for the actors, and watching all the rehearsals!

One of the productions this summer is *Anne of a Thousand Days*, by Maxwell Anderson. It is the story of Henry VIII and Anne Boleyn, the mother of Elizabeth I.

The leading lady playing Anne is dramatic and passionate. To my young self, she is a great actress.

Both leads have soliloquies that are performed behind two upstage flats with oval cutouts painted as antique frames. The actors climb the ladders behind the flats, where, romantically and nostalgically lit by a spotlight, they cipher the past and future…

Many years later, having found my way to Alice Spivak's class, I decide to perform Anne's soliloquy in class.

Once I have performed my piece, Alice asks, "Where are 'you'?"

I reply, "On a ladder behind a flat with a spotlight on me."

She patiently suggests that I apply what I am learning in class—create a room in the Tower of London and deal with the sensory realities of "my" daily life under the circumstances. (I had, in fact, recently been to London and had gone to the Tower! Yet it hadn't occurred to me to re-connect with the experience I had of going through the building—being chilled to the bone, the stone walls, the size of the cells, the dimly lit, narrow, winding stairs, etc.)

Alice's critique puts me on track. I begin the work I really have to do on the piece. That work begins with time and place.

I create an environment with objects that stimulate my historical imagination: A wooden bowl of gruel, a tin tray, a spoon, pen and inkwell, writing paper, a straw-filled pallet, muslin sheets… I buy a rehearsal skirt and find a pair of shoes that ground me. I practice carrying out everyday actions with these objects replicated from my research, and I gain faith in "my" life in the tower. My research and the steps I take in rehearsal lead me to find my own identification with Anne Boleyn.

Once I began my research into the world of Anne Boleyn and started taking into account the time during which she lived, I was able to imagine the conditions fueled by time of day, month and year that affected her life and surroundings. Time influences the lighting and air quality of your space. It may be dark, shadowy, bright and airy, musty, soggy, dirty, rancid, crisp, fresh, invigorating or thick and heavy. It may be noisy, quiet or dead still. Most often you respond without thinking to scents, odors, sounds, sights, tastes, sensations on your skin and other elements in your environment. These are fleeting sensations almost immediately forgotten unless the extent of the sensation is pervasive and ongoing. In *A Challenge for the Actor* (pages 175–182) Uta Hagen provides wonderful examples of the conditions we often have to create to fulfill the given circumstances of the play. Practice these often. Experiment to find how you recreate physical sensations truthfully, without illustrating or indicating the condition. A rich understanding of the historic moment in time during which your play takes place will help you to create a visceral reality for yourself to respond to.

Not only does my story illustrate the importance of researching the time and place in which your scene is set, it also alerts you to the temptation of imitation and how it prevents you from finding your own way into the world of the play. Be aware that if you have seen a performance of a play, film, or a scene in class, it will influence you. In such circumstances, it is especially useful to find your own way into the play through research into time and place.

Place

The playwright has chosen each location where your character interacts for a specific reason. I recently found notes on the setting of scenes we studied in a class I taught. One scene from *The Melville Boys* by Norman Foster is set in the main character's aunt's Canadian cottage—a peaceful place full of childhood memories of fishing, boating and camping out in the woods. *Crimes of the Heart* by Beth Henley is set in the kitchen of the old family home in Hazelhurst, Mississippi, a small southern town that represents safety, love and loyalty. *Brilliant Traces* by Cindy Lou Johnson takes place in a spare cabin in the Alaskan wilderness, a hideaway refuge serving as an escape from the world and its unbearably painful memories. One setting in *A Taste of Honey* by Shelagh Delaney is a rented apartment representing independence and resourcefulness—a first home.

> **Eloise**. Isabella used to keep things so organized. Now...
> **Andrea**. It doesn't matter.
> **Eloise**. It's very dusty in here. Everything's just gone to pieces.
> *The Years* –Cindy Lou Johnson

Indoors or outdoors, your surroundings affect you psychologically and physically whether you want them to or not. Many are repositories of personal history.

Some surroundings make you feel on edge, in awe, insecure, powerful, comfortable, cozy, sad or burdened. Memories are triggered by small things—a wall color, rug design, curtain or sofa fabric, the provenance or condition of a piece of furniture, an odor or scent in the air or the light in the space. Absorbed as you are in whatever is going on in your life, you may not even be aware of the split-second thought, emotion or behavior a space prompts.

The Perils of Placelessness

An attractive, vivacious young student of mine is presenting her scene in class for the first time. She is naturally graceful and carries herself with ease.

The moment she begins her scene, her whole persona changes. Self-conscious, her body loses its natural vitality. Her nerves numb her. Every time she speaks her lines, her feet scuff along the floor as she shuffles towards her partner or takes a few mincing, insecure steps to nowhere in particular. In her head, thinking about her next lines, her body is just tagging along.

Their scene is set in an art gallery, and with my critique I suggest that my student and her partner visit one to do some hands on research. They do.

Based on their research, they set up a more complete layout for the rework of their scene. Both actresses know where they are. They know the name and location of the gallery, the artists whose work is being shown, how they were greeted when they arrived. They know where the street entrance is, where the bathrooms are; my student knows the route she has taken to get into the section of the gallery in which the scene takes place. They pinpoint where the paintings are hanging, where pieces of sculpture are placed. They include a bench in their layout.

Grounded with a clear sense of place, my student experiences being "in her body" and has genuine *physical destination* onstage—oh, what a difference!

The term *physical destination* comes from the exercise of the same name in Uta Hagen's *A Challenge for the Actor*. The term "physical destination" is used for discussing your physical life. Every move you make is a destination and is determined by where things are located in each place you find yourself. You can move with ease and confidence when you know exactly where you are and what surrounds you in your scene, freeing you to play.

My student began with a general idea of where her scene took place. Her inadequate preparation left her without an environment in which she could rehearse freely and function like a human being. In class, her breathing affected, it was impossible for her to truthfully engage with her partner or the *given circumstances* of her scene. *Given circumstances* (see *A Challenge for the Actor*, pages 260–262) refers to the information provided by the playwright regarding the events that take place and the conditions within which the play takes place (the time of day, the location, etc.).

Ned. This is perfect for our new offices. The room upstairs is just as big. And it's cheap.

Bruce. How come do you think?.

Ned. Didn't Tommy tell you? After he found it, he ran into the owner in a gay bar who confessed, after a few beers, his best friend is sick.

The Normal Heart –Larry Kramer

As she found her sensory connection to the place (seeing what surrounded her; hearing the ambient sounds; feeling the air conditioning on her skin, etc.), the consequences of being in a particular place at a specific time *put her into her body*. She was then able to physically support the verbal and emotional aspects of the scene.

Circumstances affect your life daily. Learn to sensitize yourself to these elements and use your imagination as you make them specific through your rehearsal process. Being alive, present, and ready is to actually *be* where you are. No matter what is on your mind or what you are doing, you are always taking in your surroundings, if only subliminally. In order to be grounded, you must have a clear and vivid sense of your surroundings—a world to take in, relate to and react to.

Build Your Rehearsal Environment   ★

As the story so clearly illustrates, creating a physical layout for your scene is one of the first things you must handle in your rehearsal process. When you are in an acting class, you provide the elements of place for your scenes. You are set designer, prop master, costumer and stage manager. Consistently working with place in class preps you for being on the job. The choices that you and your partner make creating a sense of place will determine the quality of your rehearsals and the kind of work you will be able to do.

When you are creating the environment for your scene, remember: in the course of your life, you are *always* somewhere—and that somewhere is *always* specific, absolute and sensorial.

Scout out locations to get concrete ideas for the layout of your scene when the playwright simply states "a bar", "an art gallery" or "a food court." Begin researching place as soon as you can. Knowing where you are and all the specifics that surround you provides the roots for your physical, psychological and verbal life.

As the next story illustrates, you will often wish you could fly to the country, city or town where your play takes place or to places mentioned in your play. This desire is a sign that your body is responding to your play and that it craves the sensory riches of place and time to further feed your imagination. At heart is the pull of your artistry and the way you honor the depth and nobility of your calling. Treasure those instances when you can make such trips.

Remember…

When learning your craft, you hear many new words that will become a part of your vocabulary. As you study and perform, your experiences add meaning to those words …Only through your experience do the words become yours.

Bessie. A son of Mars wouldn't blow his nose on this place.

A Perfect Analysis Given by a Parrot
—Tennessee Williams

The Miracle Worker

I happily study with the brilliant Alice Spivak for two years and then re-audition for Miss Hagen, who accepts me into her class. After I have been studying with Miss Hagen for a year, I land the role of Anne Sullivan in *The Miracle Worker* by William Gibson for a Summer Stock company in Woodstock, Vermont.

My classes have set an artistic standard toward which I strive. My all-consuming passion for and commitment to the work drives me. Before rehearsals begin, I know I must go to the famous Perkins School for the Blind where Annie received her education. Upon graduation, she was hired to teach young, deaf and blind Helen Keller.

On a day off, I buy a round-trip bus ticket to Watertown, Massachusetts and spend a wonderful day at the school, talking to teachers, walking the halls, soaking it all in and romantically imagining what "my" life must have been like while I was there. (It was, truth be told, anything but romantic.) That day I learn how one speaks to a deaf/blind person.

> Along with every actress who ever had the good fortune of playing the part of Anne Sullivan, I had already learned the American Sign Language alphabet. With my attention only on serving the play, it has not occurred to me that I am driven by my innocent sense of responsibility to telling Miss Sullivan's story. It is a state of grace.

Stuff

Life is messy. Some people are tidier than others, but life is messy—and if your life is anything like mine, you probably have plenty of stuff to accompany life's complexity. Wherever you are, objects surround you. Therefore, as you incorporate a study of *place* into your practice, you must consider the significance that material objects have in life as well.

Who you are, where and when you were brought up, how much money you have, what your profession is, what you do, or what you want to do—all these factors determine the kind of stuff you have around you, how you treat it, and what you do with it.

Solomon. This stuff is from another world.

The Price —Arthur Miller

Wherever you go, objects abound. Throughout the course of your life, you will come into contact with millions of things. Using your personal experiences with the objects in your life, begin raising your awareness of how and why they affect you.

Objects have been an important part of life since man began to roam the earth. Visit any museum to witness the magnitude of this statement. Objects, therefore, are crucial materials for actors to work with in the mastery of their craft.

Remember…

You place great importance on possessions. They represent self-worth, accomplishment and connection.

Gather Your Stuff ★

It is exciting to begin rehearsing on your feet when you have all the objects you can think of set up in your new place. Scour the text for suggestions of objects and furniture you could have for your scene. In order to create as complete an environment as possible, I recommend that you gather all of the objects that you think might be useful.

When you are searching for these objects, remember that they are not set decoration! They are part of your new *life*. The next time you go to the theater or watch a movie, pay attention to the detail of the set. Even before the show begins, what do you learn about the people who live there? Often the place is another character in the play.

By selecting and placing objects in your created environment and knowing where they are and how they got there, you seed the conditions for stimulating rehearsals in which you really explore your scene. While you actively discover what brings your scene to life by rehearsing with specific and relevant objects, you build your faith in the designated location for your scene: the social worker's office, the professor's living room, the restaurant or the baseball field. With a clear sense of place and a believable environment decked out with all the stuff you want for your scene, you can really make strong physical choices and don't have to "think" about place. As you rehearse you will live in the space and become as used to it as you are to your own home.

It is easy and logical to set up an environment even though it can be labor-intensive. Too many actors skip this phase of preparing for rehearsal or think of it as incidental or something to address later in their process. It is certainly the work most actors avoid—some even use the expression "props are crutches" to get out of doing this work.

There is no question that it is easier to sit or stand in one place, wave your hands around, point your finger a lot and say lines to your fellow actors. It is easier to never handle an object. It is easier to pace in a general fashion or move in ways that convey general emotion than it is to find specific human behavior that is a consequence of what is happening in the scene. It is easier—but it is also tedious and boring to watch.

Endow Objects ★

With Sensory Qualities

With Value: Emotional and Monetary

When you "endow" something, you invest it with a quality, trait or property that it does *not* inherently possess. You handle or relate to the object *as if it has* that property or quality. Endowing engages your imagination and sense memory, and by having faith in your choices you release spontaneous physical and emotional behavior. Refer to *A Challenge for the Actor* (pages 170–188) and *Training the American Actor* (pages 149–151) for exercises to sharpen your reflexive behavior when endowing objects.

In the world of make believe, it is obvious why you have to master this technique. You will have to handle all types of objects onstage. Some will be potentially dangerous to you, the actor. Others will hold special personal meaning to "you," the character.

Remember…

"When loved ones die, you have to live on in their behalf. See things as though with their eyes. Remember how they used to say things, and use those words oneself. Be thankful that you can do things that they cannot, and also feel the sadness of it. This is how I live without Pelagia's mother. I have no interest in flowers, but for her I will look at a rock-rose or a lily. For her I eat aubergines, because she loved them. For your boys you should make music and enjoy yourself, doing it for them."

Captain Corelli's Mandolin –Louis de Bernieres

Remember…

You have been responding to objects all your life. Trust your reflexive muscle memory and your imagination as you identify the specific triggers for your behavior. You will play with ease the more you practice.

Be vigilant when working with potentially dangerous objects. Take no chances. Some objects that are seemingly innocent could bring your scene to a premature end if you do not plan ahead. There is always the chance that a fully functional object will control you rather than you control it. Use your common sense.

You are called on to do many things in plays that you *would be insane* to do for real. You won't want to actually burn your arm with a hot iron, sniff cocaine, drink five shots of vodka, strangle your wife, cut yourself, or set cognac on fire in a chafing dish. You won't want to really sprain your ankle, spill red wine on your pants or throw up onstage.

Therefore, when the action of the play calls upon you to burn your arm with an iron, you *endow* the iron with scalding heat. When called upon to drink five shots of vodka, you *endow* five shots of water with the qualities of an alcoholic beverage—handling and consuming them *as if* they taste and affect you like hard liquor.

Endowing objects also involves investing them with value and special personal meaning. You must do this with every object that surrounds you in your scene, including the clothing you wear. Use your imagination to create stories about the objects in your scene that will affect the way you treat and handle them. Add an emotional component to some. You will be personalizing the stuff that surrounds you and sensitizing yourself emotionally.

No matter when and where you are, you will be surrounded by the stuff of life—artifacts, personal possessions, treasures or everyday, occupational tools, detritus. Raise your awareness to all of the tangible things in your life. All objects have a story. Some are "hot objects"—those which are loaded with more meaning, power, and resonance than others.

Boo. I really love this punch.

Alice. Good.

Boo. I would like to get in the bowl and go for a swim.

Blue Window —Craig Lucas

Henry Harry. And for her these things were precious. Even their little shoes were precious. I was constantly finding these little doll shoes all over the house and saving them for her, and she would be so happy to see that long lost shoe and put it on her little doll's foot.

Brilliant Traces —Cindy Lou Johnson

Remember...

Actors know the difference between the Real World and the Pretend World of the stage, film and TV better than the average person

---

Jackie. I mean, it may sound stupid to you, but that was our special place, that pie place bro, and there was a fuckin' —I'm serious— there was a sanctity to when we used to go there, you don't know, it was like, 'When it's pie, don't lie' —and she just lied the fuck all over it!

The Motherfucker with the Hat

—Stephen Adly Guirgis

The Swizzle Stick

I am teaching my very first "professional" acting class in a space called Stage 9 on Houston Street in New York City.

A young man named Robert Leibowitz is one of three students in this first class. He follows me to the HB Studio when I begin to teach there one year later. As many students do, he stays in touch even after he has stopped studying with me. At one of our "catch-up" meetings, he tells me that he has been in the hospital several times since we last met and that he has recently had open-heart surgery. He is only in his late twenties.

A year or so later, he calls me from the hospital and I visit him the next day. I assiduously avoid talking about his health. Our conversation isn't about anything important. We speak briefly about a necklace that he is wearing. It was a gift from Robert Wilson, with whom he had been working for many years.

Months later, I receive a phone call from a woman who tells me that Robert Leibowitz has passed away. A close friend of his, she says that he has left me a swizzle stick. Saddened, I cannot believe that Robert is dead, and I am touched that he thought of me and left me a token— even if it is just one of those little plastic swizzle sticks that come in mixed drinks.

I make arrangements to drop by her office to pick up the gift from Robert. When I get there, I feel extremely awkward. I know I should be feeling some kind of grief, but instead, I feel nothing. I am numb, embarrassed and guilty.

We chat about Robert for a while and then his lovely friend opens the lower left-hand drawer of her desk. She takes out a sealed, slightly bulging manila envelope and hands it to me.

Inside of the envelope is a lusciously soft-to-the-touch leather pouch, pulled tight with braided drawstrings of silk thread. I ease the pouch opening apart and look in as images of my visit with Robert start flooding over me. It is as if I am watching a slide show, projections flashing by at the speed of light. My eyes fill with tears and I break down. Inside of the pouch is the necklace he had worn about his neck, close to the scar from his heart operation—the necklace that we had talked about during my last visit. Dangling from it, an odd silver piece. Robert had shown me how it works, but he never called it a swizzle stick.

It is a whimsical piece of silver—this swizzle stick. I later learn, seeing one in Tiffany's, that it is used to stir champagne cocktails.

I wear it whenever I am frightened and need strength. It is one of the few objects in my life that reminds me I have a superstitious streak; I do feel stronger when I wear it.

Life is so very tenuous—Robert was my first young friend who died. I am grateful for this gift he left with me, which always serves as a reminder to keep perspective when overreacting to unimportant things.

I hope reading this story has triggered some of your own stories about objects that mean something to you. Your growing awareness of how every element of your physical surroundings and possessions are invested with personal connections and meaning provides your base line. Now begin to use your imagination to craft stories that will add/endow personal meaning to everything that you handle or wear for your scene.

Similar to what happens when you establish a clear sense of place, endowing objects is a useful tool because it is so *physical*. When you endow an object with personal significance, your muscle memory kicks in; your body instinctively remembers how it handles such objects. Your body is animated and your emotional life is enriched by all the endowments you can imagine and test. Practice endowing until you react as spontaneously and reflexively with your endowed objects as you do with the fully functional objects you use and are surrounded by day to day.

Working with this technique will engage your Observing Self, and you will start to discover just how speedily and imperceptibly your material surroundings affect you.

Tips on preparing for your early rehearsals

You have met with your partner and have read the scene aloud, discussed the play, and scheduled your rehearsals.

- Use **The Work** page **Objects for Your Early Rehearsals** to prepare for your next rehearsal with your partner.

- Go through your own belongings and begin gathering the objects that you could use in your scene. If you are going to rehearse in your home or apartment, remove things that will not work in your scene. Collect all the objects that you want to have at your second rehearsal.

- The objects will fall into three categories:
  - Furniture. (Consider the furniture available in class and how you might use it.)

  - Personal objects. (Objects you have on your person as well as objects you want for your *secondary life*, i.e. the activities that you are engaged in while you are talking. These activities will be determined by the given time of day, the space where the scene takes place, your immediate past and immediate future.)

  - Room decoration. (Objects that make the room feel complete or add a sensory reality to the surroundings.)

- Don't censor yourself. Brainstorm. Think of and list everything you think you might have or could use in your environment.

- Depending upon the play, you may have to research the types of objects that were used during the era in which your play takes place. Your *status* (social standing) will also have a bearing on the kinds of objects you use. You may pull out your sterling silver candlesticks, crystal goblets, and best table linens—or you may look for the shabbiest clothing in your wardrobe and distress the dishtowel you will be using in your scene.

Lisa. Real coffee?

The Girl on the Via Flaminia

—Alfred Hayes

- Plan how you will approach your research. If you don't know anything about the time period, start to familiarize yourself with information about the social, economic, cultural and political background of the play. Divide the research topics with your partner and then share your discoveries.

- Bring the meaning of an object to light by sitting with it. Objects connect you emotionally. They hold meaning and bind you to them without you even realizing it.

The next set of **Me, Myself & I** pages will get you to start thinking about the circumstances of your own life through an actor's lens. By raising awareness to your own given circumstances at any moment in time, you will begin noticing the many ways in which time, place and your surroundings influence you and your behavior.

The Work pages will help you discover the ways in which the elements of place and time impact your scene. Choose the specifics you want to work on before you meet with your partner again.

Your Current Circumstances

Stop what you are doing. Use this chart to identify your current circumstances. Write about the situation you are in right now. When and how did it begin? What are you doing? What is in your way? What are your plans for the next three hours? The next twenty-four hours?

Circumstances

Place: Where are you? Country? State? City? Neighborhood? Building? Room? What surrounds you?

Time: What is the year? Season? Month? Day? Hour?

Secondary Life: What are you doing physically?

Relationships: What is your relationship to:

- where you are?

- the objects that surround you?

- the season, the day and time, and the weather?

- what you are doing?

- your immediate past and future?

Past: What had you been doing up until the moment you began this **Me, Myself & I**? How long had you been doing it? What are the life issues that occupy your thoughts?

Present: What are you doing at this moment? What is your immediate goal? What are the things that are in your way? What are your obstacles?

Future: What are you are going to do next? What is happening next week? Next month? Later this year?

Events Leading to My Now

Here is another way to look at your immediate preceding and future circumstances. Use the first column, "My Past," to list the things you did earlier in the day or week. Use the second column, "My Moments Before," to state what *just* happened before the present moment. Use the third column, "My First Moment of My Immediate Present," to state where you are and what you are doing in the present moment. Use Column Four to list the things that are going to happen in your near future.

You Are Here ⬇ Now

My Past	My Moments Before: Immediate Preceding Circumstance	My First Moment of My Immediate Present	My Future
Example: We have been in Florida for 4 days. Our annual visit. I woke up at 7am, took a shower, got dressed. Went downstairs. Made coffee, had yogurt and banana.	Today: Friday, Aug. _ Time: 8:30 am - Sat down next to granddaughter who was at the breakfast room table eating a Pop-Tart. She ignored me. No smile. Cut off. Not her happy and cheery self. -I am loaded with questions and would like to get her to talk about how she is feeling about going to meet her 4th grade teacher for the first time. -My inner tension between my need and my wisdom stresses me because I would do anything to ease her discomfort. -Instead, I get up quietly so as to give her space. I say the AA Serenity Prayer to myself as I carry my laptop into the living room.	Time: 8:35am I am sitting in the living room with my computer. I am deep in thought with the image of my granddaughter's expression. I try to read emails. I feel my granddaughter's vulnerability. (Am I projecting my own feelings on to her?) The rest follows from the things that currently matter to me. I bounce to a problem I am having with Chapter 3. (Will my compulsion to tweak an idea never end?) I hear my son and daughter-in-law talking in the background. I keep myself out of everyone's way.	Going to my granddaughter's school to "Meet the Teacher" in twenty minutes. Filled with curiosity about her classmates this year. Will she like them? Will they like her? Are they smart? Why do I care? I am shocked by my concerns and opinions. Tomorrow is her 9th birthday, with 15 young girls attending a water slide party. We are leaving on Monday.

Events Leading to My Now (Cont.)

This example gives you an idea of how to search for an inner object before entering a scene. Every moment has moments before it, most of which we are unaware of and are incidental.

In plays, the *moments before* have to be more extreme than they typically are in real life; they have to be more meaningful to you, in order to give you true inner occupation.

Your moments before may be accompanied by a *physical state of being*, depending on the circumstances your playwright provides. For example, the moment before might have left you out of breath, with a headache, jittery, sleepy, etc. Without a clear physical state of being, a scene might not make sense. When I talk about physical states, I refer to headaches, pains, the affects of chemical substances on your behavior (alcohol, speed, sleep medication, narcotics) etc. Nervousness is not a physical state of being; rather, it is an emotional state that has physical manifestations.

You need to learn how to work on sensory conditions in an environment, i.e. your physical state of being (see *A Challenge for the Actor*, pages 175–180).

Remember…

Continue your search for the specific inner object that serves as a real springboard, trigger for your first action. Always allow whatever you, the actor, are feeling to wed with your choices. Accept the energy in your body and let it find its release into your first action.

Current Trends Affecting My Life

Use this chart to note current trends and styles in your life today, at this moment in time. Make a collage of pictures, headlines, songs, films, and world events that capture today's trends.

The Period / Decade
Music, Art, Literature, Theatre, Cinema
Science and Technology
Social Trends
History, Economics, Politics, Religion
Current Events

The Stuff in My Life

1. How they got where they are

Throughout your daily life, you move your stuff from place to place. Notice an area in your bedroom, on your desk or kitchen table and write about the journeys the objects in that area have taken.

- Look around you. Choose one section of the room you are currently in and list every object you see. What inner objects do they trigger?

- Write about why five of those objects are where they are at this very moment in time. Include how and when they got there. What feelings do they provoke in you?

2. How objects indicate time

There are times when you enter a room and can sense what has been happening in the space. You can tell the time of day and the weather because there is a sensory condition in the room. Objects in the space reveal the life that has occurred there. Different information is communicated by a full glass of wine than a glass that has an inch of wine in it. What does a burned down candle say to you? Wilted flowers? A bare space?

- Which objects in your room indicate how long you have been in the room?

- Which objects give a sense of what has happened or is going to happen?

3. An old familiar room

Choose a room from your past. Sit quietly and write everything you can remember about the room and the objects that were in it. As specifically as you can, describe the walls, the ceiling, the floor. How old were you? How much time did you spend there? What did you do there? How did you feel when you were in it?

4. Objects from my past

Continuing the exercise you just did, choose two objects that were in the room from your past. Describe each one in as much detail as possible. Note the memories and emotions these objects trigger in you. Is it the object itself or some quality or aspect of the object that affects you? Do you associate each object with a person or a specific event?

5. A meaningful object

Write your own story about an object you currently own that means something to you.

Write about another object from your childhood.

6. Situation: You have NO financial considerations.

Make a collage with pictures that answer some of the following questions.

- What kind of house or apartment would you live in? Where? Would you own or rent?

- How would you furnish it?

- What type of automobile would you buy? Why?

- If you could travel anywhere, where would you go?

- Would you start a business? What kind?

- What else would you do with your money?

- Would you fund a charitable organization? Which one? Why?

- Would you do something with a social or political organization? What? Which one?

- Would you share your time and money with anyone? With whom? How? Why?

Awakening Your Senses and Emotions

The following exercise will awaken your senses. Do this exercise as often as you can. Try it with different objects.

- Choose one object. Sit with the object for a while. Hold it, look at it, listen to it, taste it, smell it. Quietly engage your senses.

  ○ What does it feel like? Is it smooth, rough? Is it heavy, light? Etc.

  ○ What sound does it make if you tap it or shake it?

  ○ What material is it made of? What are the properties of that material? Soft, furry, hard, metallic, shiny, dull, etc.?

  ○ What does it taste like or feel like on your tongue?

  ○ Does it have a scent? What is it like?

- Now put the object down.

  ○ What sense memories do you have?

Deeply symbolic objects

The story about the swizzle stick is an illustration of the kind of attachments we have to stuff and the significance material objects can hold. Keep your Observing Self awake concerning your attachments to the things in your life.

- Do you remember an object that was lost or stolen? When was the last time you thought about it? What did you do? How did you feel? Why?

- What objects do you feel naked without?

- What objects do you take for granted? What would happen if you didn't have them any more? What are your rituals connected to objects?

What would you do tomorrow if you had…

$500.00?

$5,000.00?

$50,000.00?

$500,000.00?

$5,000,000.00?

$50,000,000.00?

$500,000,000.00?

How would you spend …

$500.00?

$5,000.00?

$50,000.00?

$500,000.00?

$5,000,000.00?

$50,000,000.00?

$500,000,000.00?

More on Stuff

Free stuff

Situation: You have no money and struggle to keep your head above water. It is Christmas or a friend's birthday. Use your imagination to come up with perfect presents that won't cost a penny.

What talents do you have? Do you write poetry? Do you draw? Paint? Cook? Clean? Organize? Play an instrument? Babysit? Do you have special skills? Carpentry? Computer skills?

The stuff in your life

Talk about all the stuff in your life.

Remember…

Life and death
are wrapped up
in objects.

- How much stuff do you have? Do you use all of it? Where is it? Did you buy it?

- Was it given to you? Did you inherit it? Do you want to hold on to it all? Why?

- Is any of it other people's stuff?

- Do you want to get rid of any of it? If you don't, why not?

- Is your stuff a true reflection of who you are?

- Does it make your life feel cumbersome, cluttered, out of control?

Collecting

- Do you collect anything? What do you collect?

- How and when did you start collecting?

- How many objects do you have in your collection?

- Is it a valuable collection? Estimate its value.

- Do you have more than one collection? What else do you collect?

Discovering Hot Objects

Do this exercise when you want to know the *hot objects* in your life—those objects that are particularly resonant for you, conjuring up many inner objects and connecting with you emotionally. Take the time to sit with an object you take for granted. The following story will give you an idea how to proceed. I recently sat with an object that has been lying around my life for years. Until I took the time to sit with it, I had no idea that it meant so much to me. It brought me back to my childhood and opened my heart. I was a young girl again, sobbing, yearning and loving—vulnerable.

The Sewing Kit

I am holding a brown, three-by-two inch, three-fold packet, made of coated fabric which creates the appearance of leather. Machine-cut, with a top flap that can be inserted into a slit to close. On the front, rubbed off by wear, is an army insignia and the words *Military Sewing Kit* stamped in green ink. The kit opens to an attached piece of felt, skewered by a sewing needle threaded with black thread. In the small pocket is a folded, stained and aged card that once held seven buttons—there are three remaining still sewn on. There are also nine loose buttons: four white – ¼", two white – ⅔", one black – ½", one grey – ⅔", and one grey – ¾".

Such a simple man who had no need or desire for much adornment. Of all the possessions my father acquired over his 81 years, why did he keep this—along with a few other items—from the time he served? Issued when and where? Ft. Sill in Oklahoma? Then it travelled across the Pacific Ocean to the Philippines, and back—and then from Philadelphia, to Miami, to Ft. Bragg, North Carolina, and finally here, to Weehawken, New Jersey.

Hardly a fuzzy, touchy-feely object, it nevertheless takes me on a journey of my imagination, creating a vivid visit with my father that I never even had.

The Work

Factual Notes on Time

PLAY: _____

ROLE: _____

DATE: _____

When a playwright sets his play will influence and determine your choices. It will take a while for you to develop your own habits with regard to this tool. The following questions are critical. Sometimes the playwright indicates the time frame at the beginning of the play; however, there are instances when time elements and references are embedded in the dialogue. With no direct indication that there is a change or movement of time, you may sense the passage of time in the text.

- When was the play written?

- When was the play published?

- What time span does the play cover? What years are covered by the action of the play?

- Act by act, scene by scene, review how the play moves in time—by year, month, day of the week, and time of day.

- When the characters talk about the past, what time periods do they mention?

- What are the political, social, religious implications of the time periods mentioned?

Time: your own notes on time

- What aspects of time in the play do you want to know more about?

- What aspects of time in the play are difficult for you to comprehend?

- What movies, DVDs, videos, picture books or biographies will help you get a better sense of the time period in which the play is set?

Muriel. Dick, you have no idea what I went through to get here tonight! My, but it was exciting! I had to get all undressed and into bed and Ma came up, and I pretended to be asleep, and she went down again, and I got up a dressed in such a hurry—I must look a sight, don't I? ...And then I sneaked down the back stairs.

Ah, Wilderness
—Eugene O'Neill

The World of the Play

PLAY: _____

ROLE: _____

DATE: _____

Use this chart as a guide for understanding the world of the play. Depending upon what time span the play covers, and whether you are working on the entire play, you might need to use a different sheet for each scene.

Research the time in which your play takes place and describe the following elements of the era:

The Period: Century/Decade
Music, Art, Literature, Theatre, Cinema
Science and Technology
Social Trends
History, Economics, Politics, Religion
Current Events

- How will the period of the play affect "your" behavior, "your" perceptions, "your" points of view and "your" status?

- What aspects of the period are difficult for you to comprehend?

- What videos or biographies would help you get a better idea of the lifestyles from the period of your play?

Rehearsal Preparation

PLAY: _____

ROLE: _____

DATE: _____

Given circumstances

Answer these questions with the information you get from your script.

- Where am I?

- What time is it?

    Month:

    Date:

- What am I doing?

- Why?

- Why *now*?

Selecting your secondary activity

- What are you doing while you are talking? Determined by the time your scene takes place, is your secondary life connected to a routine? How does the scene affect that routine?

- List all of the objects you use and describe them.

- Do you have special feelings about any of the objects you have chosen to use in your scene? Why are those objects meaningful to you?

- When you choose a secondary life for your scene, practice it alone. You may never complete the activity. It is there to provide the possibility of physical destination for your scene.

Remember…

Facts relating to place and time are some of the 'givens' in a play—information given to you by the playwright. It's good to start out with a sense of what you know and understand and what you don't know and don't understand.

Given Circumstances

PLAY: _____

ROLE: _____

DATE: _____

Use this chart as a reference for breaking down your scene. The given circumstances of a scene—material provided by the playwright regarding place, time and other relevant circumstantial information—are specific, concrete elements of a scene and provide the crucible within which the events of the play occur. Givens, such as *who* "you" are, your *background, where* you are (place), and what *time* it is, influence your *secondary life*—the physical activities you might be engaged in while you are talking. When the playwright does not specify time or place, you have to deduce them as best you can from what you sense from the text.

Remember...

Your physical life equals behavior. The consequences of what is happening in your scene are released through your behavior.

You must gather all the information about your past and future that the playwright provides. Be extremely diligent when creating a time line of actual events that occur in the play. Include events that are mentioned.

Past

Present

Future

Your Secondary Activities and Your Time Line

PLAY: _____

ROLE: _____

DATE: _____

S. You do this every fucking morning.

H. What time did you go to sleep?

Breakfast at the Track

—Lanford Wilson

Thinking in terms of a time line will help your secondary life, which is always connected to the time of day. Most often it involves certain daily routines. Ask yourself, "What am I doing besides talking?" What is happening in the scene is primary. Your secondary life is related to your physical destinations, where you move on stage. Your secondary life is unrelated to what you are talking about in your scene but will energize and ground you in your sending and receiving process.

- What time does your scene begin?

- What are your immediate preceding circumstances? How long have you been here? What have you been doing up to the exact moment the scene begins?

- What are the actions you perform in the course of your scene?

- What are the things you are going to do after your scene is over?

Experiment with creating your own timelines of what "you" have done throughout the day in which your scene takes place. Make sure you don't write another play. Stick with the truth of your circumstances. Is it Saturday, 2am? Monday, 12 noon? Sunday, 5pm? etc.

9 AM	10 AM	11 AM	
Example:			
9 AM	9:03	9:06	9:10
Wake up	Bathroom	Start coffee	

Time Specifics and Influences

The Work

PLAY: _____

ROLE: _____

DATE: _____

Use this chart to determine technical choices you must make as you rehearse. Details coming from the specifics of the time of day will influence *conditioning forces*, your *physical state of being* and your *emotional life* (I refer you to *A Challenge for the Actor*, pages 88-89). If you are working on the entire play, you might need to use a different sheet for each scene.

Time

The Decade/The Year: The Month: The Season: Cold? Rainy? Etc.	The Day: Weekday? Weekend? Holiday? Etc.	The Hour: Dawn? Morning? Afternoon? Sunset? Evening? Night? Etc.
Clothing: How does the time of the play determine what "you" are wearing?		
"Your" Age		
Conditioning Forces		
"Your" physical state of being: How is Time affecting "your" physical state of being? How are you going to work on each state of being?		
"Your" emotional state of being: How is Time affecting "your" emotional state of being?		

Craft Your Preparation

PLAY: _____

ROLE: _____

DATE: _____

What just happened that leads you into the first moment of the play

Preparation gives you the sense of urgency needed for your scene. There are immediate preceding circumstances to every scene; you always enter your scene from something that has just happened (a created imaginary event—a dream, a fight, bad news, good news—usually quite extreme and significant in your life). You always enter a room or begin a scene with expectation.

Cars won't run on an empty tank. A specific meaningful preparation is your fuel. Without it you can't energize and power your motor. Your objective is to already be in the middle of circumstances when the lights come up or you make your entrance. Your preparation puts you there.

Remember…

You are always in search of 'the hook' -- your entry point. From that point you begin doing. Include what you are actually experiencing to be a part of that hook.

Experiment with different scenarios of what your immediate preceding circumstances might be to find inner objects that trigger the first moments in the scene. Don't forget: whatever you bring from your immediate past will be affected as soon as you encounter your partner. In rehearsal you discover when, how and if your preparation feeds and provides the human undercurrents in your scene. The work you do in the next three chapters will inform your choices.

If your first moments are not full, specific and tied to your needs, there is no point in going further into the scene. It is like singing the first note of a song off-key.

Remember…

Allow yourself to continue finding deeper, unexpected variations of that entry point.

History of Events

PLAY: _____

ROLE: _____

DATE: _____

Here is another way to look at your immediate preceding circumstances. By detailing a timeline of life events surrounding the moment your scene takes place, you provide yourself with source material for conjuring up inner objects that will solidify your faith in the imaginary circumstances of the play. Experiment with this exercise for some time to discover inner objects that genuinely fill you and propel you into your scene.

You Are Here ⬇ Now

My Past: Given Circumstances= The gas station	My Moments Before: Immediate Preceding Circumstance= Filling your tank	My First Moment of My Immediate Present: Your motor is running	My Future: Expectations
	Today: Time:	Today: Time:	

"Your" Age

PLAY: _____

ROLE: _____

DATE: _____

Depending upon when your play takes place, "your" age may alter your behavior and your expectations. Your age also overlaps with the work you do in Chapter Six, *Who Am I?* Age is a state of mind. Age-appropriate behavior (whatever that is) is influenced by your upbringing. Do you have opinions about appropriate behavior for different age groups? Where did you get those ideas?

- Are you older or younger than the new "you"? Are you the same age?

- If there is a difference in age between you and your character, how does it serve you? Or does it work against you? What can you do to find your adjustment for the new "you"?

- What year were "you" born?

- Who else was born on "your" birthday?

- What is "your" astrological sign?

The Description of the Set

PLAY: _____

ROLE: _____

DATE: _____

Make notes on the description of the set if there is one in your script, or even copy it outright. The description may be very detailed or quite vague. What things in the description puzzle you? What elements stimulate your imagination or trigger memories? Begin looking for pictures of furniture and spaces that reflect your ideas. Make a collage.

Facts on Place Gathered from the Text

PLAY: _____

ROLE: _____

DATE: _____

Where a playwright sets his play is vital information as you continue your work on **Place**. It will take time for you to develop your own habits with regard to this tool.

- What information does the playwright provide concerning place? Act by act, scene by scene, break the play down into the locations in which the action of the play occurs.

- What country are "you" in?

- What state? What region?

- Are "you" in an urban, suburban, rural, residential, commercial, resort location? Other?

- What has the playwright omitted?

Your notes on Place

- Make notes of things that you are not certain about regarding Place. Also notice what the author has not specified.

Rehearsal Set-up

      PLAY: _____

      ROLE: _____

      DATE: _____

Draw the physical layout you are using for your rehearsals.

The Work

Planning Ahead

PLAY: _____

ROLE: _____

DATE: _____

What changes do you need to make for the shift from your home to your acting classroom? What classroom furniture will you be using? What will you bring to class to make the space feel more specific?

Your Apartment

The Classroom

Planning Ahead (Cont.)

List the objects you will be taking to class.

Scouting Locations

The Work

PLAY: _____

ROLE: _____

DATE: _____

As you begin creating your environment for your scene, remember that when you go into any public place, it has been deliberately created to have an effect on the people who pass through. Notice what happens to you the next time you go to an unfamiliar place. Notice your expectations of the public places you go to frequently. This next assignment should help as you scout locations for your scene.

Let's say your scene takes place in a restaurant:

Go to a couple of actual restaurants. With each place, answer these questions.

- What street is it on? How is the outside decorated? Can you see inside?

- Where is the door located? What kind of door is it? What is the entryway like? Is there a second door that you must pass through?

- Is there a receptionist station? A sign? A place to sit?

- What is the juxtaposition of the receptionist, the bar, the coat check, the main dining area, the bathrooms? Sketch the layout.

- Describe the ambience. What is the lighting like? What colors have been used to decorate? Are there plants? How close are the tables to one another? What is the sound quality of the place? On a scale of one to ten, one being hushed to ten being music blaring and talking volume very loud, how would you rate this restaurant? What is the price range of the meals served?

- Attend to the details of the table setting: table covering, china, glassware, silverware, candles, napkins, salt & pepper, candles, flowers, etc. Also notice the menu design, size and weight and if a wine list is also offered.

- Ask if you can borrow a couple of menus and some of the objects on the table.

The Rest of the Apartment or House

PLAY: _____

ROLE: _____

DATE: _____

You always need to have a sense of the entire structure of the building where your scene is set. Where is the room in relationship to the rest of the house, apartment, or hotel? This is necessary to have faith and purpose in your entrances and exits. Always knowing that you are going into another room or hallway—and not going offstage—keeps your life in context of the given circumstances of your play. It also affects how you talk to someone in another room. Often your first beat involves an entrance, and you need to tie your immediate past to the first moment when you come on. Part of your preparation involves knowing where you are coming from and why you are coming into the room in which your scene takes place. You always enter a room with expectation. For instance, consider the opening of Scene Two of *Dinner With Friends*[7] by Donald Margulies:

Beth is in her bedroom. Somewhere in the house, the family dog, Sarge, barks. Tom comes into the bedroom from the hallway. Both actors have to know:

- The architecture of their home: Two-story? Ranch?

- Where the bedroom is in relation to the front door, the hallway, the children's rooms

- Where Sarge is: Downstairs in his crate? In the kitchen? Somewhere else?

- Where their bedroom is in relation to the sound of the dog's barking

- How often the dog barks: At night? What triggers his barking?

- If you can distinguish between his barking at a stranger or at a member of the family

- Sarge's breed, color, size, age, etc.

- How his barking affects you: Are you concerned that he will wake the kids?

If you are playing Tom, you must ask yourself: Did you come in through the front or back door? How far did you have to walk from the cab to the entryway or the back door? Did you pass Sarge? Did you come straight up to the bedroom? Are the stairs carpeted? Did you take the stairs two at a time?

Objects for Your Early Rehearsals

PLAY: _____

ROLE: _____

DATE: _____

One aspect of your technique requires that you work with real objects. Continuing the work you have been doing in this chapter, take concrete action to prepare for your early rehearsals. Begin considering all the objects that will help you create your environment and find physical destination for your scene. Through active selection and confident use, you will create a fully expressive human being who is alive physically, verbally, and emotionally.

- Make a list of objects you would like to have at your first rehearsals. The list will come from the given circumstances, including:

  ○ What time it is

  ○ Where "you" are

  ○ Where "you" are coming from and what you have been doing

  ○ What "you" are preparing to do in the immediate future

- Go through your home and gather the objects you think you might want to use in your scene. Select objects that you feel will further your faith and will be fun to work with in rehearsal.

Mrs. Peters. ...I wonder where I can find a piece of paper, and string.

Mrs. Hale. In that cupboard, maybe.

Mrs. Peters. Why, here's a birdcage. Did she have a bird, Mrs. Hale?

Trifles —Susan Glaspell

Hot Objects

PLAY: _____

ROLE: _____

DATE: _____

Later in your rehearsal process you may come upon the need for a "hot" object, one that "cooks" you and connects you emotionally to some specific aspect of your circumstances. Experiment. You will discover how very powerful some objects can be. Bring what you have learned in the **Me, Myself and I** exercise **Discovering Hot Objects** to your selection of an object for the new you.

- For instance, if you are playing Andrew in *The Years,* by Cindy Lou Johnson, you may keep in your pocket the phone number of a lawyer whom you are going to consult about your will. If you think you have been diagnosed with HIV, you may also carry a small pill container with your meds for the day.

- You may wear a piece of jewelry that a former lover gave you, which triggers memories of them and a time past.

- You may carry a note written by a loved one who has died. How does their handwriting affect you?

Stanley. And what have we here? The treasure chest of a pirate!

Stella. Oh, Stanley!

Stanley. Pearls! Ropes of them! What is this sister of yours, a deep-sea diver? Bracelets of gold, too!

   A Streetcar Named Desire –Tennessee Williams

Making Objects and Activities Your Own

PLAY: _____

ROLE: _____

DATE: _____

As you read your play time and again, be alert to the information about all of the things you do. You will learn that you use objects connected to everyday life, work, your interests or skills. You will often have to do activities onstage that you have never done before in real life. I worked on a play that took place during a canasta game. I gathered my decks of cards and all the paraphernalia that went with the game's ritual. I started practicing dealing four hands and playing every day; I taught myself how to keep score. Here are some other examples of how to make objects and activates your own:

- You have been cast as Agnes in *Ludlow Fair*.[8] You read the play and discover "you" do crossword puzzles. If you don't do crossword puzzles, begin. Do a puzzle from the *New York Times*; you will get a sense of how smart Agnes is. Do the puzzle every day. How long does it take you to complete one? Create a ritual around them. Is it a treat for you? Do you have a favorite pencil? A particular eraser? Do you do them in pen? How old is your dictionary? Is it a crossword puzzle dictionary?

  If you are not a crossword puzzle devotee, you can begin finding your own connection to the activity. What games are you currently addicted to? When and why do you turn to them? What satisfaction do you derive from doing them? Talk to friends who do crosswords. How did they begin? What are their routines? Ask them to save daily puzzles in the *Times* for you so that you have plenty for rehearsals.

Making Objects and Activities Your Own (Cont.)

- You have been cast as Henry Harry in *Brilliant Traces*.[9] In the text, you say you made some soup. You are a cook on an oilrig. You research this, and discover that cooks on oilrigs really know how to cook! Start cooking. Collect recipes. Bake bread.

  You also need to brainstorm how you spend your time when "you" are off from work. What is your daily routine? How do you make your bed? Where do you keep your clothes? Where do you keep your clothes for the rig? Your clothes for the cabin? Do you drink? How much? When? What is your source of light? How do you prepare for winter? What supplies do you bring in? What tools do you need? How do you store your food? Get water? What heat source do you use? What books do you read? Do you have a calendar to keep track of time? Games? What objects will give you a sense of your life?

  How do you get back to the rig? Do you have a phone? Any means of communication?

  Hot objects: A photo of Annabelle hidden somewhere? A little doll that she loved?

Alert: Throughout the workbook, you will encounter the word "you" in quotes indicating that I am referring to "you, the character." Do not stress the "you" to differentiate it in your mind from you. If you do, you are unconsciously separating yourself from the new you and defeating the purpose of using the first person singular in all your work. When you read a sentence like <How do "you" spend your time when you are off from work,> read it exactly the same as <How do you spend your time when you are off from work?>

Chapter 4

Wanting, Needing, Obstacle and Doing

Dracula

The drama teacher at St. Anne's School in Brooklyn Heights, New York announces that the spring production is to be *Dracula* by Deane Hamilton and John L. Balderston, from Bram Stoker's novel. Our son is thirteen years old. He has loved the Dracula story since he was five or six when a friend of ours gave him the book one Thanksgiving.

Our son unabashedly goes after the role of Count Dracula. We hear that as he changes classes or eats lunch, the script, pages fluttering, is always in evidence. He spends all of his spare time in the library where he reads everything that he can find about the famous legend. He then dispenses his discoveries to any and all, whether they are interested or not.

Hearing how our young son is approaching this project fills my heart. I am reminded of the excitement I had as a young girl whenever there was a chance to audition for a play. His conviction and commitment inspire me; I savor his lack of guile—knowing the challenging life lessons we face when auditioning in the "real" world.

> In the class that I am teaching, I talk about Jules' determination. He has a very clear objective: he wants that part. Furthermore, he is not hiding his desire from anyone as he takes one action after another to prepare for his audition. His pursuit is infused with the joy, hope and excitement that anticipating working on a play—any play—can generate. And he landed the role!

Children are wonderful teachers. Whenever you have the chance, observe a child pursuing an objective—something that the child wants or needs. Watch their persistence and inventiveness. Their actions have extraordinary variety and intuitive range. Abruptly switching tactics, their actions are unpremeditated and often very dramatic. Their involvement is complete and unselfconscious.

As we are socialized to accommodate the circumstances in which we are raised, some of us lose our body, our voice and our versatility. We cease to surprise ourselves. Allow yourself to tap back into that childhood spontaneity, inventiveness and intuition as you head into the next part of your process: working with *objectives*, *obstacles* and *actions*. Half measures are not nearly as satisfying as whole ones. Go all out to do everything in your power to prepare yourself when you want a role, when you are working on a role, and, of course, when you are performing. This state of youthful enthusiasm may come and go as you move through the phases of your training and career—but rest assured that you will have times when you can recapture the innocence and optimism, joy and playfulness you had back in the days when you didn't know any better.

Here is the bottom line: *never go onstage without purpose*. Knowing deep within you what you want to achieve gives you that purpose. Lack of intention—not knowing what is behind the words you are saying, lacking real purpose of pursuit—is the element shared by failed performances and dull theater.

Live with the Play ★

The playwright has embedded *objectives*, *obstacles* and *actions* into the dialogue of every character in your play. These are inextricably linked to the play's circumstances, and are hardwired into the characters and their relationships. Thoughts about some aspect of your process should be with you continually. When you find yourself thinking about the play or rehearsals every day, feeling the urge to check out a passage in your script, you are on the right track. When you realize that you haven't truly found a specific inner object for a reference, ask more questions that might lead to discovery. To increase your subjectivity, continue particularizing as you become aware of the specifics you haven't yet considered. Be sure to pinpoint the sources for your answers to the following questions throughout your rehearsals:

What do I want/need? (Objective) What is in my way? (Obstacle) What am I doing to get what I want? (Action).

The questions are simple, but you, the actor, should never deal with them as if you were taking a test and had to come up with the "right" answers. An *Objective* (n.) is something toward which effort is directed: an aim, goal, intention or end of action. An *Obstacle* (n.) is something that impedes progress or achievement; that which stands in the way of what you want. An *Action* (n.) is a thing you do to get what you want; an action is a doing.

Your will to live and your optimism move you forward in life. The infinite things you do are who you are. The vector that moves you to action is guided by your deepest yearnings. Like a stone thrown into a pond, the ripples not only appear on the surface of the water. In descent, it creates deeper rippling beneath. Unique to each individual, wants, needs and wishes are connected to specific targets (objects of need and desire) and thoughts of what they will provide.

> Remember…
>
> Be careful: Avoidance can become your objective.

The Objective

You will surely relate to the following list of wants and needs that we human beings share the world over. They can provide a way to frame "your" new objectives. Notice how some of these wants might never be realized and by their very nature create anguish, frustration and inner turmoil.

You Want –

- Situations and people to be other than what they are
- Situations and people to stay the same
- Possessions and things that you don't have
- Things to be done your way or a certain way
- To be liked, cherished, loved, appreciated, respected, obeyed, believed, etc.
- To do good deeds and be of service
- To be other than what you are

> Remember…
>
> As an artist, you must
> - Think for yourself
> - Speak your mind
> - Cultivate your own taste
> - Make extraordiary mistakes
> - Find your voice

You Need –

- Basic elements of survival: air, water, food, shelter, clothing
- Affection: love, care, attention, intimacy, sex
- Companionship
- Money

- Safety

- Physical assistance

- Faith, hope

You Need/Want –

- Knowledge

- Food

- A home

- Health/ Well-being

- Clothing

- Comfort

- Friendship

- Things to be a certain way

You Have to – (comes from external or internal authority, implying no choice)

- Obey and follow directions, rules or orders

I will use the words "want," "need" or "intention" when I am talking about objectives. Your *wants and needs* provide your lifeline through the play. They link you to the other characters in the play, because you usually want to do something to them, want something from them or want something for them. Find the words in your script where you actually state what you want or need. Find the words in your script that intimate what you want or need.

> **Mangan**. ...I want to be near your friend Mrs. Hushabye. I'm in love with her. ...
>
> **Ellie**. I want to be near your friend Mr. Hushabye. I'm in love with him. ...
>
> *Heartbreak House* –George Bernard Shaw

To find common ground with the new "you," living with and led by your script, extend your curiosity to understand the specifics that drive "your" new wants. Heightening your awareness of, and admitting to, your own needs, wants, challenges and doings will provide a deeper empathy with "your" new wants. Most likely, however, this will not be sufficient—research and conscious observation of the world around you are necessary aspects of your process as well.

Wonder—What Makes People Tick? ★

Your passion to act must be driven by an insatiable curiosity about people—people from all walks of life, people who live in other places and at other times. Nurture a boundless fascination with life. Need to know why people want the things they want and what makes them do the things they do. Wrap your mind around why their wants matter to them. Marvel at how they cope with and overcome the range of life's challenges, whether trivial or life-threatening.

Recognize the mass of judgment you carry around with you regarding the people you hear, read about and encounter on a daily basis. Once acknowledged, put your judgments aside so that you can get to work—learning, observing and absorbing. Imagine what the traffic cop in the intersection, or the man with the gigantic plastic bag of cans slung over his shoulder, or the child screaming in his mother's arms all want out of life; imagine what each does at the end of the day, where they shop, what their homes are like, what their most pressing needs are, if they pray, etc. The more you wonder about others, the more you stimulate your imagination as you cast your curiosity far and wide.

> **Doctor Lvov.** I am your wife's doctor, and you are killing her! I knew people were sometimes stupid, unbalanced, crazy …but until I met all you people here, I never imagined they could be consciously criminal, deliberately evil.
>
> *Ivanov*—Anton Chekhov

Think Person, Human Being ★

Never for one moment forget that *your process melds every aspect of your craft.* All of the elements of your craft lead you to thinking of your character as a person, a whole human being. The sources that give rise to human behavior aren't easily parsed out, whether in your own life or your character's. Use your actor's tools to direct your attention both into your own life and into the world of the new "you."

In your rehearsals through the lens of "your" point of view, you unearth and then absorb the needs and wants of the new "you." Your own needs and wants are directly tied to the people in, and spring from the immediate circumstances of, your life. This is true of all the characters you will play as well.

Mothers and fathers are by definition guilty of creating in their children the need for approval, love, success, and power. So, too, other people in your life kindle your needs and wants, often becoming the targets of those very needs and wants.

> **Remember…**
> The freedom of your childhood when you were never burdened by, "I have to, I must, I should." -- when you just went after what you wanted, you just pursued.

Circumstances define your needs as well. Your brother may be autistic. Perhaps your mother was an alcoholic and you became the adult in your family when you were seven. Or maybe your father was in the army, served in Iraq, and returned home a different person. Or possibly you got everything you ever wanted yet never felt satiated. Or perhaps you developed anorexia when you were fourteen.

Choose Uncomplicated, Simply Stated Wants ★

Remember that your pursuits and the targets of those pursuits, whether you achieve them or not, are at the heart of the story you are telling. Your wants and needs spring out of who you are, your point of view, what matters to you, the people with whom you interact and the circumstances in which you find yourself.

Your objectives must be straightforward and measureable. Before you even get on your feet, there is a litmus test to see if you are on track. Will you be able to execute your choices? How will you know if you have achieved your goal?

1. State what you want or need from the other person.

2. Ask yourself how you will know when you succeed in getting what you want. If you can't answer that question, reword your want or need until you can be sure of the intention behind your pursuit and that you will recognize your success or failure.

3. Always state your objective in the affirmative. If you say, "I don't want so and so to leave," rephrase your objective to "I want to keep so and so here" or "I want so and so to stay with me."

4. Make notes on how you will actually go after your objective—what you will do physically and verbally. Many times you know what you want but you are not sure how you are going to get what you want. Speculate upon and write about as many options as you can. Use **The Work** page **Verbs/Actions/Doings** to launch yourself.

5. Consider your expectations. How do you think your fellow actors will receive your actions? What will they do in return?

Keep in mind that you, the actor, are *consciously* doing homework to find the *unconscious* needs and wants that drive the new "you." You must always have an objective when you enter onto the stage; when it comes to pursuing objectives, understanding human behavior is crucial. You always enter a room with expectation: "I am. I want. I do."

Herbert Berghof (1909-1990) was a renowned actor, teacher and director. Born in Vienna, Austria, a young leading actor in Max Reinhart's Berliner Ensemble, he fled the Nazis and came to New York in 1939, where he launched a successful career as a Broadway actor and director. In 1945 Berghof founded HB Studio as a place for actors to train and practice their craft free from the pressures of the commercial theater. He married Uta Hagen in 1957, and ran HB Studio alongside her until his passing in 1990. How we function in the real world can be summed up with the phrase that Herbert Berghof used to keep our work on track: "I am. I want. I do." You, the actor, seek to identify and verbalize your choices—what you want and what you are doing to get it—because you need to know what you are doing onstage within the circumstances of the play. As you practice your choices, trust your muscle memory and don't think about what you are doing. Simply do.

Keep the Change in Your Pocket   ★

Your objectives are like change in your pocket. You know your money is there; you don't think about it unless you need to buy something. It is inhuman to constantly think about objectives when you are acting, so don't try.

The following life example should clarify how you can expect your selected objectives to work in your character's life.

The Objective: To Get Home

Your technique class is over and you are going home to drop off your props before you go to work. You work as a bartender and have a long night ahead of you.

Your immediate objective is to get out of the building. You put on your coat, find your iTunes music on your phone, plug in your earphones, slip your phone in your pocket, grab your bags and head out the door.

At the corner you run into your current scene partner from your scene study class. You had texted him to set up the time for your next rehearsal with no response. He tells you he lost his cell phone yesterday. You stop, pull off your earphones, untangle the wires from your backpack straps, get your iPhone out, tap to your calendar and thumb in date/ time for your rehearsal. You tune back into your music, plug in, hug your partner and off you stroll—home.

You pass a market and remember that you need a quart of milk. You buy it.

Three blocks from your apartment, your cell dings—a text. Walking along, you check the message. It's your agent, clearing you for an audition tomorrow. She will email the sides for the audition, time, location, etc. You get back to her on the dot.

You are closer to home…

Now, what happens if we bump up the stakes and add obstacles to these circumstances?

Now you have to get home after your class because you have to meet your brother to get the five hundred dollars, cash, that he borrowed from you.

Your brother has procrastinated paying you back and he is now forcing you into meeting his time frame. He has to get to the airport to catch a plane, and he has warned you that he won't wait more than two minutes if you don't answer the bell immediately. You have no doorman and it is pouring out. You need your money.

> Leaving school, you fling your hoodie over your head and charge down the block, body hunched protecting you from the rain. You certainly do not stop to make plans with your scene partner. He has to keep up with you as you race for the subway, etc. Forget the milk.

These added circumstances increase your purposefulness enormously. They trigger *inner objects*—images or thought fragments, noise in your mind—about getting your money back: questioning yourself for naively trusting your brother, swearing to never lend him anything again, your brother's dominance in the situation and in your life, your annoyance with him, his inconveniencing you, etc.

Notice that you don't literally think about your "objective." You know where you have to be. You know when you have to be there. You know why you have to be there on time. Once you know these things, in your body, actions follow. As you can see, raising your stakes is an essential aspect of your craft. When crafting stakes, you tap into the highly personal things that matter to you—small or large.

Remember…

The acting vocabulary used in this book will mean different things to each actor. They are not useful as intellectual ideas or obligatory rules to be followed. They have been chosen because they are part of the human experience. They are already in you. You know what it means to want and need.

Create Stakes—The Courage to Go All the Way   ★

As you tune in to your character's needs or wants, you must also consider the consequences that await if "you" do not win and do not get what you want or need. Ask yourself what will happen if you succeed or fail in getting what you want. Craft personal inner objects of what will happen if you get what you want, don't get what you want or arrive at something quite unexpected. Find your connection to the risks "you" are taking and the consequences you might face: what you have to lose or gain. Needs, wants and their consequences must genuinely matter to you.

What you risk, *what is at stake*, fuels your need to go after what you want against all odds—when everyone, including you, says that you're crazy. Like wanting to be an actor. Like asking for a raise. Like quitting your job. Like coming out of the closet. Like telling the truth as you see it. Like asking for help. Like doing something you know is wrong. Like needing to look gorgeous on your wedding day. Like wanting your grandfather to know how much you love him before he dies.

Remember…

Put the need in your belly. Use everything you've got to create stakes that matter.

How courageous are you in your own life? I am a wuss most of the time, but when I am responsible for someone who is not able to care for him or herself, I like to think that my bullish nature makes me ready to take on whatever I must.

Playwrights create circumstances in which their characters are at turning points in their lives; these are moments in time when the characters' lives will change forever, whether or not their wants and needs are fulfilled. These are circumstances in which the stakes matter because the characters' lives will never be the same again.

Intuit, Sense: The Actor's Way of Knowing ★

As you ask your new self "What do I want?" and "What do I need?" never settle for answers that have no visceral meaning for you, however good they may sound. Take your attention off of the how and what you are doing. This will help keep you out of your head, present in your body and tapped into your unconscious intuition. When you are awake to what is *actually* happening and are responding truthfully in rehearsal or performance, it is possible that you will not even realize that you are living through the circumstances of the play. You will be fully engaged.

The Actor's Way of Knowing is an intuited and sensed knowing—often referred to as instinct. Have you ever responded to a teacher's critique, saying, "That was my instinct," or, "that was my impulse"? If so, you were likely misusing these two words to justify something that you did in a scene. Why misusing? Because neither word applies to any action that is consciously self-generated. Over time you will recognize, honor and trust your intuition. Since it is an unconscious part of your process, it is not something you talk about mindlessly.

Be honest. Admit when you haven't identified or connected to your character's wants or needs. It's okay.

The Obstacle

Conflict and Obstacle: Unforeseen, Unexpected ★

You engage and capture the audience through the struggles you encounter in your play. An obstacle is anything that you don't expect, that interrupts or stands in your way of getting what you want or need. Obstacles create conflict—inner and outer.

Before proceeding, here's a word to the wise as you begin incorporating obstacles into your work. Be vigilant: *you might fall into the trap of playing the obstacle instead of fighting to overcome it as you pursue your objective.* For example: You wake up exhausted. You don't feel like going to work. However, instead of staying in bed, you exert extra

> **Lopakin.** But keep in mind, the cherry orchard is going to be sold. On August twenty-second! You hear what I'm saying? You've got to think about this! You've got to!
>
> *The Cherry Orchard*—Anton Chekhov

energy, one step at a time, as you pull yourself together to get out the door. You bully yourself. You encourage yourself. You bribe yourself. You ridicule yourself. You do all this so that you don't give in to your exhaustion—rather than acting exhausted, you take actions to overcome or move forward despite your exhaustion.

Obstacles energize. The inevitable consequence of encountering an obstacle is *action*. The word "no" is the most familiar obstacle in your life. It is the one word that arouses an instant reaction within the breast of every man, woman and child that hears it—one of challenge, curiosity and defiance or avoidance.

As soon as you state what you want, list what is stopping you from getting what you want. You have various names for the obstacles in your life: him, her, me, them, it, wall, rut, fear, block, stuck, barrier or trap. Often we experience obstacles as conflict or failure and think of them as burdensome.

> **Remember…**
>
> The moment when you think you have nothing more in you, could be just the moment to continue.

But obstacles are neither good nor bad. They just *are*. They can be very immediate and incidental in scope—a misplaced phone number, a sprained ankle, an unwanted touch, a teacher's frown, the tears of a loved one, a missed train, an angry friend. Many can have long-range consequences—being fired, being promoted, having a baby, getting married, cheating on your girlfriend, life-altering accidents and natural disasters. Some are produced by hugely catastrophic events such as a bombing in a public place, massive flooding of your home or a severe chronic illness.

When crafting and particularizing the obstacles you find in your scene, always think of the immediate consequences they pose if you can't overcome them. Consider this as well: obstacles also exist when experiencing something positive or fantastically fresh and life affirming—the air after a storm, the crunching sound of walking on new snow, the soaring, heart-stopping notes from *Sogno di Doretta* in Puccini's *La Rondine,* joyful celebrations of marriage and birth…Although they are beautiful and you appreciate and love them, they are fleeting, unpredictable and soon forgotten. Recall the times when you couldn't jump high enough, yell or cheer loud enough, sail, dance, sing or glide long enough, hold someone tight enough, share deeply enough or remember an image clearly enough. And then, recall the times when you did.

Types of Obstacles

Obstacles in the form of conflict are written into every play. The playwright embeds conflict into your character traits, relationships and the situations you are in. When you go onstage you must not only know what you want or need; you also need to have identified the things that make it difficult for you to accomplish your goals—large or small. Obstacles heighten the risks you must take to get what you want. You do this *in* rehearsal.

You may develop a better understanding of life's hurdles as you work with the **Me, Myself & I** pages in this chapter. Reflect on how you tackle the things that are in your way by first listing them and then assessing them. Is something in you creating them? Are they situational? There are some obstacles you may never be able to control completely—personal compulsions, terminal illnesses and extreme weather conditions, to name a few.

You always think you will beat the odds and fight the good fight until you face the moment of absolute depletion—with no more energy left to battle, you experience that like Don Quixote you have been fighting windmills. Without the fuel to resist, you accept.

One thing is certain—it is only when you encounter life's trials and tribulations that you truly learn about who you are and what you are capable of.

Consider these different types of obstacles:

Obstacles from Within:

- Your thoughts or ways of thinking or the way you phrase a thought
- Your attachments
- Your habits or obsessions
- Your personality traits
- The assumptions you make
- Your points of view
- The things you want
- The things you fear
- The things you dread
- The things you need
- Stress, tension and nerves
- Physical impediments or disabilities; illness
- Mental or emotional disabilities

Obstacles From Without:

- Things you can't control. People, places, and things fall into this category.
- Natural forces
- Time
- Circumstances or situations in which you find yourself

Obstacles: Comedy and Tragedy

Obstacles are at the heart of comedy. No one knew this better than Lucille Ball and Carol Burnett. Rent a DVD of *I Love Lucy* episodes or *The Carol Burnett Show*. Both women constructed brilliantly riotous situations on their respective shows. Lucy jumped into every situation with innocence and determination to do whatever it took to gain control. Each attempt to overcome a disaster was hilarious.

Obstacles are also at the heart of tragedy. Characters often experience enormous, heart-wrenching loss as they take on overwhelming obstacles and challenges. Sometimes many lives are at stake, sometimes rights or identity. Obstacles teach us what really matters in our lives and our characters' lives. Today we are bombarded with news of mass shootings, family members experiencing the sudden loss of a loved child, disastrous images of the aftermath of uncontrolled tempests and wildfires. Alas, it numbs us to view such tragedies as entertainment. Through your work as an actor you *re-sensitize* yourself to suffering and tribulation, by looking at the obstacles inherent in your script and digging deep to uncover identification with the events and actions with which you must cope, overcome or succumb to.

Allow Yourself to Be Vulnerable; Value Discomfort ★

When pursuing "your" new wants and needs you will encounter many challenges that get in your way. *Thank goodness!* These obstacles make theater vital and engaging. So, dive into the circumstances the playwright provides. When you are acting, if you do not encounter any problems and are not fighting for what you get—as either actor or character—take that as a signal that you are taking the easy way out and have not actively committed to your choices.

Make everything that happens to "you" in your play—what "you" gain or lose—as personal as if it were happening in your own life. Discover how the given circumstances matter to you and therefore affect you. You can allow yourself to be even *more* vulnerable than you are in daily life; your actor's training requires that you remove the protectors and drop the masks you have created to survive in the real world.

Take on the discomfort or ecstasy that the unfamiliar provokes in you. This is how your character will teach you more about your capabilities. By stepping out of your comfort zone, using your imagination to justify your wants and needs and finding actions that keep you moving forward, you will discover behavior (doings) you never imagined.

Susie. Oh, sure, that's easy for you to say, but I am, in my heart—see—sick of everybody being mad at me because I'm just trying to live my pathetic little life, you know, and fulfill a few of my ridiculous—I know they are—dreams—but if I have wanted something, and it's in my head, like what am I supposed to do? I can't help how I feel?

Those the River Keeps —David Rabe.

Contacting your vulnerability requires desire, stamina, courage and skill. Your vulnerability is always connected to love and caring. In the imaginary circumstances of your play, let yourself care, love and face personal truths. Learn to work from deeply personal places within yourself, places you mustn't share with anyone. *You are the mystery in your work.*

Being Where You Are – The Energy Flow

During a session of The Hagen Core Training program at HB, a lovely young actress is receiving a critique on her scene from *Ludlow Fair* by Lanford Wilson. She is playing Rachel, who thinks she is losing her mind. In the scene, everything Rachel does to overcome this feeling only makes matters worse. Rochelle Oliver is teaching the class.(Rochelle Oliver, actress and teacher, was 17 when she began studying with Uta Hagen and has been teaching at the HB Studio since the 1970s. She made her Broadway debut in Lillian Hellman's *Toys in the Attic*, played Honey in the original production of *Who's Afraid of Virginia Woolf* with Uta Hagen and appeared in many of Horton Foote's plays and films.) The actress playing Rachel is extremely frustrated. She is completely committed and has been working hard, but she doesn't understand what is being asked of her. Her frustration dominates the critique. Overwhelmed with feelings of confusion and her inability to pitch herself subjectively into the circumstances, she begins to cry. Rochelle cuts off the discussion to capture this authentic moment in which the actress is fully connected to herself. Rochelle eagerly tells the actress, "Begin the scene. Now!" The actress does, and she is completely, truthfully connected to the first moments of her scene. However, she does not trust the full use of her actual feelings to guide her to what she needs to do and soon finds herself unconnected to the scene. She gives up after three lines and does not follow through on what has been an authentic and effective way into "Rachel's" circumstances.

Erik Singer, the Speech teacher for the Core program, happened to be observing the class that day. It inspired him to write me this note:

It's a basic Alexander Technique principle: you can't *not be* where you are. You can't censor something that you're feeling or experiencing. If you do, as an actor, you just end up cut off and stuck. You have to acknowledge and accept where you are and what you're experiencing.

What I don't often hear acknowledged is what happens next. A magical thing happens when you *allow* energy/emotion, when you give permission for it to happen, and to be the *character's* experience, because *you are* the character. The energy/feeling state then becomes accessible and *malleable*. It will *change* into what you need it to be, i.e. what the character is experiencing and sending out at that moment (presuming you've done your work and are present for the character).

Energy and emotion are fluid things. They move and change. This is especially true if they are released, if they are sent out of us. This then creates room for further energy and feeling states. It has to be a river, not a pond, in other words.

Why bother acting if you don't crave or can't tolerate the self-confronting, uncomfortable challenges you face? If you only wish to reduce everything to a generic idea of being "natural," get out of acting. Your choices and the way you commit to them will release more creativity than you can consciously know or control. Exploring the exercises in this chapter will guide your discoveries. Learning to probe and question will deepen your rehearsal process as you find your through-line from the beginning of the play through every scene to the end. Throughout your rehearsals you muster and pursue new goals and ways of doing—doing even those things that, in your own life, you hate and despise.

Remember…

Obstacles

• Deepen your involvement

• Challenge you

• Engage you

• Teach you

Whether you want them to

or not!

Learn from Obstacles ★

You learn about who you are from your responses to life's challenges. You may have moments of giving up when you throw in the towel. You may quit. You may discover a surprising inner strength that you never knew you had, a resource never before needed: character. Depending upon the nature of the problem, it can fog or cloud your vision, toss you about like a leaf in the wind—literally and figuratively. When an obstacle gets the better of you, how do you feel? Extremely unhappy, insecure, deeply moved, saddened beyond words, exceedingly vulnerable, stuck, depressed, dissatisfied, angry, frustrated or lost? Obstacles are things you can't control or hold on to.

As they appear unpredictably in your life, you handle them and improvise your way through or around them to the best of your ability. *Obstacles force you into action.*

Action

Think Action ★

You have found your intentions, and have found and crafted meaningful obstacles that you must overcome. As you craft your preparation and strengthen your needs and stakes, you create urgency with which to begin your scene. You find inner objects that fill you with sensations of rage, fury, frustration, self-pity, hilarity, ecstasy, playfulness, vindictiveness, disgust, hatred, adoration to name a few. Your point of view, your needs and relationships fuel these feelings. Your feelings must find their release; otherwise, they will paralyze you or you will swim in the muddy waters of emotion. You release your feelings through your actions.

Aldo. Let's just drop this shitload, this weight a sorrow, these sandbags on our necks from a million years ago, and try to talk to each other about now.

Italian American Reconciliation –John Patrick Shanley

You want to have feelings, I repeat. Otherwise, why act? But your feelings must be released into the actions you play in your scene. You communicate with your words, your voice and your body. That means that your actions are carried and released through your words, your voice and your body.

Since acting is *taking action*—doing—the sooner it becomes second nature to you to think in terms of actions, the better. The minute you start talking about what you think you are feeling, ask yourself what that feeling makes you do. Otherwise, you could be working to produce a general emotion, not an action.

Remember that in life, emotions are the *surprise consequences* of your circumstances. They occur when you encounter obstacles that interfere with you getting what you want or need. They occur because people do things that affect you. They occur in every situation. Therefore, the minute you wonder what you think you should be feeling, replace that speculation with the question, "What is happening?" "What is the word for what I am doing to get what I need or want?" "Am I threatening him?" "Am I coaxing him?" "Am I groveling?"

Actions can be repeated again and again. Feelings are the unpremeditated consequences of complete circumstances affecting you. You can choose to *do* something. If you choose to *feel* something and push for it to happen, you create physical tension that works against you.

Begin to build your own vocabulary of verbs. Your action vocabulary will kindle your imagination, bring you to life and provide the possibility of new, unexpected behavior. It will put a positive spin on your work. Use the **Verbs/Actions/Doings** page in **The Work** pages of this chapter as a jump-start. Continue adding to the list. You will achieve the greatest clarity in your work when you think in terms of *doings*.

There are many theories about the types of actions you should use. Draw on sources that have meaning for you, that make sense to you, be they literal transitive or intransitive verbs or metaphors. You might find that corporal verbs that involve actions about the body serve you. For instance, you might say you will achieve your objective "by pinning him down," "by twisting his arm," "by pulling his leg," "by pushing him around," or "stepping on his toes." Your actions can use images. For instance, "by lifting her above all others," "by praising her to high heaven," or "by dancing on her grave." You can test literal behavioral verbs such as "by plopping down," "by slouching," "by creeping away" or "by pounding the table." Try out expressive metaphorical verbs like "by blowing my stack," "by soaking in the moment" or "by soaring above the clouds." Find your own. You will have fun.

Actions can be physical, verbal, psychological or a combination of all three. Your actions emanate from who you are, all of the given circumstances in the play, what you want, the things that are in your way and what the other characters are doing to you.

When influenced by these elements, the physical action of sitting down on a chair might result in flopping down, crumbling into, collapsing into, jumping onto, lunging for or carefully lowering yourself onto the chair.

The more sensitive you become to language, the sooner words and images will capture your imagination and prompt your body. You have many possibilities when choosing actions. Play them fully. Send them fearlessly. When something happens during a rehearsal, find the word that matches what you just experienced yourself doing.

Leave No Room for Second-guessing   ★

The moment of your greatest belief and involvement in your circumstances is when you play your action all the way. In other words, if you play your action 100%, you have no room to speculate or worry about yourself or your acting. You will see that you fully believe in what is happening in your scene. After the fact you can reflect on areas that need more fine-tuning or adjustment.

It is so easy to talk yourself out of playing an action fully. "It feels unnatural. It is uncomfortable. It is too over-the-top. It feels like a caricature and not real." Have you said these things to yourself, your teacher or your director?

Could the reason that you doubt yourself be that you are more focused, more motivated, more invested than ever before? Could it be that you are living on the edge and sending with real commitment? It feels different from the way you are in life, right? Well, it should. You have to be seen and heard when you are in a theater, and it really doesn't matter if the space holds 2,000 souls or 30.

Remember…

You don't know what's possible until you do it.

So …Just do it.

It is more productive to test your work fully and be told that, yes, you are over-the-top, pushing, or not being truthful than it is to get feedback that you are playing one note. How do you know what is possible if you do not step out of whatever box you may have created for yourself?

Send with Expectation ★

Whenever you take any kind of action, you have expectations about how things will turn out or what will happen next. Expectations grow out of your life experiences. Some become reflexive in certain situations or with certain people you know.

In the context of your craft, sending an action with expectation is an acting tool that keeps your performances fresh and alive. Sending an action with expectation ties "your" needs and actions to your relationships with the other people in your play (Chapter Five) and to your background (Chapter Six).

You expect to get what you want or you expect to lose. You expect to be heard or you expect to be laughed at. You expect to be ignored or to be followed. You expect agreement, disagreement, an argument, a fight, a battle, a welcoming embrace, understanding, success, praise, criticism, cynicism, failure or disaster.

When acting, you have to take this usually unconscious human reflex and select the expectations you bring into your interactions with the other characters in your scenes or plays.

By creating expectations that are other than what you actually receive from the other characters, you create the landscape for surprise. Fully committing to expectations that connect to your needs, you will be able to genuinely receive your fellow actors' behaviors and words as if for the first time. You will have filled yourself with inner objects and will cease anticipating or waiting for the actor's next lines.

Remember…

Actors sometimes make conscious choices that in human terms are most often unconsciously sourced in life. The terms we use can get stuck in the actor's head. You rehearse to find them in your body. The new you isn't 'thinking' the choices you have made for your objectives, obstacles or actions. Since you are the character, let yourself trust what you discover in rehearsals and performance.

Your expectations come from your past relationships or experiences. Notice what happens when you send with expectation. Your imagination thrives. When you work on your relationships in Chapter Five, you will see how *endowment* and *transference* are integral in the formation of the expectations you establish in your relationships.

There are times when you are treated as you expected to be, or things go the way you expected them to go…then you are right. When that happens, celebrate.

When you ask a question, don't you anticipate the response or answer you would like to get? When you tell a joke or a story, don't you have an idea of how you want the person to respond? Your expectations are linked with your needs or wants. Unless you have trained yourself not to have expectations of any kind, you anticipate or have expectations about most of what is going to happen in your life—yet rarely does life meet your expectations.

Find Your First Action   ★

What Am I Doing at, and When Did I Come to the Window?

It is our final dress rehearsal for *Angel Street* by Patrick Hamilton. I am playing Bella Manningham. The stage manager calls places. I am standing at the window waiting for the curtain to go up. There is some delay and I am in position for quite a while.

I catch myself thinking impatiently about when the play will begin, and this makes me realize that I haven't done my homework leading into the first moment of the play. I don't have one single inner object connected to "my" immediate preceding circumstances of the play!

Questions whiz through my brain. What was I doing before coming to the window? What is on my mind? What is the weather like? How long have I been watching for the organ grinder man and his adorable monkey? Do I have a treat to throw the monkey? How much money do I throw them? Who does the organ grinder remind me of? Why am I looking forward to seeing them today? What direction do they usually come from? Do they pass by my window every day or once a week? Are they late today? Is there a ritual or routine I am accustomed to? What songs does he usually play?

I can't begin to tell you how foolish and exhilarated I feel. The questions have always been there. Clearly, I had not been ready to ask them until now.

Approach your work knowing that you are stepping into a life already in motion at a precise point in time. There is life before a play or scene begins— this is the past. There is the life we see onstage—this is the present. There is life after the play or scene ends—this is the future.

The events that transpired before the start of a scene ignite your first action by tying your immediate past to the first thing you do. There will always be a time in a play when you provide the past that leads to the first moment the audience sees. There will always be the time at the end of a scene or play when you connect to the future that the audience will not see.

Let's consider the elements that are involved in finding your first action and your final action in a scene.

- In one sentence, describe the event (what happens) in your scene ("I quit my job", "I discover…").

- Craft and particularize your immediate preceding circumstances. What just happened before your scene begins? Find the immediate happening that triggers your first actions (physical and verbal).

- Craft your future circumstances. Where are you going? What will be happening in the next twenty minutes?

- Name your immediate objective. Your wants and needs come from the depth of your being, your unconscious. Only when your obstacle is extreme (e.g. you are paralyzed and have to relearn how to walk or talk) will your objective be at the forefront of your mind.

- Speculate about and imagine when and why your needs and wants began. Why are they important to you now?

- Pinpoint the target of your pursuit. Set your sights on the person or circumstance that will give you what you want. What will satisfy you, and how?

Once you ask yourself what you want, you invoke the next question: what is in your way? This then sparks the final question, *what are you doing to get what you want?*

Gert. Now get out of my house. Because brother or no, I'm through with you.

A Young Lady of Property – Horton Foote

Know Your Action

I am playing Paulina in William Shakespeare's *A Winter's Tale* and find myself quite miserable every time we rehearse the trial scene in Act III, Scene ii. During that scene, Hermione, who has been put on trial, protests her husband Leontes' treatment of her and their children, nobly declaring her innocence and what she stands for.

I don't know what to do with myself during this scene and I am very frustrated. Listening isn't enough. I unfairly fault the actress playing Hermione for not including me when she is speaking.

At last, in one of those glorious moments in the creative process, like a gift from the gods, it comes to me.

I have been way off base searching for the solution to my problem. So self-involved, I haven't asked myself the right question—*what am I doing*? I don't have an action to play in the scene. I am expecting my fellow actress to do my work for me, by helping me in a way that has nothing to do with the primary event of the scene—Hermione confronting Leontes, publicly standing trial after having been imprisoned, her newborn child taken away from her and left to die in the woods.

My objective is to protect her, watch over her and do whatever she wishes me to do. My obstacle, as her lady-in-waiting, stems from my position: I have to keep quiet! I also have to do my job and take care of her. She is more important to me than anything. In her weakened condition, I don't know if she will be able to make it through the trial. My actions, therefore, are to serve her, to stand by her, to watch out for her well-being and to catch her if she faints.

Once I have my actions, because they are so simple, pure and doable, I love rehearsing and playing the scene. The solution is so simple. It always will be. It's getting there that is the challenge!

Keep searching. You will find your action. When you do, it will feel as if it was always there and it will be easy to channel your energy into and through it towards your target.

Action Your Scene—A Way to Begin ★

This is an idea that is confusing for many. There are times when a teacher will ask you to write an action for every line in your play. It is an exercise to analyze your script, to see what the lines tell you about the interactions you are having with the other characters. You practice thinking about what you might be doing in the scene. You consider the currents that run under your lines. You will never be able to remember all the actions you write, so don't try!

When you meet to rehearse with your partner, some of the actions you wrote may work for you. Most may fall away. Your partner's actions will replace your ideas and spark your responses. You will discover actions that you didn't foresee as you let your partner affect you.

A dictionary and thesaurus are the best references you can use as you work on this chapter. As you *action your scene,* read every line of text wondering what waves of intent and need ripple under your lines. Notice when the subject matter changes. When you are on your feet, learn to recognize the difference between the sensations you have when you are sending an action as opposed to the sensations you have when you are holding onto and playing an emotion.

Never evaluate an action's effectiveness while you are sending it. Always send an action with an expectation of what it will do to the other person and how that person will respond. How does your action land? Your actions will almost always be motivated by your fellow actors' actions and your own needs.

When you have finished a rehearsal, check in with yourself immediately. If parts felt great and you feel some actions worked, ask yourself *why* they worked. What was I *doing*? You won't be finalizing a score, but you will be on the way to finding one.

When you are more concerned with feeling something or worried that nothing is moving in on you, you can be sure that you are not playing actions—you are not *doing*.

Talk with Purpose, Intention ★

Dialogue is never conversational. There is always a reason why "you" are talking. There is always purpose behind your words. You send a *verbal action* with the playwright's words. The greater your command of your speech and vocal instrument, the greater the range of verbal actions you can play. Often

[handwritten margin note: there is always a reason you say a line!]

the text informs the nature of the action. *Tone*, *intonation* and *articulation* are elements used in sending an action. All are physical.

For example, your line is "Hi." Depending on your circumstances, your action may be greeting, smothering with kisses, welcoming, scolding or questioning. A verbal action is often accompanied by a psychological action. With the line "Hi," you might belittle, humiliate or dismiss.

Your verbal and psychological actions could be accompanied by a reflexive physical action. Once again, depending upon the circumstances, you might offer or withhold your hand, jump up and down; turn away from, hug, or size up the person, or double-check to make sure you know them.

As you see, behavior is a sequence of interrelated physical, verbal and psychological actions. You have been "behaving" all your life. Your actions will be the inevitable consequence of all the work you do on your given circumstances, your relationships and your "Who Am I?" in Chapter Six. What you do will always be the consequence of what you want, what obstacles you encounter and how you receive what happens to you or is done to you—psychologically and physically.

Because life moves so swiftly, you condition yourself in rehearsals to respond "in the moment." You have no time to think or worry about the actions you are playing when you are onstage. A scene becomes very troublesome when you don't know your action. You become free when you do.

The Actor's Way ★

Choosing Life Actions

My friend Susan consistently applies the craft of acting to her life. She has a talent for sizing up a situation and coming up with many interesting and inventive ways of handling it. Not only does she do this for herself, she freely shares her ideas and insights with her husband, children and friends. She thrives on helping people she loves. Susan has played an important role in many of my life decisions.

So smart, Susan always talks about events coming up in her own life—whether at work or with her family—and then mentions the action that she is going to use during the event. Assessing her mother's temper, anticipating a colleague's power play, she then chooses the actions that will get her through.

Having learned from Susan, when my mother comes to live with us we apply her technique. We encounter many unanticipated obstacles and desperately seek new actions to help us live in harmony. We indulge her, include her, hug her, jolly her along, stand up to her and entertain her. We take her to the mall, on outings and doctor visits. We get our little dog Millie, who brings more laughter into the house. And through all this, I come to know my mother.

> The sad irony is that my dear, precious friend Susan dies even before my mother. I still continue to be inspired and moved by the way she lived her life and the example she set.

After all these years, I have come to realize that acting will inform and enrich your life much, much more than your life will inform your acting. Acting tools are powerful. You want to be at the ready to use them. When you responsibly use these tools in the real world, you will find you are able to change many things in your life.

During this phase of the work, as you action your play, you will undoubtedly become more aware of your own life actions. As an actor you will always be testing new actions—actions that you may have never played or actions that you have always dreamed of playing. As a theater artist you are a student of human behavior. Man is capable of wondrous and staggeringly beautiful actions, as well as stupid, horrific, unconscionable deeds.

From the moment you enter this world, you are on the way to leaving it. In between, you live, love, want, dream, create, destroy, plan, work, play and sleep. You are always moving forward in time toward something. Your wants, needs, desires, cravings, fancies, covetousness, hope and faith keep you going. Your aspirations and sense of purpose emanate from deep within you.

Georgie. ...What an amazing fucking snow job you all are doing on the world. And I bought it! We all buy it. My family —they're like, all of a sudden I'm Mary Tyler Moore or something. I mean, they live in hell, right, and they spend their whole lives wishing they were some- where else, wishing they were rich, or sober, or clean; living on a street with trees, being on some fucking TV show.

...

Spike Heels —Theresa Rebeck

Your deeds and accomplishments sprout from seeds planted early in your life. As your life situation changes, you may attain more than you ever dreamed you would. On the other hand, your dreams may dissipate or change as you make life choices and decisions. You may encounter hardships or events that send you off-course, actually defeat you or set you on a new path.

Of course, the more you want, desire, cherish or value something, the greater your investment. The greater your investment, the more you risk. The more you risk, the more you have to lose.

How you go after what you want is a reflection of your sense of need or entitlement or your sense of inadequacy. It requires your ability to risk, to put yourself on the line when success is not guaranteed.

You have a relationship to risk-taking. Your experience will be a result of your stamina, sense of humor, willingness and preparedness to take on the challenges you meet.

Your ability to evaluate, negotiate and actively work with the people, places and things you encounter will also influence the quality of your experience.

You do not walk around thinking about what you want 24 hours a day. Your pursuits are most often motivated by an instantaneous thought, sense or drive. Not all are good for you—some are life-threatening. All your pursuits are determined by your circumstances. Most major pursuits require time, commitment, tenacity, experience, ability and good fortune. Expect instant results only from Lipton Soup.

You have the chance to find, build and create both your voice and your body—and to use both well. You have the opportunity to discover the glory of language, from Shakespeare to hip-hop. You have the chance to discover the breadth of the human condition. You have the chance to find your own humanity.

Paul. ...That's my life. Ben, that's all I want, just a home, Susan, some kids, just what I can see and touch.

Loose Ends —Michael Weller

A Self-Assessment

This exercise asks you to look at the relationship you have with your pursuit of what you want, or say you want, in your life. There are no right, wrong, good or bad answers.

- Are you an over- or under-achiever? Why do you think so?

  over - competitive

- Write about keeping your word. (For example, "There are times when I know the minute I say something that I have no intention of following through.")

  a problem for me

- When you say you will do something, how much of the time can you be counted on?

  ☐ 100% ☑ 75% ☐ 50% ☐ 25% ☐ 0% ☐ other?

- How would you assess your ability to estimate the kind of time you require to complete a particular goal?

  good

- What could you do to increase your dependability, your reliability?

  Keep my word

- Do you make To Do lists or do you remember things you need to do in your head?

  remember in my head

- Are you organized or disorganized? Does your clutter bother you or is it your form of organization? How does the clutter in your life eat up time?

  I am organized

- Rank your accomplishments to date: those you are proudest of, the most difficult, the most rewarding.

  PhD
  Michael
  myself   my career   now

  Me / Myself & I (triangle diagram)

- How do you handle roadblocks or obstacles?

  go around or over, never accept them

- What is your relationship to compromise?

  not great at first, then good

- When you negotiate with another party, do you take their side into account?

  not often enough

- Talk about a time when you have been torn between two desires or obligations.

- Are you a multi-tasker? Are you able to multi-task effectively and efficiently? Do you prefer working on multiple projects at one time (juggling many projects) or focusing on only one before beginning the next?

  I multi-task well but also can focus on one project well

- Are you a long-range planner? If so, how far ahead do you plan? Are you short-range planner or a combination of both?

  both

- How do you handle deadlines? Discuss your history of procrastination and excuses.

  I meet deadlines

- How do you make decisions? Look at your history of important decisions you have made. How and why did you arrive at those decisions?

  I make decisions quickly

Your Needs, Wishes, Dreams & Desires

- Write about things you need right now in the following areas:

  ° Your presentation

  ° Your financial situation

  I am very lucky that I have a very good finac. situation

  ° Your job/employment situation

  so → not necessay

  ° Your living situation

  I love my living situation and don't need to move as I own my apt

  ° Your relationships

  I have met the love of my life Michael + we are comuted to eachother

- List some things you would like to have, have happen or do in your life right now. Next to each item in your list write about actions you have taken toward attaining them. List actions you can take toward attaining those goals.

  • Be in a play
  • get maried to Michael
  • Have M make it

A letter of recommendation

Although you may feel intimidated by this exercise, it is a great way to consciously acknowledge your strengths, training, skills and accomplishments on paper. Notice the feelings and thoughts that arise as you do this. Which thoughts are productive and enhancing? Which are belittling and self-defeating?

Pretend you are a teacher or director with whom you have worked. You need a reference from them because you are applying to a theater school or theater company. Write the letter of recommendation.

An introductory e-mail to an agent or casting director

- Choose an agent or casting director you wish to contact. Research their agency.

- Do you have a contact address for them?

- What do you want to achieve with your e-mail?

- How do you plan to follow up? How often?

- Write the e-mail, but don't send it.

- Get some feedback on your e-mail from someone who has more experience in the biz than you do.

- Send it online with your photo and resume. Follow up.

A difficult phone call

- Think of a phone call you have to make. Why do you have to make the call? What do you want to accomplish? How will you know if you get what you set out to achieve?

- Outline the points you have to cover. How can you acknowledge or take care of the party you are calling? What would be the ideal outcome of the call? What would be an outcome that you could live with?

- Pretend to make the call.

- Do the same with a pretend Face Time or Skype exchange.

Your life and acting

- Do you find it easier or more difficult to determine, state and pursue what you want in a scene than you do in your daily life? Why?

- Do you find it easier or more difficult to be courageous and more assertive in a scene or in your daily life? Why?

Where Your Wants Come From

With the next exercises, you look at your past, present and future wants. You excavate the sources of your goals. Acknowledge your past accomplishments and what it took to attain them. Other exercises will give you the opportunity to re-assess, adjust and shift goals.

My past wants

Make a list of things you wanted in the *past*. Note the details you recall regarding time, location and situation. Write about what you did to attain those things. What were the results? Was it worth it?

Inherited wants

List some of your objectives. How did you come to have them? What wants and needs have you inherited? Write about your parents. What drove each parent? What do you think that they want or wanted for themselves? What do you think that they want or wanted for you? How judgmental have you been of your parents' ways and desires? What characteristics and desires do you share with each parent?

Remember…

The only disability in life is negative thinking.

–Scott Hamilton

New wants

Part of life's journey is finding the things that you truly want, and actively choosing them. You may find that when you ask yourself what you truly want, you come up with a resounding, "I don't know." Daydream. If you could, what changes would you make right now? Let the sky be the limit. What is preventing you from those new pursuits? Write the reasonable, realistic but perhaps defeating thoughts that arise as you delve into this difficult question.

My Objectives

Here are exercises to assist you in your ability to clearly and simply state what you need, want or desire. You may set many small goals in pursuit of your objective. It is helpful to state a goal or objective in the following manner. Make sure that it is specific, measurable and accompanied by a time factor. Notice the positive declaration: I will do three scenes in my scene study class (name them)

_____

by (write date) _____.

Knowing your own life, have you set an unattainable objective for yourself? Have you stated actions you know you won't take? Given yourself an unrealistic time frame?

Old desires and dreams

Tell a story about when you were little and you wanted something. What happened?

A life-altering event or moment

Events like 9/11/2001, Hurricane Katrina and the Sandy Hook storm can change your life forever. As a result of such an event, your needs, wants and desires can be dramatically affected. Talk about a personal event that affected you and changed what you thought you wanted out of life.

Your future

- What will you be doing and where will you be five years from today?

- What will you be doing and where will you be ten years from today?

- Choose a goal. Set a date for achieving that goal.

Your needs

- Write about the things you need right now.

- Write about past needs.

My Objectives (Cont.)

Accomplishments

Every now and then, it is helpful to give yourself a reality check. My husband gets furious at me when I end a day saying that I didn't accomplish anything. Often, when I make that sweeping generalization, I am lying and in many ways undermining myself. I can reflect in a positive, affirming manner. Even if I didn't complete the projects as planned, I can honor and acknowledge the time I have spent and the work that I have done that day.

- List everything you did today.

- List everything you did last week.

Planning

- What would you like to accomplish by the end of this course? This month?

- What do you want to achieve in your lifetime? Is this question relevant?

What you want

Talk about what you want…

- From a friend

- For a friend

- From yourself

- For yourself

- From your family

- For your family

- In class

- For the world

Albertine. You said you were in trouble. Do you wish to tell me about it?

Toys in the Attic
–Lillian Hellman

Use this worksheet to gain clarity on an objective you want to pursue.

Goal Worksheet

My goal is to:

To achieve my goal I need to:

To achieve my goal I could try:

Your Goals in Acting Class

When you do a scene for class, what do you want to achieve? Here are some ideas…

- I want to blow the class away with my work.
- I want everyone to rush over to me and tell me how great the scene was.
- I want everyone to want to work with me.
- I want my teacher to like me and praise my work.
- I want my teacher to treat me gently.
- I want my teacher to be honest with me.

Now write your own.

When you answer the following questions, you might reveal some thoughts that stand in the way of achieving your goals.

- Do you worry about pushing, illustrating, indicating or "going over the top"? What will happen to you if you do any of these things?

- Does fear of doing some of the "no-no's" of acting affect your work in class? How?

- What can you do to take more responsibility for what you get out of each class?

- Are you afraid of looking stupid? Being wrong? Failing? Your character probably is, too. NO

Remember…

A little bit goes a long way.

Easy does it.

Your Artistic Aspirations

Write about the kind of work you want to do and how you wish to be perceived in the theatre, film or TV community. How far are you willing to go to achieve your aspirations? What sacrifices are you prepared to make? What sacrifices are you not prepared to make?

Go for it!

- Write about how you feel about going after things you want.

- What are you afraid of?

- What is holding you back?

- What is the best thing that could happen to you if you went after what you want?

- What is the worst thing that could happen to you if you went after what you want?

Remember...

Do you want to be heard? Do you want to be seen?

Go back in time. Think about something you wanted really badly and what happened when you got it.

Go back in time. Now think about something you wanted really badly and what happened when you didn't get it.

What do you need to achieve your professional goals?

- [ ] A new haircut
- [ ] New pictures
- [x] To do more plays
- [ ] Another acting class
- [x] Work on my voice
- [ ] More Shakespeare
- [ ] To get out of the city
- [ ] A windfall
- [x] An agent
- [ ] To network

- [x] To become a member of an acting company
- [ ] To find a mentor
- [ ] To write my own material
- [ ] New clothes
- [ ] Work
- [x] To be in a lot of plays and films
- [ ] To work with actors more experienced than I am

- [ ] To work with actors who are more talented than I am
- [x] To work with brilliant directors
- [ ] To play leading roles
- [x] To play roles in great plays
- [ ] To live my life fully and deeply
- [ ] Other _____

What Do I Have to Lose?

Stakes

Having something at stake means having an investment in something. Fear is an obstacle that raises your stakes. Check off and explain the following obstacles and fears if they apply to you as you work toward your goals:

- You might fail.

- You might humiliate yourself.

- You might succeed.

- You might be exposed.

- You might not get what you want.

- You might look back with regret and say, "If only…."

Prince. …Never look away from a problem, Benny.
Stark. I never know when you're serious.
Prince. When you look away from the problem, it don't disappear. But maybe you might disappear!

Rocket to the Moon
—Clifford Odets

Risk

You are most familiar with risk in relationship to the stock exchange, gambling, marriage, medical treatment, surgery, travel, war or standing up for your beliefs in a hostile environment. When you don't follow the rules—be they the law of the land, the policies of your employer or the rules of your family—you run the risk of being caught, found out and held accountable for your actions. Denial can put a person or a nation at risk. Some risks have more dire consequences than others. People have varying degrees of tolerance for risk-taking.

- If you don't audition, you never have to face or experience rejection.

- If you don't work in class, you will never discover your strengths or weaknesses as an actor.

- If you don't practice, you won't develop tools and habits necessary to do your job.

- If you don't ask, you might not get….

The Obstacles in My Life: Obstacles from Within

The Seven Deadly Sins: Avarice, Envy, Gluttony, Lust, Pride, Sloth, and Wrath

The Seven Virtues: Charity, Chastity, Patience, Humility, Kindness, Moderation, and Zeal

WARNING! The **Me, Myself and I** exercises on the next five pages probe profound life issues. They are not intended to solve your life problems or to make your life better.

Instead, they are designed to enhance your empathy for the characters you will create. They should stimulate your imagination and give you the courage to face the things you need to face from your character's point of view. They should open your ability to intuit the things that could be blocking, stopping, challenging, or blinding your character. When you intuit using your senses, sensation is transmitted to and through your body. When you *really* see, hear, taste, touch and smell, you will experience something that you rarely experience in the course of your own life—giving your total attention to another.

You do not have to do all the exercises. You certainly should not do them all at once. When you feel overwhelmed, take a break.

One last word: *Under no circumstances should you share or "act out" any of the results with colleagues, friends or family.*

Phillip. The Greeks believed that it was a citizen's duty to watch a play. It was a kind of work in that it required attention, judgment, patience, all social virtues.

Our Country's Good —Timberlake Wertenbaker

Obstacles from Within (Cont.)

My thoughts and the way I think or phrase a thought

- Choose a day this week when you will write down your thoughts and the things you say throughout the day.

- Review your notes at a later time.

- Did you:

- ☑ bully yourself or someone else?
- ☐ blame someone?
- ☐ second-guess yourself?
- ☐ excuse your behavior?
- ☐ think you were wrong?
- ☐ think you did badly?
- ☑ wish you could take back something you said or did?
- ☐ put thoughts in someone else's mind?

- ☐ judge yourself or someone else?
- ☑ criticize yourself or someone?
- ☐ attack yourself or someone else?
- ☑ defend yourself?
- ☐ think you were bad?
- ☐ complain?
- ☐ think something was impossible or hopeless?
- ☐ Other? _____

- How many thoughts did you have that acknowledged your accomplishments? How many thoughts were encouraging and optimistic?

Some perceptions can cause great discontent

- Is the "grass always greener" somewhere other than where you are? Where?

  no

- Do you think there is a secret to success? Do you think others know it? Who?

  NO

- Do you think that people who "have it all" are happy and carefree? For instance?

  NO

My attachments

- Talk about your attachments to your possessions, your home, your family, friends and work. What would your life be like without them?

My habits, obsessions or addictions

- Do you have to have things done your way?

  yes, sometimes too much

- Do you have to do things the same way all the time?

  never

- List your addictions. Do you smoke? Drink? Watch Internet porn? Clubbing? Work? Rehearsing?

  eating sugar chocolate

- Write about your obsessions. How many times a day do you wash your hands, shower or bathe?

  eating when depressed

Obstacles from Within (Cont.)

My personality traits

Are you:

- ☐ disorganized
- ☐ chronically late
- ☐ rigid/inflexible
- ☐ defensive
- ☐ protective
- ☐ stubborn

- ☐ obtuse
- ☐ insensitive
- ☐ overly sensitive
- ☐ vulnerable
- ☐ slow
- ☑ impatient

- ☑ negative
- ☑ critical
- ☐ resentful
- ☐ methodical
- ☐ indiscriminate
- ☐ cynical

- ☐ invasive
- ☑ aggressive
- ☐ Other? _____

Do you:

- ☑ take things personally
- ☐ have unrealistic expectations of yourself and others
- ☐ see things as "if only…."
- ☐ never complete what you begin

- ☐ have too many irons in the fire
- ☐ always give in
- ☐ complain
- ☑ give advice
- ☐ ask for advice

- ☐ deprive yourself
- ☐ indulge yourself
- ☐ Other? _____

The assumptions I make

- How often do you find yourself saying, "But I thought _____."
  This statement is the result of a mistaken assumption you made.

  NO

- In order to achieve a goal, do you believe that things have to happen in a certain order? Give some examples where you think an order is necessary.

  No

- How often do you think that something is impossible, hopeless, unrealistic or unreasonable?

  Rarely

- True or False: Winning the lottery would solve all your problems.

  F

- True or False: If I lose weight, more people will like me.

  F

The things I want

- Think about a person you know. In what ways and why do you want them to be different? *Do not run to them with this information. This is really about you, not them.*

- Do you find yourself wanting things that someone else has? Think about what that person has and why you want those things for yourself.

  NO

- Do you want things when you can't have them? What do you do to have things your way?

  NO

- Do you want your life to be other than it is? Why and how do you want it to be different?

  NO

- Do you want to be other than you are? Why and how do you want to be different?

  NO

- Do you want to:

☐ be famous	☑ be liked	☐ help others	☐ live abroad
☐ be popular	☑ get an agent	☐ write a novel	☐ Other? _____
☑ be happy	☐ study French	☐ have your own home	
☑ be healthy	☐ get married	☐ please everyone	
☐ be wealthy	☑ work	☐ gain weight	
☐ have children	☐ have a partner		

Obstacles from Within (Cont.)

The things I fear:

- [ ] unknown cultures, ways and beliefs
- [ ] success
- [ ] failure
- [ ] being wrong
- [ ] not being liked
- [x] abandonment
- [ ] not being loved
- [ ] intimacy
- [ ] sex
- [ ] not knowing
- [ ] dying
- [ ] ghosts
- [ ] anger – yours or another's
- [ ] losing control
- [x] violence

- [ ] aging
- [ ] emotion – yours or another's
- [ ] responsibility
- [x] being alone
- [ ] regretting
- [ ] your blind spots
- [ ] illness
- [x] gaining weight
- [ ] drugs
- [ ] addiction
- [ ] loss
- [ ] asserting yourself
- [ ] making a fool of yourself
- [ ] sounding stupid
- [ ] blowing an audition
- [ ] Other:

Choose one and write about it.

George. Who's afraid of Virginia Woolf …

Martha. I … am … George … I … am …

Who's Afraid of Virginia Woolf —Edward Albee

The things I dread

In some situations you anticipate the impending events or activities with terror in your heart and soul. Contemplate one or two at a time. When did these dreads arise? Where does your mind go when the event is near at hand?

Are you afraid of:

- ☐ public speaking
- ☐ being alone
- ☐ phoning agents
- ☐ being fired
- ☐ entertaining
- ☐ getting on the scale
- ☐ sex
- ☐ reading out loud
- ☐ waking up in the morning
- ☐ going to school
- ☐ competition
- ☐ birthdays
- ☐ New Year's Eve
- ☐ taking exams

- ☐ flying
- ☐ being late
- ☐ getting sick
- ☐ going to the doctor
- ☐ going to the dentist
- ☑ depression
- ☐ visiting someone who is terminally ill
- ☐ getting in touch with your feelings
- ☐ resentment
- ☐ dying
- ☐ my parents dying
- ☐ auditioning
- ☐ Other _____

Choose one and write about it.

Me / Myself & I

Obstacles from Within (Cont.)

The things I need

The following things are necessary for survival or add to the quality of your life. Some come from early life experiences and some have become habitual.

I need:

- [x] to be right
- [ ] to have things my way
- [ ] to avoid confrontation
- [ ] to be good at _____
- [ ] comfort
- [x] to be heard
- [ ] to be accepted as I am
- [ ] to be wrong
- [ ] to be criticized
- [ ] to love
- [x] to be loved
- [ ] to fail
- [ ] to get ahead
- [ ] to suffer
- [ ] to be liked
- [x] approval
- [ ] family
- [x] friends
- [ ] shelter
- [ ] exercise

- [ ] fresh air
- [ ] attention
- [ ] to be taken care of
- [x] work
- [ ] to play more
- [ ] to take better care of myself
- [ ] to do good deeds
- [ ] assistance
- [ ] quiet
- [ ] solitude
- [ ] my faith
- [ ] music
- [ ] literature
- [ ] art
- [ ] food and water
- [ ] beauty
- [ ] nature
- [ ] joy
- [ ] Other _____

Choose one and write about it.

Stress, Tension and Nerves

This is an opportunity to assess the causes and manifestations of stress, tension or nerves.

How would you categorize yourself?

- [ ] easy-going
- [✓] confident
- [ ] ADD/ADHD
- [ ] hyper

- [ ] insecure
- [ ] bipolar
- [ ] nervous
- [ ] calm, cool and collected

- [ ] obsessive compulsive
- [ ] anxious
- [✓] Other? _impatient_

Talk about the stressors in your life: family, work, illness, loss, etc.

My tension

- What makes you tense or anxious?

- How does this manifest in your behavior? (Do you stop breathing, shut down, tune out, etc.?)

- What circumstances create tension within you? How do you experience it?

- Do you hold your tension in a particular part of your body? What part?

- How do you release your tension?

- When you are in class, what role do the following play in producing tension in you?
  - ° Being corrected in public
  - ° Not "getting it" in public
  - ° Feeling "wrong" in public
  - ° Wanting to do it "right"
  - ° Your desire to be "good" ✓
  - ° Taking criticism personally and automatically thinking you are in the wrong
  - ° Wanting to "fix" and make changes without processing or rehearsing

---

Ken. Small things can look big when they all come at the same time.

Hot Line –
Elaine May

Remember…
A thought is only a thought.

Stress, Tension and Nerves (Cont.)

My nerves

- When do you get nervous?

- What are your default habits when you are nervous? (Do you talk faster, laugh after everything you say, mumble, fidget, hyperventilate, etc.?)

- Do you have a way of calming your nerves? What do you do?

- Is there any time when your nerves serve you? How do they serve you?

Remember…

Life is one long improvisation.

The Obstacles in My Life: Obstacles from Without

Things I can't control

- People, places, and things

- The transient nature of life

- Natural beauty, individual difference, man's nature, permanent and impermanent materials

People. Think about the people in your life who:

- argue
- don't listen
- cheat
- lie
- attack you
- go behind your back
- tease you
- don't take you seriously
- want you to be other than you are
- criticize you
- have a hidden agenda
- worship you
- befriend you

- advise you
- fight you
- belittle you
- protect you
- shield you
- are attracted to you
- expect and ask too much of you
- disrespect you
- see you a certain way
- look up to you
- want for you.
- Other _____

Choose one and write about it.

Joe. Of course I believe you. Living is an art. It's not bookkeeping. It takes a lot of rehearsing for a man to be himself.

The Time of Your Life
—William Saroyan

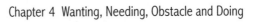

Obstacles from Without (Cont.)

There are also people who:

- you admire
- you advise
- you envy
- you love
- you respect
- you put down
- you manipulate
- you want to be other than as they are

- you shield
- you criticize
- you cheat on
- you protect
- you trust
- you idolize or worship
- you emulate
- Other? _____

Choose one person and write about them.

Do not share your insights with the people involved!

Places – public and private

- Holy places
- Work places: farms, factories, offices, homes
- Natural spaces: woods, mountains, lakes, beaches, islands, oceans
- Public places
- Homes of all sorts from cardboard boxes to castles, ghettos and slums
- Hazardous waste sites
- Conditions of the place: crowded, desolate, luxurious, isolated places, poorly ventilated, odiferous, heated or cooled, dark, noisy, dilapidated, dingy, monumental, imposing, solid, pristine, historic, antiseptic, claustrophobic, polluted

Things

- heirlooms
- personal treasures
- antiques
- basic life necessities: food, water
- tools and supplies
- flowers
- money
- homes
- clothing
- education
- art, music
- books
- TV, film
- automobiles
- toxic substances

Natural forces

- global warming
- natural disasters
- weather
- germs
- viruses
- man
- poverty

Bill. Supposed to get up to seventy today.
April. Two more weeks and everything will stink.

The Hot L Baltimore –Lanford Wilson

Obstacles from Without (Cont.)

Circumstances or situations in which you find yourself

There are times when you find yourself inundated with obligation or responsibility. Because of the nature of your work or because of where you live this could be a chronic situation.

- You may have too many things to do and not enough time to do them.

- You may have to do something that is difficult and complex.

- You may want to or have to do something that requires knowledge or skill that you don't have.

- You may have to do something on the spur of the moment (improvise) without adequate preparation.

- You may be pulled in many directions by family, friends and work.

Cliff. Hey, I need to hold you.

The Woolgatherer —William Mastrosimone

More on Obstacles in My Life

My fears

- Name them. What fears do you have yet to name?

- What happens to you when you experience them?

- Which fears shut you down, wake you up, keep you working?

- Travel back. Talk about something that became a buried secret and caused you shame.

- Consider your relationship to Trust and Truth.

- What do you do when a fear surfaces?

Obstacles now

- What are the obstacles stopping you from doing the things you say you want to do?

- List the current obstacles preventing you from doing the things you need to do.

- List the obstacles you face from your upbringing or culture and today's world.

A current situation

Write about a difficult situation you are currently facing.

- How did you get into the situation in the first place?

- Who was responsible for the situation? How did it begin?

- Write the perfect ending. How would you like it to be resolved?

- Write the worst possible ending.

- Write an ending you could live with.

More on Obstacles (Cont.)

- Discuss all the obstacles in your path.

- Is something stopping you or holding you back from taking action?

- What is standing in your way?

A past situation

Write about a difficult situation you faced in the past.

- How did it begin?

- How did you get into the situation in the first place?

- Who was responsible for the situation?

- How many parties were involved? Who were they?

- What was your part in the situation?

- What role did shame play in the situation?

- Describe how the situation was resolved, if it was resolved.

- Was the situation resolved to your satisfaction?

- How would you have liked it to have been resolved?

- Could it have ended worse than it did?

- Discuss all the obstacles that were in your path.

- How did you overcome them?

- Do you still have strings left dangling from the situation?

- What would give you closure? Do you believe closure is even possible?

lady in blue.

one thing I don't need is any more apologies.

For Colored Girls Who Have Considered Suicide When the Rainbow is Enuf

—Ntozake Shange

Tough Calls

A future situation

Think about a situation you know you are going to have to deal with.

- Write it out.

- How and why do you anticipate confronting this situation?

- Who or what are its causes? How did it start?

- How would you love it to be resolved?

- What are your concerns about not getting it resolved?

- What obstacles do you already foresee?

- What obstacles do you think you haven't considered?

- Using what you learned about *actions* in this chapter, think about what you might do, and have to do, to reach a mutually agreeable resolution.

Difficult decisions

Decisions all involve choice. Almost any decision you make will affect someone else. You may have to make decisions for someone you know. Rarely do warranties or guarantees accompany your choices. For example, you may have to make a decision:

- To have a surgical procedure
- To determine the medical treatment for a chronic or life-threatening condition
- To have an abortion or carry a baby to term
- To take a job that separates you from your family
- To determine proper care for aging parents
- To marry someone in spite of disapproving parents
- To buy a house
- Other _____

Tough Calls (Cont.)

Think of tough decisions you have had to make. List them. Write about some of your difficult decisions.

Selecting Actions

Your relationship to language is very personal and highly subjective and is a vital ingredient when arriving at your actions for a scene. Don't treat choosing action verbs as a guessing game, or think your choices have to be right. Look for words that mean something to you, and therefore energize and activate you within the context of the scene. Test your actions in rehearsal. Put them in your belly.

Here is a scenario requiring you to make a decision and take action:

You have been arguing with a friend because, although he has been complaining about not feeling well for a few months, he has not gone to the doctor. You have been concerned but haven't said anything to your friend in all this time. You are now at the point where you can't keep quiet any longer. You decide to confront your friend.

What actions could you play that might induce him to go to the doctor?

Turn the page to see other possibilities to go with those you have thought of.

Catherine. What am I going to do, just kick him in the face with it?

Beatrice. Look, honey, you wanna get married, or you don't wanna get married? What are you worried about, Katie?

Catherine. I don't know B. It seems wrong if he's against it so much.

A View From the Bridge —Arthur Miller

Your Additions

Now incorporate your verbs with the list below and place each action in the order you might try them.

- [ ] Beg him
- [ ] Challenge him
- [ ] Dare him
- [ ] Stand up to him
- [ ] Defy him
- [ ] Question him
- [ ] Put your cards on the table
- [ ] Plead with him
- [ ] Take exception to everything he says
- [ ] Throw down the gauntlet
- [ ] Offer to make the appointment for him
- [ ] Offer to go with him
- [ ] Make the appointment for him
- [ ] Wash your hands of him
- [ ] Other _____

Which would you choose to test first? Second? Third? Why?

You and Your Actions

Your life actions

One way to begin thinking in actions is to begin taking stock of your everyday actions. Use **The Work** page **Verbs/Actions/Doings** to help you describe the actions you catch yourself playing.

What are some of your most common life actions?

- Do you cheer yourself on when the going gets tough?

- Do you stick to a task until it is complete?

- Do you put other people's needs before your own?

- Do you take initiative?

- Do you find the best in every situation?

- Do you put yourself down?

- Do you complain a great deal?

- Do you have excuses for why your life is the way it is?

- Do you blame others?

- Do you whine and feel sorry for yourself?

- Do you stop yourself from doing certain things?

- Do you minimize your accomplishments?

- Do you criticize others?

- Are there some that you would like to change? Why? What are they?

- What could you do to make those changes?

- Is there someone whose behavior you admire? How do you think they got that way? Do you think they are that way all the time?

You and Your Actions (Cont.)

Your coping skills: actions and people

- List five people in your life. When you are with them, what actions do you find yourself playing again and again? What triggers your actions/behavior?

- What actions would you rather be playing with them?

A daily routine

- Choose a daily activity or routine. Detail each action you take as you complete the activity or routine.

An incident

- After you have an encounter with someone, try to describe a part of what happened by writing what the other person said and did and what you said and did.

Actions you can't imagine yourself ever playing

So many of us have restrained our behavior because of our upbringing and attitudes about other people's behavior. Our belief systems also determine our feelings about appropriate civilized behavior. I think of myself as a pacifist and think I am always polite and considerate, never pushy. Yet, when I am driving in rush hour through the Lincoln Tunnel when four lanes are merging into one and other drivers are ruthlessly butting ahead, I become equally aggressive and enraged.

- Name actions that surprise you when you catch yourself behaving in unexpected ways.

"My" Objectives

PLAY: _____

ROLE: _____

DATE: _____

Write your objectives in the scene

Begin to write "your" Objectives in the scene. If you are not sure or think there might be more than one, write them all down. As you continue to rehearse, add to your list or highlight those objectives that continue to be valid and check those that you feel connected to.

- Do "your" Objectives change during the scene? How do they change?

- Do "you" want something for yourself? What do you want?

- Do "you" want something for someone else? What do you want?

- Do "you" want something from yourself? What do you want from yourself?

- Do "you" want something from someone else? What do you want from that person?

- What is "your" Overall Objective for the scene? The play?

- What is "your" Immediate Objective at beginning of the scene?

- If the scene shifts and "you" abandon your initial Objective, or something happens that introduces the necessity for a new Objective, write what "your" next Objective is.

- What drives "you" through life?

> **Remember…**
> This is an ongoing process. If you are bored, you are probably not doing the work. Reevaluate your expectations.

What is at Stake?

PLAY: _____

ROLE: _____

DATE: _____

Consider what is at stake in the pursuit of "your" Objective.

When something is a matter of life and death, something is at stake. Stakes are related to the objective and the obstacle. When you have something at stake it means that if you don't get what you are going after there will be consequences that you desperately want or that you don't want to face. You have something to lose, something that matters, and you and others might suffer. This adds to the need to overcome whatever obstacles stand in your way. A categorical imperative is that when you go on stage, you must know what your character wants and what is in "your" way.

Peggy. Well, is there anything you'd like me to do?

Buddy. What?

Peggy. Do. Read a scene? Or kind of take on a character like in class. Or is just talking like this enough?

Come Blow Your Horn —Neil Simon

To be in your body, you don't have to feel or think the want: you have to *know* it. Your brain may tell you that you don't know what you want. If you have chosen a want, trust it. Your faith will strengthen when you take action.

- What will happen if "you" don't achieve your Objective?

- How does your scene end? How does the ending of your scene inform your choice of Objective?

Remember...
No good deed goes unpunished.

- What is "your" life drive? What do you want out of life?

- You may feel that your character has an Underlying Objective that is never mentioned. What is it?

"My" Objectives and Possible Obstacles

PLAY: _____

ROLE: _____

DATE: _____

List the various objectives you think "you" have in the course of the scene.

As you write possible objectives, leave space in order to note the possible obstacles that seem to be standing in the way of your getting those Objectives. Always make positive statements when writing your want:. "I want to cheer _____ up", instead of "I don't want _____ to be unhappy."

"My" Needs

PLAY: _____

ROLE: _____

DATE: _____

- What are the sources of "my" needs?

- When do they surface?

- How do they manifest in "my" behavior?

- Think of "your" needs as currents unseen on the surface of a lake. What currents run under your words? List where you sense that your needs determine your words?

Sending and Receiving

PLAY: _____

ROLE: _____

DATE: _____

Athletes train so that their reflexes are sharp. They have no time to think during the game. They train to hone their mind/body/soul connection to be able to respond to anything that happens during the game. You do the same to ready yourself for the give and take that is acting.

Make notes about what you receive from your partner. These should be in your own short-hand.

- What gets to you? Their tone of voice? A particular word? A facial expression? An attitude toward you or what you are talking about? A piece of information?

- What do you do in return?

- Write about what you see your partner do and how it affects you. What do you do in return?

- Name the actions your partner sends you. What do you do in return?

- Write about your partner's tone of voice and how it affects you. What do you do in return?

Cory. Hey, Pop … why don't you buy a TV?

Troy. What I want with a TV? What I want with one of them for?

Cory. Everybody got one.

Fences
—August Wilson

Identifying Obstacles

PLAY: _____

ROLE: _____

DATE: _____

Obstacles strengthen your faith in your circumstances and give you verbal will. Remember, Obstacles exist within the play and within "you."

Obstacles exist in every situation, good and bad. When you see a sunset, you may want to hold onto it, to remember it forever. Its beauty is the obstacle, as is your desire to hold onto something so transitory.

List the obstacles "you" encounter in your scene.

Patricia. When I listen to you, I hear this — you're always looking for something that isn't there — something better — as opposed to reality. Who someone might be instead of who they are.

Where Do We Live —Christopher Shinn

Playing Actions

PLAY: _____

ROLE: _____

DATE: _____

Go through your script carefully, line by line. Try to find the actions that are actually indicated in the text and note them with a pencil.

Possible Actions

PLAY: _____

ROLE: _____

DATE: _____

With the new "you" in mind, write the kind of actions you feel "you" might take in the situations in your play. What actions are unfamiliar to you? (Return to this page frequently as you work with Chapters Five and Six.)

Verbs / Actions / Doings

The Work

A
abort
absorb
accuse
acquiesce
act out
add
admire
admonish
adore
align yourself with
analyze
answer
apologize
argue
ask
attack
attend
attract

B
back away
back down
back off
back out
back up
badger
bang your head
  against
bargain
barrage
bash
beat
beg
belabor
belch
belittle
bellow
berate
beseech
besiege
bicker
bite
blow your stack

bombard
boss
bray
browbeat
bulldoze
bully
bumble
bump into
burp
butter up
buy time

C
cajole
calculate
calm
capitulate
caress
cave in
cavort
celebrate
center
change
cheat
check out
check up on
cheer
cheer on
cheer up
chill
claim
clam up
clean
clean up
coax
coddle
collapse
collect
come on to
commend
compare
compel
compete
compliment

congratulate
conjure
consider
contain
contradict
constrain
convey
convince
count
cover up
crawl
crumble
crumple
crush
cuddle
curse
cut down
cut out
cut through
cut up

D
dance
dare
daydream
declare
defy
demand
demean
demolish
demonstrate
destroy
dig into
direct
disagree
dismiss
distract
dive into
divert
dodge
dream
drop
drop out
dry

E
ease
egg on
embellish
embrace
encourage
entice
envelop
exaggerate
explore

F
face
faint
fall apart
fall down
fall in with
feign
fight
fight off
finalize
finish
flirt
follow
follow through
follow up
fool
forge on
freak out

G
gag
gallop
gape
gargle
gasp
get back at
giggle
give in
give up
goad
go on a rampage
grab
grill
grin

Verbs / Actions / Doings (Cont.)

grind
grip
groan
grovel
gulp
gurgle
guzzle

H
hail
hamper
hand over
hang in
harass
heckle
help
hide
hinder
hiss
hit
hold back
hold down
hold off
hold on to
hold your nose
hold your own
holler
hop to
hug
hum

I
idolize
ignore
illustrate
imagine
implore
indicate
initiate
insist
instigate
interrogate
interrupt
introduce

investigate
isolate
issue

J
jab
jam
jar
jest
jog
joke
josh
jostle
jump
jump for joy
justify

K
kick
kill
kiss
kiss the ground
kvetch

L
lash out at
laugh
lead
lead on
leave
let go
lie
limp
linger
link
list
listen for
listen hard
look down on
look through
look up to
lounge
lurch

M
make a scene
make fun of
mall
manage
mangle
massage
mend
mimic
mince
moan
model
move in on
mull
munch
muscle in on
muse

N
nag
neck
needle
negate
nest
nip in the bud
nose around
notice
nudge

O
obey
object
obliterate
obsess
offer
organize
operate
oppose
order

P
pamper
pass by
pass over
pay back

pitch
pity
plan
play
play down
plead
plod
plop down
plot
plunge in
poke
pounce
pound
practice
prance
preach
pretend
probe
propose
prove
pry
puke
pull
pull away from
pull back
punch
punish
purr
push
put down
put your cards on the
   table

Q
quiet
quit

R
race
rack your brain
rail
rally
rant & rave
recoil

regale
regurgitate
relate
relax
repeat
reprimand
resist
rest
retaliate
retreat
rip
rub out
ruminate
run
rush

S
savor
scatter
scheme
scream
scrounge
sell
sell out
set straight
settle
settle down
shadow
shift
shout
shove
show your hand
shrink
shush
sigh
simplify
single out
sip
sit down
slam
skip
slap
slink
slither

slow down
slurp
sneak
soak up
soften
soothe
sound off
speculate
speed
spin around
spit out
stand up for
stare down
stare straight ahead
steer
stir up
stop
strike
strip
stroke
stroll
stumble
suggest
swallow
sway
swear
swing

T
take back
tamper with
tantalize
taste
taunt
tear apart
tear up
tease
tell
tempt
test
testify
throw in the towel
throw out
throw yourself into

throw yourself on
throw up your hands
throw up to
toast
top
torment
torture
toss
tramp on
trample
transport
trick
trip
trot
trust
tug
turn around
turn in
turn over

U
uncover
use

V
validate
vent
veto
voice
vomit
vote
vow

W
wade
wallow
wash your hands of
watch
whimper
whine
whisper
whistle
wince
wind
wink

wipe
wish
wolf down
woo
worry
worship

Y
yawn
yell
yelp
yodel

Z
zip
zoom

Sending with Expectation

PLAY: _____

ROLE: _____

DATE: _____

List some of the actions you play in your scene. Write how you expect the other actor to respond to those actions.

List the sources of your expectations. Refer to Chapters Five and Six.

Make sure that your expectations are counter to what you receive.

Here are some examples of expectations and what actually happens:

- You think your boss is going to fire you. He gives you a raise.

- You think your father is furious at you. He bursts into tears because he is so proud of you.

- Your sister tells you she has news. You think she is getting a divorce. She is pregnant.

- You have been robbed twice before. You come home to find the front door unlocked. When you enter you hear a noise in the bedroom. You grab the floor bar that locks the door and ready yourself to take on the intruder. You expect a muscular, six-foot drug addict, who is in withdrawal and desperate, to come out of your bedroom with a gun. You move to attack—and scare your girlfriend out of her mind.

Rick. We're here from Utah.

Paul. Do they have any black people in Utah?

Rick. Maybe two. Yes, the Mormons brought in two.

Elizabeth. We came to be actors.

Rick. She won the all-state competition for comedy *and* drama.

Six Degrees of Separation —John Guare

That First Beat

PLAY: _____

ROLE: _____

DATE: _____

In your early stages of rehearsal, take the time to focus on the first beat or bit. Be curious. When you are on stage or when you make an entrance, you have to create circumstances that put you in your body before the lights come up. In process explore how you bridge using (i.e. not denying) your present state of being into your immediate need. Explore how actions manifest and shift as you deepen your experience. Here is an extreme example:

The overall circumstance: You have arrived at your sister's house, running to get away from your abusive husband who is trying to kill you. You are in flight or fight survival mode. Craft your preparation:

- What time is it?

- The Past: Where were you when your husband beat you up? What provoked him? Exactly what did your husband do to you – where specifically did he hit you? Did he kick you? Hit you with his fists? Throw you against a wall? How hard were the blows? How did you try to defend yourself? What part of the house were you in? What images, sounds and sensations do you recall? Of him? Of the floor? Of the blows as they landed? Of his voice, his words? How did you get away from him?

- How many friends have you gone to for help? Where did you go first? What happened? Where did you go next? Or did you go straight to your sister? How did you get there? Did you drive? Did you run a red light on the way? Did you think that your husband was still chasing you?

That First Beat (Cont.)

- What is your physical state of being? What is your emotional state of being? Do you think your husband was following you? Do you think that you just saw him as you ran to the door of your sister's kitchen?

- What is your most immediate need? To get to safety? To get off the street? To get in the house.?

- Your expectation: You know your sister doesn't want you. You are not sure she is home. You hope you can convince her to help you one more time.

- Your need: to stay alive.

- You burst through the door, shut it fast to block him out, lean against it to catch your breath, feel the safety of your sister's kitchen. You are weak, but manage to get yourself to the kitchen table. Lower yourself into a chair and know you have achieved your first goal.

- No matter what your sister says, she will have to take physical action to get you out of her house.

Remember…

Everything that happens to you goes into your body.

Rehearsal Notes/Class Notes

PLAY: _____

ROLE: _____

DATE: _____

Make notes after rehearsing or presenting your scene in class. You may remember some of the things you did and the sensations that you experienced when you did them. Don't be surprised if you only remember snatches of a scene.

For example, you may remember a moment in your rehearsal. Reading the next description will take longer than the actual doing:

> You and your partner were sitting at the table drinking coffee. You were bringing your coffee mug to your lips as he called you a liar.

> You remember that your inner attention flashed on your partner's tone of voice, a momentary expression on his face, the fact that the coffee was lukewarm and what he thought you were lying about. His intensity surprised you. You felt his distrust. He seemed to be ending the relationship.

> Your inner objects (the sensations and thoughts that raced through your mind and body) caused you to swallow, very deliberately put your coffee mug down on the table, stand up, turn and face your partner, and then deny his accusation.

Chapter 5

Creating Relationships: Complicating Life

On asylum earth, people complicate your life and you complicate theirs. Your attachments, circumstances, needs, desires, hopes, cares and love bind you to all the people in your life. Your conscious and unconscious ties to family, friends, colleagues and acquaintances are the source of your vulnerability and strength. This is no different for the characters you play, whose relationships are just as varied and complex as your own.

> **Titania:** … We are their parents and original.
>
> *A Midsummer's Night Dream* —William Shakespeare

To prepare for developing "your" relationships to the other characters in your play, you will look at your own relationships—past, present and those you desire. Allow your Observing Self and the **Me, Myself & I** pages to heighten your awareness of, and lead you to revelations about, yourself and your relationships. Do this from now on, whether you are working on a role or not. As you learn to examine the relationships in your own life, you find source material to draw from when crafting relationships for the stage. Tapping into what matters to you deepens your faith in, and vulnerability to, "your" relationships.

Be prepared for what lies ahead. Finding the new you can lead you to unearth aspects of your personal relationships and the sources of your interactions that would otherwise remain deeply hidden within your subconscious. You may contact areas that could in some way be painful, hurt deeply or fill you with fear and uncertainty. As you navigate your character's relationships in pursuit of your objectives, your choices may lead you into experiences of loss, sacrifice, or grief. Proceed carefully and deliberately but without fear as you meld real life into your imaginary life. As you live through the circumstances that each play brings you—and as you come to greater consciousness of the significance of your own relationships—you will grow to be a more insightful, mindful, present and loving companion to the rest of us here in the asylum. The characters you play are your teachers—in humility, respect and gratitude.

Ginott

Michael (my husband) and I are lost and desperate. Our son, Jules, is in the 3rd grade. He has a horrid teacher and has developed a math phobia. In an effort to get his homework assignments completed, Jules and I default to a mode of engagement where we butt heads every night. When the nightly shouting match begins, Michael flees. He hates the yelling. Who can blame him?

I have a simple want in my relationship with Jules. When it comes to his homework, I want him to cooperate and do what I ask him to do without arguing. The obstacle is clear: he doesn't do anything I want him to.

Beth. I'm finally feeling whole, finally feeling like I'm on the right track, for the first time in my life, and what do you do? You undermine me!

Karen. I'm not undermining you, I'm only thinking of what's best for you.

Dinner With Friends —Donald Margulies

Life after dinner is hell. Our relationship torments me, fills me with shame and confuses me. Michael and I are supposedly the adults. Why do we feel as if we are being tyrannized by a seven-year-old?

One afternoon when I am picking Jules up after school, I see a simple flyer posted on the wall. It reads, "Tired of fighting over homework?" "Tired of yelling to no avail?"

"Do you want your children to listen to you?" The words on the flyer, purporting to offer a solution to these problems, sound too good to be true—but I write the number down. Later that evening, I ask Michael if we can sign up for this class. He agrees.

Our first "How to Parent" class takes place at Jules' school in a 2nd grade classroom. Our teacher is sitting at one of the small tables sized for the six-year-old second graders. Picture us: Brobdinagians—6'3" Michael, me, the two other sets of parents and one mom—in Lilliput, all sitting on diminutive chairs that make us feel like underdeveloped children. We are all in the same boat, feeling confused and miserable, thrashing and having hassles with our spouses, our children and their teachers. Our familial roles reversed, we are now second graders who have failed in parenting, attempting to learn how to nurture the most important relationships of our lives—our relationship with our children.

The course is based on the work of Haim Ginott, and it is through this work that I begin to really learn about playing actions. We have weekly assignments along with reading the book, *How to Talk So Kids Will Listen & Listen So Kids Will Talk*, written by two of Ginott's disciples. We are learning how to shift aspects of our relationship with Jules. We change our "flying-off-the-handle" mode. At least, years earlier, I had stopped my reflex of gently slapping our son when he did something wrong, because he quickly learned that hitting was okay and started hitting me back.

With the course we are taking, instead of yelling at the kid, calling him names, making empty threats, spanking, hitting or attacking his character, we learn to handle our anger and frustration by playing new, more effective actions which put us in control. We can hurl a value and walk away. For instance, we can say with a firm voice, "In our family we come to the table when called." We can go into the bathroom and lock the door until we calm down. We can express our anger in a way that does not attack the child. We can send "I" messages. We can take care of the child's feelings and not dismiss them or minimize them. We can give our child choices which are acceptable to us and, in so doing, teach him how to make decisions. We learn to praise in a constructive, specific manner.

When he catches on—and he does—it infuriates him. He realizes that the old ways aren't going to work anymore, and that he will lose, so to speak. I know how he feels but I know in my heart what he is spared—he doesn't know that, had we not taken the Ginott class, he could have been hit, could have been forced to deal with many fits of rage and temper and could have experienced character assassination on a daily basis.

This story reveals how intertwined the aspects of your craft are: even though the chapters of this book are divided for the purpose of focus, you see that you cannot talk about relationships without identifying your *needs and wants* within that relationship, the *obstacles* that evolve within the relationship and the consequent *actions* that result. Additionally, the nature and dynamics of any relationship are inextricably linked to and affected by *time and place*— the era, the culture, your age, even the time of day and the day of week.

The Tangled Web of Relationships

Take this moment to reflect on just how many relationships you currently have in your own life. Some are inherited, some chosen. Some have lasted and some have vanished like smoke. Consider, too, your technologically facilitated relationships via social networking sites.

Your relationships range from formal to casual, steamy to frigid. Some are comfortable, nurturing and loving; some awkward, unpleasant or disturbing. Some can be so horrifically painful that your psyche, triggering its natural coping mechanisms, propels you into denial, defense, justification and secrecy.

Martin. And you're not really cousins?

Eddie. No. Not really. No.

Martin. You're—her husband?

Eddie. No. She's my sister. My half-sister.

Fool for Love –Sam Shepard

Relationships that matter to you are complex. Their complexity lies in the fact that people are complicated, and circumstantial variables are constantly shifting the nature of each relationship you have. You play many different roles with one person depending upon the time of day, the day of the week, your levels of vulnerability and everything else going on in your life. There are moments when you may worship the person, others when you may loathe and despise them and, still yet, other moments when you seek their comfort. Your circumstances, the behavior of the other person and your perception of them at any given moment affect the actions that person pulls out of you.

Consider: which relationships really matter to you? You have some relationships that you neglect and some that you nurture. In some relationships you give more than you get. In others you get more than you give. Some are hard, fatiguing, intolerable, calamitous or oppressive. Some are easy, straightforward, effortless and uncomplicated. Many are work related. All have periods of stasis. All are subject to overt highs and lows or hidden ups and downs. Finally, as an actor, you have your actual relationships with fellow actors and the relationships your character has with the other characters in the play.

Mary. Having you for a sister is all the adventure I need, Loretta.

The Melville Boys –Norm Foster

Excavate What Matters ★

Who are the most important people in your life? Why do they mean so much to you? Are those relationships based on pleasant or painful memories? What moments in time or place come to mind when you contemplate these individuals?

When people talk about outgrowing a marriage or a relationship, what they are really saying is that they have outgrown the original roles that they accepted at the beginning of their relationship. This is a good way of looking at all of your relationships. What role or roles do you play in each relationship that you have?

Read for Relationships ★

Plays deal with relationships at a particular moment in time and place. Each time you read the play you will be more primed to receive the information you need. Although my suggestion to read the play so many times is not an order, I do hope that you find a way to be with your script all the time. I hope that that you live with it, that you continue to wonder about what is happening in the play, about what you want and the interactions you have with the other characters. Always read with intention and curiosity, allowing yourself to continuously receive the play. This time around, read the text to flesh out the following aspects of your character's relationships. They are the birthplace and repository of your deepest emotions:

- **Name** the relationship. (See Appendix D)

- **Identify the basis** of "your" relationship: Circumstance? Coincidence? Common interests? Family? Work? Need? Attachment? Love? Other?

- **Background/History**: If you are not strangers meeting for the first time, search for particulars that open you to a shared past. If you are strangers, how and why do you find yourselves in the same place at the same time?

- **Standing**: Are you in a superior, equal or inferior position to the other person? What puts you in the position you are in? How do you feel about it? **Status, Culture, Trust, Control and Intimacy** influence your standing in every relationship.

- **The Benefits and Costs** of the relationship to you. What do you gain from it? What do you give up by being in that relationship? Admit to your challenges in the relationship. Your choices should cost you something: you may expose yourself to uncomfortable insights that cause you pain, regret, sorrow, shame, embarrassment, or humiliation. You may also find deep wells of gratitude, appreciation and respect.

Know Where You Stand: Status/Class, Culture, Control, Trust and Sex ★

You can distill the dynamics of any relationship by considering: are you on an equal footing with the other person, above them or below them? Or is your relationship on shifting sand?

You

- Do you treat the person as an equal?

- Do you *look up* to the person because of their kindness, intelligence, skill or values, or are they elevated by birth or their position at work?

- Do you *look down on* the person because they are of lesser birth, intelligence, position, wealth or accomplishment?

Mother. Harry, your son is going to get married.

Father. No one tells me nothing. All I get is pushed.

Alan. Dad, I don't know how to say this to you—but—well, you were so right about so many things. I was a bum.

Come Blow Your Horn –Neil Simon

The Other Person

- Does the person treat you as an equal?

- Does the person *look up to* you?

- Does the person *look down on* you or does the person have an edge on you through intelligence, birth, job, gender, wealth and age?

Status/Class

[the relative social, professional, or other standing of someone | high rank or social standing: those who enjoy wealth and status. | the official classification given to a person, determining their rights or responsibilities.]

Attaining a higher status in life can be a life drive for some people, which consequently affects the way you pursue certain relationships. Other people are born privileged and cannot imagine life any other way. Your status will influence your point of view and your expectations in connection to your relationships. Do you aspire to attain the status and influence of wealth, education, class or success? What will you do and how far will you go to achieve it? Who are the people you will seek out to help you? Are you stuck in a dead-end job with no possible means of improving your lot or that of your children? How does this influence your relationships? Are you used to having the best of everything?

Remember...

Place no head above your own.

–The Buddha

Status and class are affected by—and indeed, stem from—cultural class systems, power structures, traditions, norms and expectations. They are also affected by, and intersect with, gender, race, age, sexuality and physical and mental ability. Status and class differences between two people affect the power dynamics within any given relationship.

Culture [the customs, arts, social institutions, and achievements of a particular nation, people or other social group.]

How does the culture you are in, or the one you grew up in, affect you and your interactions with others? Are you trying to escape it? Are you proud of it? What are the traditions inherent in the culture?

Miles: Must be... difficult. I mean, you grow wheat and corn out of the dirt, out of literally nothing, then you cut it down and sell it. You raise animals, feed them and house them for years, name them; and then you kill them and eat them.

The Drawer Boy –Michael Healey

Culture is a main determinant of how status and class affect your life and relationships. Within some cultures, status and class are rigid—you are born into a class from which you cannot leave. Other cultures popularize rags-to-riches stories—consider the myth of the "American Dream." Some cultures make claims of classlessness and equality for all. As cultures have changed throughout history, so, too have the prevalent class systems. In this way culture, cultural systems, class and status are rooted in time and place.

Culture impacts how and to what degree the intersecting elements of gender, race and class affect your life, your status, your wants and your needs. Your status and the culture in which you were raised influence your point of view. They influence literacy and the way you speak (your regional dialect). Thus, Joseph Chaiken, in his great book, *The Presence of the Actor*, wrote,

> An actor should visit and inspect patients in hospitals, and he should go to night courts, Buddhist services, A.A. meetings, draft boards, ghettoes, Bowery flophouses, and public bars of different kinds; otherwise he has only a partial understanding of the dimension of his study. An actor must also have exposure to different group-identity situations such as prisons and criminal organizations. Without this kind of inquiry into other forms of living, the actor is simply working off the top of society's crust where very special advantages are on display.[10]

Let's add: work on a farm, drive a truck, work in a sweatshop, be a cook on an oil-rig, a security guard, visit with cultures unfamiliar to you, etc.

The Drug Culture

I am planning to direct a reading of *Burning Desire* by William Mastrosimone. The main character in the play is a successful model. She is also a heroin addict whom the protagonist wants to save. I need to know the world of the play, and so I begin an odyssey that starts at a hospital in East Harlem, goes to a needle exchange storefront on Manhattan's lower East side and ends in a rehab facility in Vancouver, British Columbia.

My first encounter is with a social worker in an outpatient methadone clinic in a part of New York that I have never been to. As a middle class white woman, I am totally out of place ascending the stairs to the area where I am to meet my informant. I pass the caged area where patients are lined up waiting to get their daily treatment. There is no reception area and I am not sure I am in the right place. I find a folding chair leaning against a wall in the bleak, cheerless hallway, sit down and wait.

Soon a young Hispanic man comes to get me, introduces himself and invites me to his desk in a cubicle in a small room with about three other cubicles and desks. He asks me to tell him about myself. I tell him why I am there. The social worker then tells me about himself.

As his story unfolds, I start to feel conventional and foolish. He had asked me to tell him about myself—something I would never have dreamed of doing! He, on the other hand, tells me his personal story in detail. Just as one does in a Twelve Step program, he shares with me the depths to which he had plummeted through his own addiction. He describes his descent—how he finally ended up pimping his own wife, and how his living conditions went from bad to abysmal. The final straw was when, in order to stay in a rehab program even though he was still using, he burned his arms with a hot iron to cover the track marks.

Leaving the hospital, I acutely feel how ignorant I am of the world I just entered—though I know what I saw was but the tip of the iceberg. My education continues when I am put in touch with a man (a user and activist proponent of the needle exchange program in the United States) who takes me to a needle exchange on the Lower East Side. As I enter the storefront, chills run down my spine. I don't need to wear a sign; all know I am an outsider. While waiting for my contact, a couple of people come up and talk to me. I watch people coming in, replacing old needles for fresh ones, and leaving. Some are drifting on their high in the safety of the place.

I sense the world of Mastrosimone's play and have glimmerings into his characters' lives. I am in touch with a level of honesty and directness to which I am unaccustomed. No one wears a social mask. The tolerance and acceptance of the drug addict makes the space feel totally safe.

I stop working on this project when I get another job. Although I don't work further on this play, my voyeuristic glimpse into the drug sub-culture has brought me closer to understanding the power of heroin and how it destroys lives.

I have had a taste of another world.

Control. Status, class and culture largely determine the degree of control you have in your relationships and in your life. Do you have control over maintaining your own identity and your personal boundaries in your relationships? Have you identified, and are you able to deal with, the aspects of your relationships that you can and can't control? How hard is it for you to get what you want, whether it is worldly possessions, understanding, acknowledgement or love? For what reasons and in what areas do you have or lack control—over yourself, over others and over aspects of your life and relationships? Are you granted or deprived of control for reasons relating to physical prowess, mental capacity, class, status, race, gender, or temperament?

Andrew. You have class issues.

Suzanna. No. I have a newly sobering view of how much money it takes to get by in America since my dad died.

Becky Shaw —Gina Gionfriddo

Trust. Trust involves risk. There are risks whenever you commit to or confide in another person. Your ability to trust another person is often related to your sense of control as well as the power dynamics within the relationship. Trust is an essential element of intimacy and a key ingredient of healthy sexual relationships. The betrayal of trust is a common theme found within drama throughout history. Also consider: how much can you trust others if you do not trust yourself?

Sex/Intimacy/Love. Matters of sex, love and intimacy are game-changers within any relationship. Feelings of love can turn power dynamics on their head in an instant. We relinquish control and bestow trust when we enter into intimate relationships with others. Love and sex create some of the deepest bonds and most complicated relationships. They also result in the worst rifts and heartbreaks.

> **Mary.** I wouldn't believe him if he swore on a stack of Bibles.
>
> *Long Day's Journey Into Night*
> —Eugene O'Neill.

How do relationships change when sex enters the equation? How do the powers of attraction effect the class and status dynamics of a relationship? Are your sexual relationships and preferences accepted by culture and society? What happens within different cultures around the world and throughout history when sex and intimacy occurs across boundaries of class, race, faith and between members of the same gender?

Sex, intimacy and love are, of course, heavily influenced by status, culture, control and trust. Cultural expectations circumscribe sexual norms and accepted gendered behavior. Status, control, and trust can be exploited to take advantage of others within intimate and sexual relationships. Love and an intimate understanding between two people can also give rise to equality where there previously was none.

All of these factors—status/class, culture, control, trust and sex—affect your relationships to varying degrees; sometimes their effects are obvious, sometimes they operate in a more clandestine manner. The degree to which they matter is associated with your upbringing and to what is happening in your play—or in your life. Know that these are specific, visceral, core elements that remain embedded in you until aroused. They color your needs, point of view and actions. Your need for control or status may be driven by long-forgotten personal events from your childhood.

> **Joe.** What did he ever do for you?
>
> **Lorna.** . . . He loved me in a world of enemies, of stags and bulls! . . . and I loved him for that.
>
> *Golden Boy* —Clifford Odets

Many characters you play will have trust issues or experience heart-breaking betrayal. All relationships will have someone who is controlling, perceived as controlling or in control. Culture permeates all aspects of life and relationships and can take you on the most vivid, possibly heart-warming or disheartening, journeys of all.

Investigate the Past and Background of Your Relationship ★

The origins of your emotional needs reside in your past. Crafting key incidents, alliances or memories gives "your" relationships history. You can do this alone or with your fellow actors by asking questions such as: Where did we meet? How long have we known each other? How close are we? What do we know about one another that no one else knows? And so on. Be careful about writing a background that sounds good but has NO meaning to you, or no basis in the text! When you do find a personal connection, be wary of dissipating its energy by talking about it with anyone. Protect your imagination. Keep your secrets close to the vest.

Ismene. He was our brother, of course. But he's dead; and he never loved us. He was a bad brother. He was like an enemy in this house. He never thought of you; why should you think of him?

Antigone adapted by Lewis Glantierre from the play by Jean Anouilh

Accept—Work off of Your Fellow Actors ★

Your approach to developing your character's relationships with the other people in your play is straightforward. Always begin by working from yourself and taking in your fellow actors *exactly as they* are so that you remain present and immediate as you rehearse.

Be honest with yourself about your actual chemistry, but don't share your thoughts with your partner. Since you *are* the character—living the life the playwright has established, saying the words that the playwright has you saying—it naturally follows that your partner *is* the character who is talking to you and whose behavior is affecting you.

Before imposing anything on them, be responsive to what they send you. See the behavior that accompanies your partner's words. Hear your partner's tone of voice and the intention behind the words. You can't do this if you are rushing to say *your* words. If you are simply getting to your next line and not breathing, you are not in your body. In the early stages of your process, be alive and alert to your partner. Do not obligate yourself to a result.

But don't forget: moments fly by. You can't catch them. How many times have you held onto or extended a moment during a scene for emotional impact (or self-satisfaction)? Living truthfully in the immediate present means that you never sink into any moment because you are always inescapably in the next with each breath you take.

Play Your Best Game ★

Athletes train so that their reflexes are sharp. Their training and practice creates a body-mind connection that enables them to respond reflexively with spontaneity to whatever happens in the game. When a ball or puck is part of the game, it is hit, thrown or kicked at lightening speed. There is no time to stop and think about what to do. As an actor, you must do the same to ready yourself for the give and take, sending and receiving that is acting. Words and actions – yours and your partner's – are the objects in play. The playwright provides the words that you send and receive. You provide the intension and behavior that fills and carries those words.

Create within yourself an appetite for working off of and being affected by your partner – of taking what you receive from your partner very personally. Be alive to the chemistry between you. It sparks your relationship in your play.

Be there for your partners. William Hickey taught his students to make the scene about their scene partners. Listen, hear, watch, see all the things your fellow actors do and say. Stay on your toes, alert and responsive to whatever they send you. What you receive generates your thoughts, feelings, words and actions.

Open yourself to taking things personally. Don't build armor that your partner can't pierce.

Most often, you will be able to identify with or relate to your relationships with the other characters and the circumstances of your play. However, there may be aspects of the circumstances or your relationships that you don't quite get. This is when you need a means to connect to those particulars that are not within your grasp. You do so with the most personal tools of the actor's craft: *endowment* and *transference*. You only use these tools after you have been in rehearsal with your partner and have uncovered the areas in your play for which you desire a deeper, more specific connection to your relationships and circumstances. When you use endowments or transferences they affect your sending and receiving as well as your expectations. They are tools that employ and challenge your imagination and lead you deeper into discovery.

Endowment – the Magic "As If" ★

Although the words "Endowment" and "Transference" sound intellectual, they are not. They are active in your everyday life, you just have different names for them.

You go to an audition. You are sure the redhead sitting across from you has the role in his/her pocket. S/he exudes a quiet confidence. The Casting Assistant greeted her/him with warm familiarity and didn't even glance your way.

What has happened? In a nanosecond, you have *endowed* the other person and, without knowing it, undermined yourself.

You are familiar with the concept of *endowment* by these more common names:

- **Opinion:** I liked the play I saw last night. My partner is a really good actor. That man is really stupid. My congressman is a liar and a cheat.

- **Fact:** The man sitting next to me reeks of tobacco. Global warming is happening. I paraphrased most of my scene.

- **Suspicion:** Babette is on the verge of a nervous breakdown. Harry has been talking behind my back.

- **Speculation**: I can convince my husband to go with me even if he doesn't want to. Bill has Asperger's Syndrome.

- **Assumption:** You know what I am talking about; we discussed it yesterday. You love chocolate; you eat it all the time.

- **Expectation:** My boss is going to criticize my weekly report; he always does. My teacher is giving me an F; she warned me that my work was disappointing. Maggie's party is going to be great fun; I met some very interesting people at her last one.

Jean. … Mum turned and said, "That man's judging us by the way we look now." She settled back into her chair and said, "The truth of people isn't where they are now. It's in the space between that, and where they came from."

Play Memory –Joanna Glass

- **Prejudice:** People who check themselves every time they pass a mirror are narcissistic. Cheerleaders are stupid. Students who are habitually late don't care. People who whine feel sorry for themselves. People who don't pay taxes are freeloaders.

- **Projection:** So and so is a fantastically secure person.

- **Feeling:** I feel stupid every time I get a critique and know I am a failure.

Isn't your mind frequently filled with unchallenged thoughts such as these? How often are you preoccupied with thoughts about someone you know, used to know, someone you want to know, or someone you have never met but heard about? Your point of view determines how you see someone and, consequently and most importantly, how you behave when you are with, or talk about, that person. Indeed—your point of view also determines your perceptions of the situations you encounter and how you see everything that surrounds you at any moment in time.

As you work on this chapter, reflect upon how routinely you endow people in your life. It is an unconscious reflex.

Remember…

You must be working off of your partner before you even think of using a transference

Choosing a simple endowment might, by consciously or unconsciously leading you into a deeper connection, stir the other technique for rooting your relationships: *transference.*

There is a slight difference between endowment and the next tool in your actor's arsenal, transference. When you endow someone, you imagine that they possess *an isolated quality or trait* that you don't think they have, or you embellish a trait that you do think they have. Transferring, on the other hand, is an imaginative act of conveying *some aspect of a whole person, place or situation you actually know* onto another. When you practice transference, you deal with your partner *as if* they are someone you actually know or want to know—a particular person about whom you have a point of view in your own life. You transfer some aspect of the person whom you know onto your partner, rather than just a single selected quality or trait.

Transference and Your Imagination ★

Knee-Jerk Reactions: 1950-2010 Beaver Lake

Ellen has a huge appetite for food and life. She had a troubled childhood and as a young adult experienced emotional trauma brought on by her parents. She is profoundly obese, weighing about 400 pounds for the last forty years of her life. Her corpulence has led to many other medical conditions that in turn have led to a dependency on pain medication. She has grown facial hair due to her hormone imbalance and has to shave.

A kind, outgoing and wealthy woman who is razor-sharp smart, she is also overly sensitive, often irrational, emotionally incontinent, impulsive and prone to excess in all matters. Don't accept my description of Ellen as accurate; she triggers too many reflexive reactions in me for me to see her objectively.

Reclining on her electrified La-Z-Boy chair, she enlists anyone and everyone to run errands for her. (Fact). I am always wary when I have to see her about some business because I am sure she will ask me to do her a favor—and she always does. (Expectation).

She spends her money like water. (Opinion). She orders 20 flats of blueberries in season. (Suspicion). A knitter, she has hundreds of skeins of yarn stowed in plastic containers in her living room. (Fact). When she dies, the three freezers in the basement of her house are filled with food. (Fact).

In conversation, she only refers to people by their first names with no concern as to whether I know who they are. (Fact, Judgment). Her overall appearance fills me with terror. (Projection).

I am always voicing my negative opinions about her. It is my way of handling my fear that she is killing herself and my inability to change her. I am not proud of my attitude.

Of course, the feelings that I describe in this story say much more about me than they do about Ellen. I never asked myself, "What's my problem?" "Why am I so reactive to Ellen?" "How are my opinions bolstering my ego?"

If I had to play a part where I felt entitled to treat someone with disdain, I might choose to use Ellen as a transference. I would imagine that my partner is her size. In the context of the scene, I would treat my partner as if he or she has this trait. I would not try to literally see Ellen when I look at my partner. Rather, I would see my partner while a *sense memory* of Ellen's shape flashes through me. The image might create a degree of revulsion within me, which becomes stronger when I ridicule, dismiss, rail at, lash out at, plead, beg on my hands and knees or defy my partner.

Please keep in mind these are tools that you use in service of the play, to strengthen the new you and "your" relationships. The consequences of your choices release inner objects and behavior that place you *in* the circumstances of the play. (Transference in the context of acting should not be confused with the medical definition of the term. The definition of transference when used by therapists is "the unconscious experiencing of someone from your past life as someone in your present." This definition is not appropriate for your work as an actor.)

> **Roberta**. An when she's not prayin, she's lookin around like she lost somethin but she ain't lookin for anythin an SHE WON'T LOOK AT ME!
> *Danny and the Deep Blue Sea*
> —John Patrick Shanley

Begin by naming the person, place or situation you would like to use as your transference. You can discover possibilities for your transference by noticing the flashes of images that pop into your mind or sensations that are aroused in your body as you rehearse and live with your play. You may find yourself saying, "This is like so and so" or, "This reminds me of when I…." Experiment to discover and build your secret cache of personal inner objects that connect you to your endowments or transferences. Your memories are connected to specifics of time and place.

Respect the Tools of Your Craft ★

Accidental Lessons

The day I first audit Alice Spivak's class, a student, upon completing a presentation of his scene, mentions that his "substitution" worked. I am really impressed with the actor; his substitution—whatever that is—worked!

I join Alice's class and begin working on scenes. Although I have no idea what a "substitution" is, having recently divorced, I attempt to use my ex-husband, Paul, as a substitution in every scene I rehearse for class. In doing so, no matter the play, no matter what is happening in the scene, I cry. I am extremely self-indulgent but don't know it. Rather than using the tool correctly and appropriately, not knowing any better, I am using it to manipulate my emotions.

A couple of years later, I begin rehearsals for a new play that is being performed at the HB Playwrights Foundation Theater. The director sets up an improvisation to build the relationship between me and the other female character in the play. We are supposed to be best friends, so I decide to deal with the actress as if she were my very best friend, Jenny.

During the improvisation, I experience a rush of jealousy and envy of Jenny. Appalled and shocked by my feelings, I am bewildered and upset. How can she be my best friend if I am jealous of her? Thrown by my new unsettling insights, I later realize that I wish I could be like Jenny, who is accomplished, smart, tall and sophisticated. She is admired and adored by all the people we know. She exudes a self-confidence that I know I will never achieve. She draws people to her in ways I never will.

When using Jenny for my transference, I stepped on a buried landmine—the first of many others I later encountered in my work. This landmine was the first time I realized I might have underlying feelings about a person that I have never admitted to myself. Thus I began to learn what a dangerous and explosive tool transference can be. Be aware that when you consciously work with your own transferences you will encounter your own landmines scattered across the terrain of your life.

Reading about endowment and transference, as you are now, is risky business—you may develop a false sense of understanding these tools, just as I did when I first heard about substitution and used it inappropriately so many years ago. Reading about something which, at its essence, functions through deeply ingrained autonomic (involuntary or unconscious) behavior can give you the false impression that all you have to do is make some choice from your life and that will be that. Not so.

Both tools channel to your unconscious, defying logic, common sense and explanation. Therefore, be mindful of even uttering the words *endowment* or *transference*—you cannot assume that you understand what they are and what they mean. They cannot be known or understood intellectually, for successful endowments and transferences tap into your unconscious and channel viscerally through your body. When you use these tools correctly, you direct your attention off of yourself and onto your partner. Using them correctly, you will see and hear your partner with crystalline clarity. You will not see anyone else.

Remember...

Protect your choices. Don't talk about them!

When working for you, the endowments and transferences you test will often have unexpected, unanticipated results. Your discoveries are sure to unsettle you and push you off-balance, as mine did with my friend Jenny. They will disturb your comfort zone and take away your sense of feeling "natural"—but haven't you been training to build your stamina and appetite for feelings of uncertainty and discomfort? You have certainly learned that there is nothing "natural" or "comfortable" about what happens in a play. Allow yourself to feel unsettled.

Not to be taken lightly or casually, get ready to experience the effects of your choices physically. Your choices will release sometimes seemingly illogical feelings that must manifest in your behavior—energy that flows through your physical, verbal and psychological actions. With your choices you justify your actions.

Test in Rehearsal ★

In rehearsal, experiment with endowing your partner when you feel the need to strengthen some specific aspect of your relationship. The **Me, Myself & I** pages will give you ideas. When selecting an endowment you wish to test, ask yourself what happens to you in real life when you encounter someone with that particular trait. For instance, I become sharp and sound harsh when a student is defensive or argues with me during a critique. Their behavior catches me off guard because it is counter to my expectation. Engrossed in the work, I assume that they want to hear what I have to say and that they know I only want the best for them. I react by cutting the person off, confronting them and overpowering them. I feel they need to hear what I am saying. Thus, in order to elicit or source these specific actions, I may endow my partner with this quality of being defensive.

It is also possible to test an endowment for which you have no particular awareness of your own reactions, in order to see how you react and to discover what actions it pulls out of you. For example, you might treat your partner as if they have a gun in their jacket, as if they had told your acting teacher that you have been refusing to rehearse, or as if they had informed you that their dog died yesterday.

When you test an endowment or transference, always link it to your partner. It will take a second to invest your partner with your choice. Don't feel obligated to arrive at any specific outcome. Let it go. How does *your partner* with this imagined trait affect you? How do *your partner's actions* affect you? Accept and work off of whatever your fellow actors do or don't do. Be as alert to them as you would be if you were playing a championship game of tennis. You will always affect one another and adapt and adjust as you both change. Fully engage with one another in the world of the play. Allow yourselves to meet in the work.

Filling your treasure chest with effective endowments and personal transferences is your quest. You need not match sex, age or relationship when you make a choice.

Work in the moment with spontaneity. Respond to your partner impulsively without watching yourself. Your choice of an endowment or a transference must always be linked to what you want from your partner and how you go after your wants and your expectations. It gives you permission to pursue your wants and needs fully. Your partner's actions become the triggers that bring you to life. How many times do you have to fall in love with someone you really don't like?

Without actual rehearsal, my theory about using Ellen's size is only an untested idea. In rehearsal, when I treat my partner (who is in reality extremely sweet, svelte and pretty) as if she is as obese as Ellen, I hope to find new inner objects and actions triggered by what my partner does. No longer thinking about Ellen's size, knowing my discomfort and shame, I must freely and fully play the actions that I had squelched in my own life when dealing with Ellen.

Remember…

Live in Discovery

You will only know if your choices work after you play the actions your endowment triggers in rehearsal. If you haven't succeeded in getting your attention off of yourself, and if you are not spontaneously responding to your partner's behavior, you can be sure your choice has not fulfilled its purpose. You may still be in your head second-guessing and not trusting the spontaneous release that puts you in your body.

Practice and experiment to refine your personal use of these tools until you discover how they work for you.

The actions that begin to manifest in rehearsal may have no resemblance to your recollections of how you behaved with your transference. That is as it should be. You are in the imaginary circumstances of the play and are not confined by the restrictions that are a natural part of real life. You can do things with your scene partner that you would never have done with the person you use as your transference. Latent feelings that you buried or never admitted that you had might also erupt. On the other hand, you may behave the way you always did with that person. Either way, you are selecting an aspect of a past relationship for a purpose. That purpose is to fulfill the demands of the play by releasing a truthful action and opening your vulnerability to your partner.

Since you always work off of your partner, you must make sure that you really receive what your partner sends. You will ultimately decide how the "new you" is affected by your partner's actions. Your transference could help support your choice.

You will usually be aware of the aspects of your own life that you want to tap into, but there are times when something in the play triggers something from your past that is still raw. You then face the dangers inherent in using past experiences, particularly if you have never spoken to anyone about them.

When you identify with a role or with the circumstances in the play, or when the relationships you have with the other characters in the play seem to come effortlessly, more than likely unconscious transferences are at work.

Even though transference always happens unconsciously in real life, the **Me, Myself & I** pages in this chapter give you the opportunity to think about the people in your life more specifically and make you more aware of the workings of your relationships.

Guidelines for the use of these two techniques:

- Experiment with them *only* after you have been rehearsing for some time.

- Know why you are choosing a particular person from your life as an endowment or transference: Do you want to motivate and justify a stronger action? To release a deeper emotional connection? To access greater vulnerability to the relationship? Greater intimacy? To provide a more specific history to fuel or give more traction to the relationship?

- Test your *as if* choices when you don't know what you are doing in a section of the play.

- *Never* talk about your choices with anyone! If you do, you will dissipate your faith in them. If you can talk about them easily, they are not personal enough.

- Once you find your action, you no longer have to consciously think about your *as if* choice. The person in your life does not replace your partner.

- If you work with your endowment or transference correctly, you will be more alive to your partner and see them better than you ever saw them before.

- Always work directly off of your partner *as if* they were that person.

- When you identify with a role, transferences are already working unconsciously.

- You may have more than one endowment or transference for a fellow actor, situation or circumstance.

- It is unlikely that one choice will get you through an entire play.

Respect Limits ★

Warning: Just because you have an impulse, you never have permission to hurt yourself or any other actor on stage. An endowment or transference can quickly trigger overwhelming unexpected sensations in you, unleashing the impulse to rage, hit, kick, and throw the nearest thing at hand. A real feeling does not give you an excuse or permission for endangering yourself, your colleagues, the set or the props on the stage. You can never justify losing yourself so deeply in your emotions that you break anything, punch a brick wall or throw objects directly at your partner.

There is a reason why knowledge of how to use and execute stage violence is so important for the actor. It is all about safety. With proper training in stage combat, you are free to source hugely powerful emotions and allow aggressive energy to course through your body, without posing a danger to yourself or your partner—you are able to channel it with control. In this case, rules are your tools. You must always choreograph onstage violence, or anything that requires physical engagement with other actors, with a stage combat expert.

Protect Your Secrets ★

The Pocketbook

My father is serving in the army; I am in elementary school living in Miami Beach with my mother. I have a friend named Norma Brower. We both have birthdays in April. Norma's birthday comes before mine. We are best friends. One birthday, we make a pact to buy each other the same present.

We go to a store that has a lot of black and white round patent leather pocketbooks, about six inches in diameter. The words "I Love You" are stamped in red around the base of the purse. The lid is attached to the handle and has a round mirror on the underside. We both covet that purse.

As soon as we make our pact, I go out and buy Norma's present. I have fun giving it to her on her birthday. I spend the rest of the month looking forward to my birthday, knowing what my friend will be giving me!

When she arrives at my party, she casually says that the purses were sold out when she went to buy one for me. I can't believe that she has not kept her word and that she so clearly has no sense of what our pact means to me.

Yet how could she?

She doesn't know I am a bed-wetter and awake many mornings, huddled under the army quilt that covers me, the sheets wet beneath me, awaiting the metal coat-hanger beating my mother's fury, frustration and rage will launch on me. She doesn't know that the expectation of the "I Love You" purse has been a ray of light streaming through the clouds that shroud me...

I have risked sharing a deeply humiliating secret to give you a sense of where your own treasures may be buried. I can't tell you how or if this will serve me in rehearsal. It will depend on the play, the scene in the play and my fellow actor. I do know that in recalling this story, I surprised myself as I faced my deep-seated shame and fear. The story led me to memories that opened the floodgates, and out poured the primal experience of having felt, when I was seven, that my mother wanted to kill me. Even though I, now sixty-eight years later, understand her frustration and have compassion for us both, I can access the seven-year old girl within me at will.

Remember...

Respect your feelings – they are yours whether shame, hatred or embarrassment, love, fury, or tenderness, etc. They are the most important part of you and gold for your acting.

As you probe your own memory bank and recall your own stories, you will be surprised, too, by the deeply buried feelings that surface.

The people in your life and your personal experiences are *yours*. Through transference and your imagination, you mine and discover depths of emotion that you never knew existed within you and that you don't tap into on a daily basis. You might literally find a new voice. Working with transference is extremely private work.

Don't discuss this work with anyone—your colleagues, your acting teachers or your directors. Respect and protect your privacy. Be full of secrets.

Having said that, you should know how very serious using this tool is. If you have not done any kind of therapy or if you have long buried secrets of past life experiences known or unknown, you may uncover painful, deeply disturbing realizations about yourself and people very close to you. Therefore, I recommend that you not test or work with any choice that you have never shared with anyone else, preferably someone trained, to help you find your way through it.

Remember...

Acting can be very **therapeutic**.
But it is not **therapy**.
There is a difference.

In line with the story about the Shaman that you can read in Chapter Six, let's say you are working on a scene in which your character deals with the loss of a child, an abusive girlfriend or boyfriend or a cheating spouse. At the same time you are going through a rough patch in your own life. You have to protect yourself. Create a safety zone in your life during your rehearsal period. Know that you have a very different life than the new "you." While you are rehearsing, take even better care of yourself, look your very best and seek out people who support rather than undermine you. Find your ability to step into the cauldron and step out.

With every scene or play you will have the opportunity to add to your stockpile of personal transferences that work for you.

Waiter. Cheer up, sir, cheer up. Every man is frightened of marriage when it comes to the point; but it often turns out very comfortable, very enjoyable and happy indeed, sir – *I* was never master in my own house, sir: my wife was like your young lady: she was of a commanding and masterful disposition, which my son has inherited. But if I had my life to live twice over, I'd do it again: I'd do it again, I assure you. You never can tell, sir: you never can tell.

You Never Can Tell —George Bernard Shaw

In conclusion, you, the actor, already have many relationships that fill your life. Each relationship is with a specific person whom you can describe and with whom you have some kind of history. I invite you into the workbook section of this chapter to begin looking at the tangled web of relationships you have been weaving throughout your life, as well as the webs within the world of the play in which the new you is caught.

The People In My Life

Use this page to begin reflecting on your relationships. Notice how some of the questions trigger memories.

Remember…

This workbook may seem daunting because the work could go on forever. There is no such thing as completing the book 100% … It's like life … it ain't over until it's over.

If you feel you are shutting down as you go through this exercise, stop. Select only the topics that interest you. Remember that you do not have to answer all these questions in one sitting! Come back to the questions as often as you want to. Add to them. Save your notes. You can never tell what will inspire you.

- Who are the people you care about?

- Whom do you adore? Why? Write about one person you adore.

- Whom do you admire? Why?

- Whom would you want to be like? Why? When did you discover them?

- Is there anyone in your life who scares or intimidates you? Who? Why?

- Do you hate anyone? Who? Why?

- Are you are jealous of anyone? Who? Why?

- Who doesn't understand you? Why don't they? Do you think they ever will?

- Is there anyone who has hurt you badly? Who? When? Why? How?

- Have you hurt anyone? Who? When? Why? How?

- Do you think some people don't like you? Who are they? Why don't they like you?

- Are there some people you think would never accept you? (They might like you but not accept you.)

- Are there people in your life you feel totally accepted by, comfortable with, free to be yourself with? Who? Why? Do you feel that someone can't accept you as you are? Who? Why?

- Who do you boss around? Why? When?

- Who embarrasses you? What do they do? When? What do you do then?

- Have you ever protected, defended or taken care of anyone? Who? When? Why?

- Have you ever abandoned anyone? Who? When? Why?

- Has anyone ever abandoned you? Who? When? Why?

- Has anyone ever betrayed you? Who? When? Why? What was the nature of the betrayal?

- Has anyone disappointed you? Who? When? How?

- Is there anyone you would hate to disappoint? Who? Why?

- What happens to you when you are with _____? How do you change?

- What relationships have you nurtured? Why?

- What relationships could you nurture more? Why haven't you?

Risks I Take in Committing to Relationships

Use this page to think about those relationships to which you have committed. Commitment is not the same as being faithful or being loyal—although those involve risks as well.

You risk being disappointed if someone you have committed to betrays you or fails to live up to your expectations. If a friend, relative or partner suffers and you are unable to ease their suffering, you could have feelings of inadequacy or betrayal of the trust they have in you. If that person dies, you suffer the pain of loss. If you never commit to a marriage-type relationship, some might say that you also risk a great deal. You risk becoming extremely self-involved and you deprive yourself of the challenges that can only be had in a long-term day-to-day relationship. Others might say you spare yourself the everyday hassle of living with someone.

Reflect upon your experiences with a committed relationship.

Where You Stand

The following grids may help you untangle the various elements that make up your relationships.

Use this chart to examine your status in relationship to people in your life. Decide where you stand, then briefly describe why you are above, equal to, or below each person in status.

	You are Above	You are Equal to	You are Below
Family members 1. My mom 2. My sister	In education level In kindness warm authenticity	In intelligence as siblings + human beings	In artistic ability + singing voice In not having children & cooking
At work 1. My boss 2.			
Friends 1. 2.			

Check the boxes to see how you feel about your position in relationship to another regarding the following areas.

Name of person: ___Michael___

	You are Above	You are Equals	You are Below
Intelligence		✓	
Background	✓		
Education	✓		
Social	✓		
Financial	✓		
Attractiveness		✓	
Personality			✓
Religion N/A			

Family

Use this page to reflect on the people who have had a major influence (positive or negative) in your life.

Write about your relationship with your:

Mother	*negative*	Mother(s)-in-law
Father	*negative*	Father(s)-in- law
Brother(s)	——	Brother(s)-in-law
Sister(s)	*negative*	Sister(s)-in-law
Husband(s)	*negative*	Godparent(s)
Wife(s)	——	Stepmother(s)
Son(s)	——	Stepfather(s)
Daughter(s)	——	Stepsister(s)
Grandmother (s)	*positive*	Stepbrother(s)
Grandfather (s)	——	Other
Grandchildren	——	

Siggie. I am married to your daughter and when you do this little thing, you do it for me and her together.
Golden Boy
—Clifford Odets

- Choose one person from this list and talk about stages you have been through or are going through with that person. What is ideal about the relationship? What aspects of it leave you dissatisfied? What would you change if you could?

- Do you have a relationship that needs healing? Has someone left you because of divorce, death or marriage without your having been able to resolve your differences? Is there any way that you could still find resolution (and forgiveness) in that relationship?

- Did you ever give up a child for adoption or are you a child who was adopted? What are the unresolved issues you face? Have you ever searched for your child? Have you ever searched for your birth mother? What happened?

- Did you ever have a miscarriage or an abortion? Did you name your baby? Did you ever mourn your loss?

- You can track your history with every person or pet in your life, can't you? You can also describe the nature of each relationship you have and what you want from each relationship. What does mother/daughter mean to you? Father/son? Brother/sister? Twin? Step-father? Friend? Partner? Boss? Etc.

Your Aversions and Attractions

This exercise is a way of beginning to pinpoint other people's characteristics, traits or habits that produce responses in you. You might find that you need to flip the lists.

AVERSIONS

List things to which you have an aversion.

For example:

- Bad breath ✓
- Obesity
- Body odor ✓
- Perspiration
- Cruelty ✓
- Sad sacks
- Liars ✓
- Complainers ✓
- Explainers
- People who never smile
- People who avoid eye contact
- People who are extremely reactive ✓
- People who finish your sentences
- People who only talk about themselves ✓

ATTRACTIONS

List things that attract you.

For example:

- After shave lotion
- Honesty ✓
- A warm smile ✓
- Kindness ✓
- People who are easy-going
- People who are upbeat ✓
- People who are smart ✓
- People who agree with me
- Young people
- Free thinkers
- People who are deliciously articulate and have a sense of humor ✓
- People who are interested in the world around them ✓
- People who are needy

As you proceed to the next section, the items you have listed may help you understand *endowment.*

Mrs. Cheveley.
Wonderful woman, Lady Markby, isn't she? Talks more and says less than anybody I ever met.

An Ideal Husband
—Oscar Wilde

My Closest Relationship

Set aside time to reflect on your most intimate relationship in order to gain insight into what matters to you in a relationship. Note the little annoying and enthralling things that person does. It is the little things that often create the tug of war in a relationship. Sometimes there is a struggle for control when you want the person to do things your way or vice versa. Somehow you have to handle their resistance to your desires or your resistance to theirs. These little things create a push and pull which often conceals larger matters, or which can become a larger matter over time.

Whatever you do, don't go running to the people you have been thinking about and share this information with them. This is for your eyes only as a means of sourcing specifics you might want to use in the course of your work.

Things in my relationship I like, treasure, adore, respect, emulate, admire:

Peter. . . . I almost didn't tell you, except that I thought I'd go crazy if I didn't—

Phoebe. At least, Mother.

Peter. You can't be serious. She knows less about my life than strangers passing me on the street . . . .

Eastern Standard
–Richard Greenberg

Things in my relationship I dislike, wish were different, abhor, frighten, embarrass me:

People Whom You Have Endowed In Your Life

Use this page to think about people you know and traits you may have endowed them with that they might not inherently possess. Choose one or two people and think about how you have endowed them. What have you projected onto them? Use the chart to help you. After you fill out the chart, try to imagine the person without those qualities. Are you able to see them in a different light?

Reminder! Don't share your discoveries with anyone!

NAME _____ DATE _____

FACT	OPINION	SUSPICION

NAME _____ DATE _____

FACT	OPINION	SUSPICION

My Scene Partner

Before you even think of using transferences or endowments, you first want to genuinely hear, see and receive what your partner sends you. You may not even need to consciously work with these tools at all. Work off of whatever your partner does or doesn't do. Accept that your partner *is* the character! You need to know what, if anything, is standing in your way of working off of your partner and preventing you from getting what he or she sends you. For instance, if you are judgmental of your partner's acting, you are putting your attention on your opinion instead of "receiving" whatever your partner is doing, "right" or "wrong".

PLAY: _____ DATE: _____

- What were your first impressions of your partner before you knew that you would be working with him/her?

- What were your first thoughts when you knew he/she was to be your partner?

- What color are your partner's eyes?

- Describe your partner.

- Does your partner intimidate you, make you uncomfortable, irritate you?

- Do you think you intimidate your partner, make them uncomfortable or annoy them?

- What traits does your partner have that dovetail with his/her character?

- What traits does your partner have that you can imagine being even stronger than they are? For instance, you may be impressed with your partner's acting career or you may think your partner is very intelligent because she went to Yale University. You can shift your relationship by treating your partner as if they were a super-star or a member of Mensa.

- What do you especially like about your partner?

- What frustrates you about your partner? Is there some way that you can channel your frustration into the scene?

Under no circumstances are you to share this information with your partner. It is private work. It is a means of attaining greater presence in your work.

"My" Relationship To The Other Characters In The Play

PLAY: _____

ROLE: _____

DATE: _____

List "your" relationship to each character in the play. Note if your relationships change in the course of the play and how.

Name of character: Relationship:

Larry. ... Since we're talking, could you have a word with your solicitor? I'm still awaiting confirmation of our divorce.

Closer

—Patrick Marber

What "I" Say About The Other Characters In The Play

PLAY: _____

ROLE: _____

DATE: _____

Go through your script and write all the things you say about the other characters in the play. These will help you isolate and identify how you feel about them. Notice the things you don't say.

- What do "I" say about the other characters in the play?

Now go through your script and write all the things the other characters say about "you."

- What do the other characters in the play say about "me"?

Rachel. We happened to have been going together for three months!

Agnes. And you didn't know a damn thing about him—

Ludlow Fair –Lanford Wilson

Rehearsal Relationship Discoveries

PLAY: _____

ROLE: _____

DATE: _____

Only answer these questions after you have been working on the play for some time. Note the immediate speculations you have about "your" relationships. However, be careful. Make sure that you continue probing, that you have specifics and that you feel personally connected in your rehearsals before you address this page.

- "My" relationship with _____ is _____.

    (Name of your partner's character)

- ☐ "I" am his/her equal. ☐ "I" look up to him/her.
  ☐ "I" am above him/her.

- Our relationship is:

    ☐ familial   ☐ professional ☐ social   ☐ personal
    ☐ sexual   ☐ casual   ☐ intense   ☐ intimate
    ☐ distant   ☐ strictly business
    ☐ new   ☐ tense   ☐ official ☐ competitive
    ☐ other _____

- "We" (know, have known) one another:

    ☐ all "our" lives.   ☐ years.   ☐ months.   ☐ days.
    ☐ a few moments.   ☐ "We" are total strangers.
    ☐ Other _____

- "We" met in (location) _____ in (month/day/year) _

    _____

- How did "you" meet? _____

- "I" am _____ years old and _____ is

    _____.

- Do "you" get along? Why?

- If "you" don't get along, why not?

- Do "you" respect each other?

- Do "you" trust each other?

- Do "you" fight? How much?

- What do "you" fight about?

- Do "you" have secrets from the person?

- What are they?

- Are "you" afraid of the person? Why?

- Is the person afraid of "you?"

- Why do "you" think they are afraid of "you?"

- What happens to "you" when they cry? Yell? Laugh? Withdraw? Are moody? Cop an attitude? When they are quiet? Peaceful? Working? Add to this list.

- What about the person excites "you?"

- What about the person worries "you?"

- What about the person intrigues you?

- How do "you" feel when "you" are with them?

  ☐ safe ☐ insecure ☐ watchful ☐ encouraged
  ☐ awkward ☐ protective ☐ protected ☐ on guard
  ☐ relaxed ☐ playful ☐ silly ☐ calm
  ☐ curious ☐ smart ☐ on top of the world
  ☐ sexy ☐ jealous ☐ disturbed ☐ free to be me
  ☐ uncomfortable ☐ oppressed
  ☐ Other_____

Remember…

You can always go deeper.
You will discover what that
means to you — it is not
something you can 'make'
happen.

The Work

Rehearsal Relationship Discoveries (Cont.)

- "I" think _____ is:
  (Name of your partner's character)

☐ delightful	☐ a nuisance	☐ illiterate	☐ pitiful
☐ argumentative	☐ sad	☐ sharp	☐ critical
☐ playful	☐ embarrassing	☐ fragile	☐ tough
☐ deceitful	☐ educated	☐ self-involved	☐ dangerous
☐ quiet	☐ slow	☐ dumb	☐ hard as nails
☐ shrewd	☐ sadistic	☐ masochistic	☐ secretive
☐ generous	☐ talented	☐ graceful	☐ intelligent
☐ beautiful	☐ untrustworthy	☐ glowing	☐ talkative
☐ busy	☐ rushed	☐ confused	☐ bullying
☐ taunting	☐ stubborn	☐ bossy	☐ domineering
☐ crass	☐ exotic	☐ erotic	☐ sexy
☐ dull	☐ exhausting	☐ too trusting	☐ naive
☐ abusive	☐ misunderstood	☐ nurturing	
☐ Other: _____			

What aspects of your relationship are you struggling with? Identify which elements you don't understand or have a difficult time relating/connecting to. What could you do to gain clarity?

Nora. . . . Don't feel yourself bound, any more than I will. There has to be absolute freedom for us both. Here, take your ring back. Give me mine.

A Doll's House
—Henrik Ibsen

You and Other Characters in the Play

PLAY: _____

ROLE: _____

DATE: _____

As you begin to get more specific about the relationships you have with other characters in your play, you may investigate the components that make up all relationships. Consider:

- How you met

- Your past or history

- Your bonds (what holds you together)

- Your class

- Your status (are you equals, do you look up to, do you look down on)

- Your culture

- How the person satisfies your needs

- The degree of co-dependency

- The nature of relationship (competitive, loving, dependent, useful, passive-aggressive)

- What you want from the other person and how you react to them

- Your honest opinions of the other person

- Your compatibility, dominance, expectations, honesty, trust, secretiveness

Dad. ... What's in a bloody word, Shakespeare said, well, there's a bloody lot. Words give life to things, and beauty and meaning. Like your grandma was a very beautiful woman, and just because she found a bit of happiness after your granddad died, just because in her grief she turned to Mary and they found a bit of comfort in each other's arms, that doesn't give you the right to call her names. How would you feel if I went around calling you a fairy, or a pansy, or a poufter?

Jeff. You do half the time.

The Sum of Us —David Stevens

Endowing Your Partner

PLAY: _____

ROLE: _____

DATE: _____

Test endowing your fellow actors. Consequences of your choices will manifest in the way you respond to your partner, just as endowing inanimate objects affects the manner in which you handle them.

Depending upon what is happening at a given moment in your scene, you might test an "as if." You might treat your partner "as if" he is "your" long lost friend or "you" might treat him "as if" he never stops complaining.

- List possible endowments you might give to your partner.

Every scene has a leader, a character whose want or need is dominant, thereby driving the scene.

If "you" are the leader of your scene, you may want to test an endowment that makes your objective stronger than your partner's, or gives you greater authority over your partner—e.g. you have specific information that they don't have, they drink too much, they lie all the time, etc.

- Are you the leader of your scene? List possible endowments that will justify the strength of your drive.

Using Your Imagination

PLAY: _____

ROLE: _____

DATE: _____

Will acting out something that happens in the play in real life help your work? As an actor, you have a vivid imagination through which you believe in the circumstances of your play. Your imagination protects your secrets. The consequences of acting out in the real world may shut you down or get you into trouble, especially when it comes to sex.

All's Fair in Art...or Is It?

I am rehearsing a scene from Ugo Betti's *The Queen and the Rebel* for class with Miss Hagen. My partner is an experienced actress. She is playing Argia, and I am playing the Queen. At the end of one rehearsal at her apartment, she offers me some of her ex-husband's clothing to give to my husband. I naively and happily accept her generous gesture. In retrospect, it seems a bit peculiar.

Over tea, after another rehearsal, I confide how badly I want to get into a theater group to which she belongs, and she says that she is going to recommend me for membership. I am so happy! She is such a kind, gifted, caring friend and I am sure that I will be invited to be in the group.

Cut to many years later. I don't remember where I was, but something occurred that whisked me back to this time of rehearsal.

I feel a stab in the gut. Oh my God. The actress had been improvising in real life. She was finding ways to win me over. She was doing to me what her character does to my character in the scene, and she succeeded. She, of course, never put my name forward in her theater company—indeed, never intended to. I have never felt so stupid in my life—manipulated and used. Such betrayal. But she found her relationship to me in the scene.

I made this discovery many years after it really happened, and yet I felt that I had been violated. I did have time to process it and work through it. In some ways, it was a benign event. It wounded my pride. It was done to me. I think it helped my partner. She won my confidence.

Be cautious when trying something "real" with your scene partner to help you understand your scene. To manipulate your scene partner in real life in order to gain status in a scene, or to sleep with your partner so as to create sexual chemistry in the play, can create obstacles you don't need and major distractions from the work at hand. It destroys the trust needed between actors to be truly safe and free in performance. Maintain professionalism

Using Your Imagination (Cont.)

and integrity, and trust that your craft and imagination will provide you with a richer landscape from which to draw. It will release you and free you.

Do you have sex with one of the characters in your play? Use your imagination to craft what it was like. You can make it as hot and steamy as you like if you think it was. I leave you to the intimate details that will give you faith in the event and specific images that bring you into relationship with your partner.

Actress. I beg you to remember, my dear Count, that I've been your mistress.

La Ronde –Arthur Schnitzler

"My" Relationship With The Other Character In The Scene

PLAY: _____

ROLE: _____

DATE: _____

Speculate on "your" relationship with the other character in your scene. Only attempt this exercise after you have been on your feet and feel that you have a subjective grasp of the scene. This assures that you have had actual experiences giving you a greater understanding of what is happening between you and your partner in the scene.

Do not feel compelled to fill in anything that you believe has no relevance to your work.

_____ is my _____

(the other character's name)   (Relationship)   _____

The Past

- Ever since "I've" known (her/him), (s)he has loved _____ and _____.

- "I" (never, always, somewhat) understood that.

- "I've" known him/her since _____.

- "We" met _____.

- "I" remember when s/he was _____.

- "Our" parents _____.

- His/her father _____.

- "I" assumed the role of _____ because _____.

- S/he has always treated me _____, _____, and _____.

- S/he has always been _____, _____, _____, _____ and _____.

- When s/he was ____, something changed. S/he became _____.

- "We" stopped _____.

- "I" always knew _____.

- "I" _____ him/her.

- "I" never _____.

- S/he was always closer to _____.

Fentry. Papa, I'm not the baby's father. ... I promised her I'd keep the boy and raise it, like it was my own. And I will, too.

Tomorrow

–Horton Foote

"My" Relationship with the Other Characters (Cont.)

- His/Her favorite _____ was _____.
- S/he rarely _____.
- S/he had a _____ reputation.
- His/Her best traits were _____.
- S/he was always _____.
- "I" remember when s/he _____. S/he didn't _____; but s/he _____.
- S/he used to _____ all the time.
- His/her parents were _____.
- S/he had lots of _____.

The Present

- "I" think s/he is _____, _____, _____, _____, _____, and _____.
- "I" only wish s/he would be _____, _____ and _____.
- "I" think s/he is the best _____ "I" know.
- Right now s/he is really _____.
- S/he looks _____.
- S/he is _____ "me" because s/he is so _____.

The Future

- "I" know s/he would be happy if _____.
- "I've" told him/her that "I" would _____.
- S/he is really good at _____ and _____ but s/he will never _____ or _____.

Transference

PLAY: _____

ROLE: _____

DATE: _____

List some of the transferences that you think might help you in developing "your" relationship with your partner. Be specific. Why are you considering this particular transference? How might it serve you? Test it. What is the result? What did you discover? What questions do you still have about using transferences in your work?

The Work

Rehearsal Notes/Class Notes

PLAY: _____

ROLE: _____

DATE: _____

Remember...

Every time you go on stage, you have to be willing to fall on your face.

Remember...

The next moment in the scene is the next moment of the character — not just the next line.

—Herbert Berghof

Remember...

A critique contains necessary information.

Chapter 6

Character: Who Am I? Stepping Into a New Pair of Shoes

The Mystery of What Turns You On

Uta Hagen assigns the Arsinoe/Celimene scene from *The Misanthrope*, by Moliere, to Susan Spector and me. Susan is working on her Ph.D. at New York University and tells me that we will not be able to do a rework of the scene until she takes the German Exam for which she is studying to meet her doctoral language requirement. That is fine for me because I have a young son and can't rehearse with my usual intensity, anyway.

We work on the scene over a three-month period and it is one of the most satisfying rehearsal experiences I have ever had. I learn the gift of time in the creative process.

Of course I know the circumstances: Arsinoe (the new me) has the hots for Alceste and is jealous of the popular Celimene (Susan), who has his love. That knowledge is all well and good, but it has no meaning for me. Perhaps I am too repressed. No matter. I know that I can use a transference of someone I am wildly attracted to in place of Alceste. However, for whatever reason, nothing works. I can feel that I am not finding the actions I need for the scene, and that consciously thinking about physical attraction to support my rich verbal life is getting me nowhere.

We do the scene for Miss Hagen, get our critique and then continue to rehearse sporadically over the next few months. The break gives me an opportunity to do extensive research on the period. When we finally do the rework on the scene, I discover just how successful this research has been: my faith in my circumstances is very strong.

However, I had not found my action when we initially presented the scene, and I am still seeking to discover it. As I read the play for the eighth or ninth time, one line suddenly leaps off the page. I wonder if it would have made a difference had I caught it sooner—would I have been ready for the information? Perhaps I noticed it at just the right time.

What I have connected to is the fact that Celimene is a "widow." This frees my point of view: the prude in Carol knows that because she is no longer a virgin, Celimene attracts admirers by sleeping with them all. "I" (Arsinoe) arrive at her door with purpose that is supported by my puritanical entitlement. I tap into the prudish side of myself—a side I don't like to admit to. This side is much more comfortable than my overtly sexual side. "I" love, thrive on and initiate all the gossip that "I" warn Celimene about in the course of the scene. My homework and rehearsals have been so correct that, during our next presentation in class, when it is time for "me" to leave, the inner object (my mental image) of "my" carriage coming down the cobblestone street is as real as a taxi showing up at my door.

The premise of developing a character is quite straightforward: a character is a person and that person is *you*—you, saying the playwright's words. When you act, *your* body moves—not the character's. Your character's words come out of *your* mouth. Your body holds the sensations that occur as you play off of the other actors and live through the imaginary circumstances of the play. However, the world of the play will most likely be different than your world, and the character you are playing will probably see their world differently than you see yours.

Confusion often arises from the idea of using yourself in your work. Let me be clear. You always begin from your own point of view, acknowledging where you actually are. But, do not mistake the idea of using yourself to literally mean being the way you are (or the way you think you are). You will find this misunderstanding extremely limiting, especially if you have a narrow, rigidly guarded perception of yourself.

Manifesting the life of another human being occurs in the process of rehearsal. Until this happens, the character you are to play is only an idea on paper or in your head.

Your lifelong practice as an actor is twofold:

- **Personal**
  - To learn how you see your*self*. To face yourself and take responsibility for your personal growth.
  - To uncover your potential, reach it and move beyond it.
- **Artistic**
  - To manifest the "new you," a human being who lives within the world of the play.[11]

Search the Attic ★

Uta Hagen taught that you have everything within yourself that you will need to draw on when finding the new "you."[12]

You are a container holding treasures that you don't even know you have. Inside of yourself (choose your image: a big cardboard box, an old-fashioned attic or a computer hard-drive) are deeply buried memories, flashes of images and ignored experiences that might be difficult to acknowledge.

Some may be humbling, humiliating or make you feel ashamed, foolish or stupid. Some may make you sob or cause you pain. And some may fill you with joy and delight. Your desire to fill yourself with the point of view of your character will direct you to the things you pull out of or add to your container. Everything you need is within you.

Some discoveries may be thrilling. You will feel, do and move in ways you never imagined. You will surprise yourself.

Your journey is the discovery of capabilities inside yourself that bring you to the new "you." This takes time. It occurs in process. *This is your process.*

Five Conduits to Find the New You

Your goal is to live through the circumstances of the play, walking in your character's shoes. Five conduits will help you embody the things "you" say and do in the play:

1. Connect the "I" of the play to yourself by literally referring to yourself when talking about your character; i.e. always use the first person singular when you talk about the character. Also, literally mean yourself when you speak the word "I" as part of your text.

2. Investigate "your" new background. It has shaped many of the things you think, say and do.

3. Find "your" point of view. How do you see and relate to everything? What are your new opinions and beliefs? From whence do they spring?

4. Learn about "your" new profession and its body of knowledge.

5. Research and choose or create the clothes "you" wear.

Strengthen these habits as you rehearse.

#1: Be Subjective: The First Person Singular ★

Still? A Classic Mistake

Even after so many years of acting and teaching, I make a classic mistake and need guidance from my teacher.

> **Serge.** You worked at Barney's in European suits.
>
> *The Food Chain* —Nicky Silver

The last critique I receive from Uta Hagen is about my work on a scene from *Lettice and Lovage* by Peter Shaffer. The fine actress and teacher Carol Morley is my partner. At the end of our scene, Miss Hagen asks if I realize that I have an image of the character. I reply that I don't. She says that I do not have enough of myself in my work. She says that whenever I use the word "I" in the scene I am not connecting it to me, Carol.

I sit down, perplexed. Within fifteen minutes, however, I understand. What she means is that I am holding onto an image of the character I have in my head, instead of letting myself be in the work. For a number of reasons, I am not actually connected to myself, Carol, during the scene. I am preoccupied with remembering my lines and so afraid of forgetting them, I am holding onto line readings that carried over from my rehearsals.

In this crucial lesson, Hagen was saying that I needed to be more subjective, to have more of myself in the "I" of my character. Being *subjective* means allowing your own personal feelings, tastes and opinions to influence or inspire the way you are in the world. *I, me, my* or *mine* are the words you use whenever you refer to yourself.

Why would the characters you play be any less subjective than you are? Mean yourself when you say the words "I", "me", "my" or "mine" in any play. Get into the habit of using those words even when you think, speak, make notes or wonder about the characters you are playing. You may feel awkward at first since you will be changing the ingrained habit of talking about the character as "he" or "she." Do it anyway.

The words *I, me, my* or *mine* ground and focus you in the world of the play. They give you your new perspective on and experience of all the things you see and hear, the things you say, think and do. They place you in the midst of what is happening in a scene or play. They make it easier for you to deal with your research tangibly and sensorially rather than intellectually or academically. Using the first person singular lets you embody your new life.

Living your life subjectively, you are rarely aware of your behavior (what you do) because you are mentally preoccupied with the things that are actually going on in your life. Think about a recent argument you had with a friend, the day your father died, your last critique in class or when you were washing the dishes this morning. What do you remember? Do you recall how you felt, or the various things you did and how you did them? Do you flash to images of a section of the room, an object or an expression in someone's eyes when you were talking to them?

Remember...

Invite yourself in the world of the play.

My guess is that you remember your feelings and flashes of images but not the small things you did—your physical actions. The same holds true for the new "you" on stage.

We live our lives subjectively, always relating to our circumstances from our own point of view. Some circumstances are so difficult and painful that we simply cannot face them. Hence, we intuitively, unconsciously protect ourselves, develop defences and live in denial. The adjustments your unconscious makes to protect you blinds you to what others can see clearly. Feelings of love, joy and ecstasy can be similarly blinding. Your characters are just the same. The new you should be as "blind" and unaware as you are in your own life.

The habit of thinking "I" will open you to the most compelling, mysterious, distinguishing facet of your craft—manifesting the character through yourself.

#2: Know Your Past, Your Background ★

You have a past, the story of your life up to this very moment. The people you have known, the places where you have lived, your family background, cultural heritage and all your life experiences affect all that you do, think and say. Everything in your life is specifically fused to *actual* people, places, events and things.

Your background is largely responsible for your drives, your wants and the tactics you use in life. Your sense of who you are and how you feel about yourself has roots in your past.

Do you trace some of the following to how, when and where you were raised?

- your interests
- your taste
- your self-esteem
- your moral fiber
- your need for success

Evelyn. I used to sit around this table with my own sisters. You know what? I remember many times we'd sit around this same room, and just talk for hours. ...We'd stay up whole nights. This house. My mother was born in it.

Independence –Lee Blessing

- your definition of success

- your prejudices

- your likes and dislikes

- your relationship to your body

- any addictions or compulsions you may have

- the kind of wishes you have

- your dreams, those that you feel are possible or impossible to achieve

- your disposition toward life

- how you process

- how protective, defensive, aggressive, passive, open, trusting, secure, self-assured, self-absorbed, self-effacing, pessimistic, negative, neurotic, narcissistic, manipulative, calculating, secretive, closeted, opinionated, outgoing, private, insecure, imaginative, curious, political, socially conscious, introverted or compassionate you are

All of you is rooted in your past. You grow from your past like plants grow from soil.

Your past determines who you are. Who you are determines your perceptions of the world around you. Who you are determines how you think, how you relate to and handle the situations in which you find yourself and how you behave with the people with whom you interact. It determines the kinds of thoughts you have, why you do the things you do and why you say the things you say.

Your background includes your cultural heritage, your class and status (which may be ever-changing), your racial identity, your sex, gender and sexuality. You may experience these identity markers as fixed, or you may have the experience of them changing and adapting over time.

What information does the playwright provide about "your" background? What information does she or he omit or leave for you to flesh out? As you rehearse, events in the play may trigger memories of an event or a person from your own past. As you particularize and make more specific choices, you will bond with the character you are creating.

As you bridge the psychological, physical, historical and cognitive gaps between you and your character, expect that "you," the character, will likely do things differently than you usually do, and that "you," the character, will likely experience feelings you have rarely, if ever, felt. Once again, isn't that why you want to act?

#3: Find New Points Of View ★

In It

It is the first gathering of the cast of *Eli: A Mystery Play of the Sufferings of Israel*, an impressionistic Holocaust play by Nelly Sachs. We are in a rehearsal hall of the Guthrie Theater in Minneapolis to see films—documentaries with footage of the Warsaw Ghetto and propaganda films shot by Hitler's SS.

Waiting for the films to begin, I am turning the pages of a book that happens to be on my table. I am still in the glow of being at "the Guthrie."

Biting into an apple, I randomly open to two pages of iconic photographs: naked bodies of dead men, women and children thrown helter-skelter into a huge pit; a pyramid of eye glasses; a mountain of human hair; their heads shaved, young skinny girls standing barefoot with the sun beating down on them; men lying in their barracks on bunks of bare wooden planks; all eyes staring lifelessly into some dark nothingness.

Suddenly feeling nauseous, I swallow the sweet piece of apple I am chewing and throw the rest away. I am horrified by the photos. I am shocked and embarrassed to be looking at them while nonchalantly eating. Far removed from the events the photos depict—and, consequently, the world of the play—I react to these photographs as the spectator I am. I am safe and naïve, and I can never know what life was like for those six million souls.

In an attempt to enter the world of the play, I use my imagination, read victims' and survivors' journals, listen to a survivor's story, research and rehearse. Even though I do all of this, however, I remain a spectator, not truly entering the world of my character as a participant.

It isn't until our opening night that I have an "Aha!" moment—a flash of what I have to do to really shift into my character's point of view. An hour before curtain, I photocopy about six images of women and children in a concentration camp and tape them around my dressing room mirror.

"I" have survived the harsh conditions of the camp. "I" knew these people in the photographs. Side by side, we breathed the same air, ate the same rotting food, slept, walked barefoot in snow, worked, endured beatings and rape and were close to murder and death every hour of every day.

My research is no longer an intellectual exercise. It feeds my imagination with specific inner objects that are a part of "my" past. I experience having a new point of view, of seeing, touching, living and standing in new shoes, and this puts me into "my" new circumstances.

Rather than recoiling from these images or finding them spectacular or extraordinary, I have found "my" point of view, making them part of my everyday life.

If I hold up a cube in my classroom with every side painted a different color, no student would see the whole block. Depending upon where they are sitting, some would see green and yellow, some only orange, some only purple and some only red. Such is the nature of subjective belief and point of view.

You see what you see. You think what you think. You believe what you believe. Changing ways or shifting perspective is hard in life, but it is what actors do for every role they play. Taping those pictures of Holocaust victims to my dressing room mirror, I started to see the Holocaust as the daily reality that it was for those who lived through it, and following the portals my imagination opened, I shifted my perspective away from that of a spectator viewing something sensational. Throughout the run of the play, I continued letting my imagination and research strengthen my actor's faith that I was a survivor.

Your particular point of view stems from your background, the morals and values you were raised with, and your life experiences. Point of view is affected by your class and status, by your race, gender, sexuality, age, nationality, physical and mental ability and your education. The way that these factors affect the course of your life gives you unique insight into and perspectives on the world. The janitor of an organization has a very different viewpoint of that organization than, say, the CEO—and in many ways, it can be argued, the janitor is privy to a much broader and intimate understanding of the true workings of the institution. In a similar way, those of us affected by prejudices due to race, class, gender, etc., are able to see aspects of life and culture that others can, in blissful ignorance, remain blind to. On the other side of that same coin, those of us with privilege may be exposed to ideas and circumstances that others do not have access to; for example, having the financial means to see a therapist and attend college, travel, or the time and space to practice meditation or yoga, join a gym or take art classes. Our viewpoint changes as we grow and change; it is the result of our cumulative life experience.

> **Princess.** ...Why didn't you marry this Heavenly little physician?
>
> **Chance.** Didn't I tell you that Heavenly is the daughter of Boss Finley, the biggest political wheel in this part of the country? ...He figured his daughter rated someone a hundred, a thousand times better than me, Chance Wayne ...
>
> *Sweet Bird of Youth* –Tennessee Williams

Your sexuality, your sexual desires, your morals, beliefs and values surrounding sex and your sexual history are all very important aspects of your background and point of view. The way you see yourself—your self-image—is impacted by your sexuality and your sex life. Sex may stir up in you fear, performance anxiety or feelings of inadequacy or numbness. Alternately, you may experience your sexuality as freeing or empowering. Consider— how do your wants, needs, and subsequent actions relate to or stem from your sexuality—your sexual desires or fears? How does your sexuality influence the way you see the world and yourself, for both you and the new "you"?

Your character will probably see the world differently than you do. However, you might also find areas where you share morals, beliefs and attitudes. Learn more about "your" belief systems. It is your job to:

- Know what they are

- Assimilate why and how they are a part of "you."

For example, imagine that your character is a practicing Irish Catholic. If you are not Catholic, you will feel the need to know more about your new religion. Your research could lead you to the core of the new "you". Learn and practice the rituals all Catholics are raised with. Go to a church, visit a Catholic School, read an elementary school text book on the Catechism, hear a Sunday Mass, get someone to teach you how to say the Rosary. Watch others say the Rosary and notice their relationship to the object. Ask someone to show you how to take Communion. Go to Confession. Every action you take will flood your imagination. Gathering specific, tangible objects and images will lead you to the questions that open you to the experience of what it means to be Catholic. You can then craft why, when and how "your" beliefs became a part of you.

When you are developing the point of view of your character, you will increase your sensitivity to "your" new priorities, opinions, values and beliefs. They will influence how you react to everything you taste, touch, smell, see and hear.

Are "your" beliefs challenged in the play? Do you change and grow? How do your beliefs affect the very heart of the play?

As you embody and espouse your new point of view, you take your place within the circumstances of the play.

#4: Get to Work—Your Profession, Your Job ★

With your first reading of a play, you may learn that your character does something to earn a living. Begin your research as soon as you identify "your" new profession or job. Apply the ideas in the above example of being a Catholic to research your character's profession. So much of your identity comes

> **Beatrice.** …You still walk around in front of him in your slip —
>
> **Catherine.** Well I forgot.
>
> **Beatrice.** Well you can't do it. Or like you sit on the edge of the bathtub talkin' to him when he's shavin' in his underwear.
>
> *A View From the Bridge* –Arthur Miller

> **Rubin.** The new job is work I've never done. Work I never even thought of doin'. Learnin' about all that God damn machinery, and how to get out there and demonstrate it. Working with different kinds of men, that's smarter than I am, that think fast and talk sharp and mean all business. Men I can't sit around and chew tobacco with and joke with like I did m'old customers.
>
> *The Dark at the Top of the Stairs* –William Inge

from your job. The playwright doesn't always tell you what your character does for a living; however, whether or not it is given, you can both daydream and take actual steps to learn about "your" line of work and education history.

Every job or profession requires some kind of education or training. Each has its own rules of conduct, pecking order, body of knowledge, tools and techniques that must be mastered. When you begin working on a role, learn what it takes to become proficient and move ahead in "your" profession. This will not only give you insight into your new job, but also into your background, history and your point of view, as you come to develop an understanding of how you ended up in your current position and what it took to get there.

> **Vito.** ...You don't know anything about me of the satisfaction I get from my job at Dillon, Auchinclaus and Simpson... I'm a vice-president with one of the best goddam companies in New York. I've been there for fifteen years. ...
>
> *It Had to Be You*
> —Renee Taylor and Joseph Bologna

At the very least, you should know about the demands, challenges, dangers and risks of "your" job. Visit the kind of place where you work. Apply for a job there. Find the building, the office, courtroom, restaurant, the examining room, the classroom, the church, the trucking company, the warehouse or store where you think you work. Talk to people who hold down the kind of job you are researching. Watch movies that deal with your character's profession.

Doing certain jobs, you may have to function in ways that are uncomfortable for you. You will have to figure out how to bridge the gap that exists between you and the status of "your" new position. What is your status in your own eyes? What is it in the eyes of the world? Did you come from humble beginnings and have to fight to get where you are today or were you born with a silver spoon in your mouth, i.e. into privilege? Ask these questions about yourself and the new "you." This will help you identify gaps between your background and "your" background, allowing you to focus your attention on those areas you need to develop in order to bridge the gaps.

> **Sammy.** May I help you into your wrap? (*The word wrap is a false glorification of her Sunday coat* ...)
> **Reenie.** Thank you.
> **Cora.** (*Whispering to Lottie*) I wish I could have bought her one of those little fur jackets like Flirt is wearing.
>
> *The Dark at the Top of the Stairs* —William Inge

#5: Get Dressed—Clothing (Not Costume)   ★

The clothes you wear affect you psychologically, emotionally and physically; because they do, you often consciously and intuitively select what you are going to wear for a wide variety of occasions. The way you are feeling, who you are going to be with, where you are, where you are going, your status, how much money you have, your gender, your culture, your job and your needs all play a role in how you choose to dress. In short, your given circumstances influence what you decide to wear at any given time.

To immerse yourself in the life of the new you, think "my *clothing*" rather than "my costume." Imagine where "you" bought your clothes, had them made or how you acquired them. Stay within the context of the circumstances and period of the play. Dress from your skin out—learn about the underwear of the time. How does wearing the particular garments you have on make you feel? Research the clothing styles of the period in which the play is set. Use research and your imagination to decide how you came by the clothing you wear.

Your wardrobe and how you treat it will reflect "your" status. All clothing will be linked to your social class and the time and period in which the play is set (see Appendix C).

Mary. ....It was made of soft, shimmering satin, trimmed with wonderful old duchesse lace, in tiny ruffles around the neck and sleeves … My father even let me have duchesse lace on my white satin slippers, and lace with the orange blossoms in my veil. Oh, how I loved that gown!

Long Day's Journey Into Night
—Eugene O'Neill

The Nails

I am in a production of *The Duchess of Malfi*, the Jacobean drama by John Webster. Set in the court of Malfi, Italy, 1504-1510, it is a fully mounted production—the director's thesis for his Master of Fine Arts degree from a noted university. I play Julia. The space we rehearse and perform in is an actual chapel called The Nave, and, even though it is small with one or two major drawbacks, it is a wonderful setting for the production.

The director also designs the set. It is mammoth and multi-levelled. The backstage area, as often is the case, leaves much to be desired. The stair risers leading to entrances are higher and narrower than normal. They are unfinished plywood and uncarpeted. Nails are sticking out everywhere. The stairs do not even lead directly onto the stage—with one step-unit, we have to make a sharp 90° angle turn in order to enter. All entrances, of course, have to appear effortless and are to be executed with grace and aplomb.

This production coincides with the creation of the Costume Collection, which is an organization that rents costumes to not-for-profit theaters. Costumes originally built for famous Broadway and opera productions make up most of the stock of this fantastic collection. My costumer/ set designer husband, Michael, tells me that they inherited costumes that go back to productions from the Twenties. My costumes for *Malfi* are magnificent Renaissance creations. They are artfully constructed. My gown for Julia is voluminous, heavy and has an outer layer of diaphanous silk.

> My gown and the staircase are mortal enemies from the beginning. I go to the director to alert him of my situation. I am not sure what I want him to do, but getting someone to hammer in the protruding nails would be a good start.
>
> He responds that I am responsible for working with my costume. Duh!
>
> A few months after the production closes, I use the character of Julia as the basis for the History Exercise[13] in Uta Hagen's *Respect for Acting*. This exercise requires detailed research into all aspects of life during the period in which the play is set. In my research, I learn something that would have had *no meaning* to me had I not struggled with (and mastered) those horrid stairs in our production.
>
> The steps of the buildings of the time were marble: the tread could be twelve to eighteen inches, the risers were about three inches and the width could easily be three feet. Women of class would have no trouble gracefully and fluidly moving up and down stairs in their garments.
>
> Ah, Illusion.

As you work on more plays, you will discover how much the clothing you wear matters for finding the new "you." It goes beyond looking good. You are not the designer, but you are responsible for *wearing* the garments your costumer provides. Learn about the history of clothing. Do your research on the period of your play to find out how and why certain styles of clothing were prevalent. Practice in your new clothing—see how it changes the way you move: walking, sitting, entering and exiting, dancing, etc.

Stepping Into New Shoes…and Stepping Out

Learn Your Boundaries –Safety and Your Mental Health ★

The Shaman

> A shaman comes to heal a sick woman, whose soul has been captured by evil spirits. He puts himself into a trance by inhaling tobacco, dancing, and beating his drum. While in this trance, his soul travels to the spirit world and does battle to retrieve the woman's soul, thus restoring her. His assistant holds the shaman by a chain so that if he gets lost or trapped in the spirit world he can be pulled back.

Victor Slezak understands how important mental health is for the actor. He uses this image of the chain as an essential reminder that you always need a way back to normalcy when you are lost, bewildered or unhealthily consumed by the chaos of your creativity or the dark sides of the character you are playing.

You have to be able to be *in* the work; you have to be able to step *out* of the work.

Your character will most likely be in extreme, extraordinary circumstances. You may someday have to play a murderer, a drug addict, an alcoholic, a rape victim, someone who commits suicide, loses a child or robs a bank. Your character may be a pregnant woman whose husband has lost interest in you. You may be abused.

With every character's imaginary journey, you engage in circumstances that cause you to experience real sensation more intensely and more frequently than you normally do in the course of your actual life. You might not get lost or trapped in the imaginary world of the play like the shaman, but you may find that aspects of the play seep into your everyday life. When this happens you may not realize that the play has been affecting you emotionally and stirring your unconscious.

Dorothea. We all need forgiveness.

Eleemosynary –Lee Blessing

Empathy is the ability to understand and identify with the feelings of others. It is absolutely essential for an actor. At the same time, it is good to remember that even when situations seem the same as yours, they are not. What's yours is yours. What's another's is theirs.

Your personal practice and your network of friends, teachers, family, colleagues—and yes, your therapist, if you are fortunate enough to have one—are the links of your chain for maintaining equilibrium when you feel off-balance, uncertain and afraid.

Don't confuse the idea of real life with life in a play. Life in a play is make-believe, pretend. Theater is a carefully controlled environment with many people doing their best to make sure that no one is in danger.

Always use your common sense when it comes to researching and understanding the characters you play. *Do not experiment with real drugs, real guns or real weapons, EVER.* If you do, you take the real risk of not being able to complete or repeat a performance and you will encounter unanticipated consequences.

Argia. The other day the police arrested me.

The Queen and the Rebels –Ugo Betti

Consequences of real life are actual and can be life-threatening, and not fun. To further emphasize this point before we continue: a Word of Warning!

Under No Circumstances!

Don't Do Stupid, Life-Threatening Things In "Real" Life!

In more innocent times, I am teaching a workshop in Toronto. A young actress is working on a scene from *Hello and Goodbye* by Athol Fugard. Her character is a tough, streetwise Afrikaner; the life and background of the young actress couldn't be more different from the life and background of the character.

> The third time she and her partner come in to present their scene, they recount a story that makes my hair stand on end.
>
> The night before class, to research the character's past, they go to a street that is in the "red light" district of Toronto. The actress is dressed like a hooker. After observing some of the other women on the street, she begins imitating them. She starts following johns as they walk down the street, propositioning them. Her partner is close at hand as a safety precaution. Animated as she tells the story, she says that she actually starts having a good time.
>
> Then a car pulls up and the actress begins talking to the driver. Her newly found confidence leads to an impulsive action.
>
> Her partner takes over telling the story.
>
> All of sudden he is watching his partner **get into the car**! He can't believe his eyes and is terrified. He goes into action. Pulling out his wallet as if it is a badge, he strides around to the driver's side, "officially" orders the girl out of the car and gives the guy in the car a warning!
>
> As they tell their story, I tremble.

Imagine what might have happened if the actress's partner had not acted so swiftly! The girl would have been trapped in a car with a stranger who expected her to give him a blowjob. What would have happened to her if she had confessed to not being a real prostitute and refused to follow through? There are three lessons to be taken from this story:

1. There are times when you have to admit that you really *can't* fully identify with your character or the circumstances of the play. It is not to be perceived as a failure.

2. *Never* use the excuse that you are an actor and need to try out something dangerous that happens in your play to see what it's "really" like! If you do, you will be *endangering others as well as yourself. People will not know that you are pretending*!

3. There are many ways of finding identification with the imaginary circumstances of a play. Let your research feed your imagination.

Don't Settle, Keep Seeking ★

Betty. It bothered me at first not knowing who killed Bert. But then I thought of all the things we don't know.

Landscape of the Body

—John Guare

Continue working in such a way that possibility can flourish. Keep an open mind. Test before you censor. Remain curious. Return again and again to refining and finding specifics that mean something to you. Don't settle. Ask questions. Keep seeking even when you think you have done all of the work.

Finding the new "you" is a process. Your continual questioning, daydreaming and speculating aid you as you fortify your point of view. Of course, you discover even more about who "you" are when you work off of your partner in rehearsal. Permit your imagination to assimilate your research by connecting specific and detailed references in your script to images and words that increase your belief in all aspects of your life in the play.

With every new role, you will learn more about yourself. You already realize that facets of your personality become more or less dominant depending upon life's variables—time, place, the people you are with and the events in which you are engaged. As you look for personal links, however small, and specific connections that are genuinely meaningful to you and release your feelings into action, you will find sides of yourself you didn't know were there. You may discover your own personal habits are restricting you in ways you never realized. As you broaden your perception of yourself, you will gain faith in all "you" do and say. You will likely learn more about your own capabilities every time you work on a new play.

> **Algernon**. All women become like their mothers. That is their tragedy. No man does. That's his.
>
> *The Importance of Being Earnest*
> —Oscar Wilde

You begin working on your "Who Am I?" from the moment you first read the play. Your questions and your quest for specificity and particulars should move you beyond your first images of the character. Keep the question "Who Am I?" alive. Give yourself time to discover the new you, your new point of view.

Allow the **Me, Myself & I** and **The Work** pages to steer the discovery of your unique alignment with the new "you." Your process, like you, is one-of-a-kind. It is yours alone and no one can take it from you. Your homework and your experiences in rehearsal lead to those thrilling "aha!" accidents when you know that you are, in that moment, the new "you".

> **Biff**. He walked away. I saw him for one minute. —How the hell did I ever get the idea I was a salesman there? I even believed myself that I'd been a salesman for him! And then he gave me one look and —I realized— we've been talking in a dream for fifteen years … I was a shipping clerk.
>
> *Death of a Salesman* —Arthur Miller

You might find some of the following **Me, Myself & I** exercises to be confronting. You may question why they are in this book. The answer is simple—even if you have never been confronted with the issues raised in some of the exercises, the new "you" might very well have been.

These exercises should stimulate your curiosity. You can't act if you are not curious, always wondering what makes a person do and say the things he does and says. The sheer number of exercises may turn you off. Don't feel that you must do them all at once. A small section of one exercise can take you on an unexpected journey of personal insight.

There may be some issues that you are not ready to tackle—and you don't have to. Notice if, when and how often you avoid focusing on one. Could your avoidance be a signal that there is something you may someday wish to address?

You are on a lifelong journey. For today, only do as much as you can. You will hone your practice forever.

Remember…

You can make your life out of

doing what you love.

My Background

Consider the following set of questions. When you come to a question that captures your interest, think about it within the context of your own life. Your own background might provide a link with "your" new background.

One or two of the following questions may stimulate your imagination as you review your own relationships with your mother, father, siblings, grandparents, teachers and friends—the people who were part of your life when you were growing up. You might begin to wonder about "your" relationships with some of the people from "your" past.

The people in my life: Family

- Talk about your ancestors and family history.

- Where did your ancestors come from?

  Vienna + Germany

- What languages were/are spoken in your home?

  Some German

- Did anyone in your family go through a catastrophic event such as the Holocaust, the Great Depression, the Vietnam War, the Iraq War?

  WWII   Vietnam War

- When were you born? Were you raised in the 1920s, 30s, 40s, 50s, 60s, 70s, 80s, 90s, 2000s?

  1950's

- Where were you born?

  New York

- Where did you grow up?

  NY, Spain, Bogota, Quebec

- Were you adopted? Did you live in foster care?

  NO

- Did you grow up in one place, or did your family move around? If your family moved, name the cities, states, or countries where you lived.

  see above

- What was/is your home like?

  lonely

My Background (Cont.)

- Who is your mother? Do you have two mothers? Have you never known your mother?

- Did/does your mother work? What kind of work did/does she do?

- Who is your father? Do you have two fathers? Have you never known your father?

- Did/does your father work? What kind of work did/does he do?

- What were/are your parents' values?

- What was/is important to each of your parents individually?

- How religious was/is your family? In what faith were you brought up?

- Did/do you come from a loving family, or was there strife and tension in your home?

- Did your parents stay together or divorce? Were they never married to begin with? If divorced, did one or both remarry? How many times? With the new marriage, what other family did you inherit?

- What were/are the dysfunctional aspects of your family?

- Was/is your family poor, on welfare, royalty, aristocracy, wealthy, educated, middle class, blue-collar, white-collar or homeless?

- Who in your family stands out in your mind as having the greatest influence on you? A grandparent? Your mother? Your father? A sibling? An aunt or an uncle? A cousin? Other? How? What were their strongest influences on you?

- Were you or anyone in your family verbally, physically or mentally abused?

- Did you experience the death or critical illness of a family member or friend at an early age?

- How many brothers and sisters do/did you have? Are/were you the youngest, oldest or middle child? Was/is there a favorite child in your family?

- What was/is your role within your family?

- Did/do you have a favorite parent, sibling, or grandparent? Who and why?

- Are you single, married, separated, widowed or divorced?

- Do you have children? How many? How old are they? Have you raised them?

Family myths

- What stories have you been told about yourself when you were little? Who told them?

- What are the stories about other family members? e.g. Uncle Jimmy, etc.

Family education

- What was the highest education your grandparents and your parents achieved?

- What were the circumstances under which each received their education?

- What was the average level of education at the time that they went to school? Were they more or less educated than the average?

My Background (Cont.)

My education

- What is the highest level of education you have achieved?

- Where did you go to elementary school? Middle school? High school?

- Did you attend a college or a university? If so, which? Did you graduate?

- Did you choose your school or did something or someone influence your choice?

- Do you wish you had gone to a different school? Which one?

- What was your major or your area of specialization? Did you choose it or did family pressure prevail?

- Did travel abroad play a part in your education? How?

- If you could do it over, what would you do differently about your education?

- What memories do you have from your school years?

- Were you diagnosed with a learning disability or special need? What happened?

- What subjects did you study?

- What were your best subjects? What were your worst subjects?

- What were your favorite subjects? Why? What were your least favorite subjects? Why?

Miss Tesman.
General Gabler's daughter. What a life she had in the general's day! Remember seeing her out with her father—how she'd go galloping past in that long black riding outfit, with a feather in her hat?

Hedda Gabler — Henrik Ibsen

Remember...
Self-discovery takes a lifetime.

- How do you learn?

- What teachers or professors influenced you the most? How and why?

- Did you have a mentor? If so, how did you find that person?

- Where and with whom have you studied acting?

My friends

- Are you still in touch with any of your friends from elementary school? Middle school? High school? University?

- Who is your best friend? What is the binding ingredient of your friendship?

- Describe your friendships.

- What kind of a friend are you? What kind of friends do you have?

- How often do see your friends? Talk to your friends? Travel with your friends?

- How many friends do you have? Do you make a distinction between friends and acquaintances?

- Write about someone you recently met whom you consider a friend.

Past

- Write a paragraph about what family members and friends said to you when you did something creative.

- Think of an incident that encouraged you to follow, or that turned you away from, your natural inclination.

What I Say About Myself & How Others See Me

The next exercises help you think about the image of yourself you create in the world.

What I say about myself

This is an important and valuable exercise. You may discover that you are not kind to yourself. You may discover that you beat yourself up and are unrealistically and, therefore, unproductively hard on yourself. You may find that you excuse your behavior and that you don't take responsibility for your actions. Then, again, you may discover that you are encouraging even when you don't feel optimistic.

Celimene. One's vision of oneself is so defective …
The Misanthrope –Molière

Carry a little notebook around with you for a day. Write down the comments you make about yourself out loud or the thoughts that run through your mind.

How I am seen in the world

1. How do you think you are perceived:

    - by each member of your family?

    - by people with whom you work?

    - by your teachers?

    - by your friends?

    - by people for whom you audition?

    - by directors?

    - by strangers?

    - Do you care about what others think of you?

    - Does it concern you?

2. How much time do you spend thinking about this?

My 'Who Am I' List

This exercise is a way of looking at you, the actor. Do not consider it a fixed, definitive exercise. Instead, add to it. Erase entries. Adjust entries. Consider it a form of meditation.

In your notebook, list at least fifty adjectives and phrases that you think describe your personality, personal traits and characteristics. Many may be contradictory. For instance, when talking about money, you may describe yourself as frugal, generous, tight and a spendthrift. As insights come to you, add them to this page. Date your entries.

You will discover that you are complex, and have sides of yourself that are at once attractive and unattractive, pleasant and not so nice. Note situations when some of these traits manifest themselves. Also note the people who bring out some of these traits in you.

Kate. All right, I'm going to tell you something else.

Jimmy. Oh, Jesus …

Kate. Two people were talking about you at a party once, and one of 'em said, "That Jimmy Zoole, he's such an attractive guy. Say, are his front teeth capped?" You know what the other one said? "Jimmy Zoole's whole life is capped!"

P.S. Your Cat Is Dead! —James Kirkwood

This list will always fluctuate. It will change and grow as you change and grow.

Return to this list after a few months have passed. How would you change your list now?

My Physicality

Because so much of the work in this book is mental, it is important to remember that your work must always manifest itself physically so that you are not acting "from the neck up."

Your body is the vessel through which your emotional life percolates. Your emotional life, in turn, affects and finds release through your voice and body.

You communicate through your body and voice. Therefore, as you tackle the other exercises in this book, always take into account how they affect your physicality.

Self-observation

- Take a shower or bath.
- Get ready for bed.
- Eat dinner.
- Come home from a great dance class.
- Prepare for rehearsal.
- Play cards.
- Get ready for a party.
- Choose a time when you attempt to pay attention to the way you do each activity above. What are your habits? What objects do you always have at your disposal? What are your routines? What are your rituals?

- What are the things that are on your mind?

- How do circumstances cause you to change the way you perform each activity?

How I move

Find the words that you think describe the way you move. Write about your physicality under several different circumstances. This may include physical habits, traits and qualities.

What Matters to Me

Here is an opportunity to ask yourself questions that you may never have asked yourself, questions about things that you take for granted, or questions that you don't want to consider.

Think about your relationship to the answers you give. Are your answers definitive or are you avoiding a committed answer? Do you have an investment in the answer?

Are there some questions you don't have an answer for? Do you judge some of your answers, even if they are accurate?

- For what or whom would I die?

- For what or whom would I make a great sacrifice?

- What gives me pleasure?

- What motivates me?

- What saddens me, thrills me, gives me satisfaction?

- What are some of my habits, routines? How do they affect me?

- What are some of my obsessions?

- What makes me comfortable, uncomfortable?

- Where is the struggle in my life?

- What turns me on?

- Am I jealous, generous, compassionate, loyal, envious, sad, happy, defeated, manipulative, ambitious, competitive, combative, spoiled or comparing? When? Why?

- What am I afraid of?

My Big Stones

Here is a story an actress shared in my class.

"My favorite professor came into class and put some items on his desk. Beginning the class wordlessly, he picked up a very large, empty mayonnaise jar and proceeded to fill it with big, colorful marbles. He then asked the class if the jar was full. The class replied that it was.

He picked up a bag of pebbles and poured them into the jar. He shook the jar a bit. The pebbles rolled into the open areas between the marbles. He then asked, again, if the jar was full. We responded, again, that it was.

So he picked up a box of sand and poured it into the jar. Of course, the sand filled up all the spaces left. He asked once more if the !&# jar was full. My classmates responded with a resounding 'yes.'

The professor then produced a bottle of red wine from under the table and poured the entire contents into the jar, effectively filling the empty space between the sand. The class laughed.

'Now,' said the professor as the laughter subsided, 'I want you to recognize that this jar represents your life. The marbles are the important things—your family, your children, your health, your friends, your intense passions — things that if everything else was lost and only they remained, your life would still be full. The pebbles are the other things that matter, like your career, your home, your important "stuff". The sand is everything else — the small stuff.'

He paused. 'If you put the sand into the jar first,' he continued, 'there is no room for the pebbles or the marbles.

The same goes for life. If you spend all your time and energy on the small stuff, you will never have room for the things that are important to you.

Pay attention to the things that are critical to your happiness. Play with your children. Take time to get medical check-ups. Take your partner out to dinner. Have fun. There will always be time to clean the house, mow the lawn and fix the disposal. Take care of the marbles first, the things that really matter. Set your priorities. The rest is just sand.'

A classmate raised his hand and inquired what the wine represented. The professor smiled. 'I'm glad you asked. It just goes to show you that no matter how full your life may seem, there's always room for a good bottle of wine.'"

Ask yourself:

- What are the "big stones" in my life?

On Temperament

This exercise asks you to consider your nature. Your nature, or make-up, is something that, up until this moment, you may have taken for granted. As you work on the exercise, do not confuse *temperament* (tem·per·a·ment, *n.* frame of mind; disposition; nature. A disposition that rebels at restraints and is often moody or capricious) with *temper* (tem·per, *n.* a tendency to become angry readily; anger, rage). They are not the same.

Temperament is related to an energy force, your passion and your commitment to your work.

Using a pencil, fill in the following sentences with whatever pops into your mind—your first spontaneous responses. Notice what thoughts are triggered when you review your responses.

- I am a basically a _____ person.

- I have always expressed my _____.

- I have a really _____.

- I usually get angry when _____.

- _____ really upsets me.

- _____ infuriates me.

- _____ makes me laugh.

- I always cry when _____.

- When _____, I _____.

- I used to _____ because _____.

- When I am with _____, we always _____.

- I am afraid of my _____.

- I think that they would _____ if I let them.

- I think people who cry are _____.

- I can't stand to see men _____.

- _____ has a wonderful laugh.

- As long as I can remember, I _____.

- I am passionate about _____.

- When I am around people who _____,
  I _____.

- When I am doing something I love, time _____.

- _____

  makes me sad.

- _____

  makes me glad.

- _____

  makes me mad.

- These fill-in exercises _____.

Me △ **Myself**
& I

Remember…

Allow yourself to begin
from where you are, rather
than where you think you
should be.

My Knee-Jerks

We all have knee-jerk reactions (an unthinking, emotional response) to any number of things people say or do. Occasionally these reactions are explosive and produce consistent consequences.

- Think about an incident when you had a knee-jerk reaction. What caused it? How did you react?

- Do you feel good about yourself when you respond to a situation, statement or person with a knee-jerk response?

- Are any of your knee-jerk responses productive or effective? Are any destructive? What do you gain by holding on to them?

- How hard do you think it would be to eliminate them? Do you think you could?

- What are your most common knee-jerk responses?

- What incidents, people, words cause them?

- What have you done to handle them?

- Talk about one time when you were able to control a response. What did you do?

- How do you feel about yourself when your knee-jerks are in control? How do you feel about yourself when you can't or don't control them?

My Relationships to...

The next exercises are designed to help you deal with **The Work** pages that follow. They can be used to contemplate aspects of your character as well.

Sex and sexuality

- Journal about your sexuality, sexual preference and your comfort with yourself in this area.

- Are you a virgin?

- When did you have your first sexual experience? Where? With whom? How did it affect you? What happened? How do you view it now?

> **Belle.** Then why don't you kiss me? Call that kissing? Here. What's the matter, Honey Boy? Haven't you ever kissed like that before?
>
> *Ah, Wilderness* —Eugene O'Neill

- How many sexual partners have you had? Do you use protection? Why? Why not?

- What do you expect from sex?

- What do you expect from a mate?

- Is there a difference between your image of yourself as a sexual partner and your actual experience?

- What would you like to change about your sexual behavior?

- Write about your sexual fantasies if you have them.

- What are your thoughts on extra-marital sex?

- Do you think monogamy is possible? Explain.

- Have you ever felt or experienced sexual rapture, ecstasy, hunger, lust, passion? What brought about these states of being?

My Relationships to... (Cont.)

- Are you afraid of contracting sexually transmitted diseases?

- Have you ever contracted a STD? If so, how has it affected you and your life?

- How have your family and your religious leanings influenced your sex life?

- What is eroticism? What things do you find erotic?

Religion/Faith

- Write about your religious training or persuasion.

- Do you hold the same religious beliefs as your parents?

- What are your religious beliefs?

- Do you believe in God?

- Are you an agnostic or an atheist?

- Have you ever felt or experienced rapture, ecstasy, hunger, or passion in your connection to your religious or spiritual beliefs?

- Do you know anyone who is clairvoyant, a mystic or who has visions? Write about them.

Love

- Is there anyone or anything that you love more than anything in the world?

- What is the nature of that love? How does it make you feel?

- What is the difference between a crush, falling in love and being in love? What feelings accompany each state of being? How long do these states endure?

Pleasure

- Define pleasure.

- What does pleasure mean to you?

- Complete the following statements:
    - I treat myself whenever _____.
    - Whenever I treat myself, I _____ for _____.
    - I get so much pleasure from _____.
    - _____ makes me very happy.
    - I make sure I experience pleasure _____ a month.
    - It takes _____ for me to feel happy.
    - I deprive myself of pleasure because _____.
    - List some innovative things you could do that might really give you great pleasure.

    - Is pleasure a satisfying or painful state of being?

Personal obsessions, addictions

If any of the following apply or have relevance, trace the history of your relationship to them. Also discuss the role family members have played.

- Eating disorders: overeating, bulimia, anorexia nervosa, binge/purge, etc.

My Relationships to... (Cont.)

- Substance abuse: alcohol, narcotics, stimulants, prescription drugs, etc.

- Other addictions: smoking, shopping, gambling, sex, exercise, spending money, TV, Facebook, Twitter, texting, Instagram, YouTube, video games, iPod, etc.

- Have you ever been in treatment for an addiction?

- Could you stop drinking? Smoking? What would you have to do to stop? What do you think would happen to you if you stopped?

- Could you go without listening to your music, texting, going online for a weekend? A week?

Substance abuse

- Do you have a substance abuse problem?

- If so, when and how did it begin?

- How do you feel about it?

- How does it affect your life? Your work? Your relationships?

- Have you ever sought help for it?

- Has anyone ever told you that you have a substance abuse problem?

- How did you respond?

- Would you know if you had a problem? Would you admit it?

Remember...
When you feel pressure working with the workbook pages —You can stop that feeling at any time by doing them when you can, when you want to, or not at all.

Fun

- Define fun for you.

- What do you do for fun?

Holidays

- What is your favorite holiday?

- What holidays do you celebrate?

- Talk about your family traditions.

- What memories do holidays conjure up for you?

- What emotional patterns can you predict around holiday time?

Travel

- Talk about vacations you've taken – the best, worst, funniest.

- What countries have you lived in?

- What countries have you travelled to?

- Where would you like to travel? Why?

- How do you travel? ☐ First class ☐ Business class ☐ Tourist class
  ☐ Third class ☐ Bicycle ☐ On foot ☐ Backpacking
  ☐ Other _____

- How would you like to travel? ☐ First class ☐ Business class
  ☐ Tourist class ☐ Third class ☐ Bicycle ☐ On foot
  ☐ Backpacking ☐ Other _____

My Relationships to... (Cont.)

My needs

- Would you say that you were high or low maintenance – emotionally, physically, socially, politically, artistically?

- How do you manage those needs?

- Do you deny your needs? Express them to friends or family?

Routine and idiosyncrasy

- Write about your routines and/or personal idiosyncrasies.

- When did they begin?

- What comfort or pleasure do they give you?

- How do people in your life react to them?

Animals

- Have you ever had any pets? What were they? What were their names?

- Do you have a pet now? If so, what kind of animal do you have?

- If you could, what animals would you have in your life? Why?

- Do you hunt? Do you fish? Write about your hunting or fishing experience.

- Do you have a philosophical relationship to the animal kingdom, i.e. Veganism?

- What animals do you identify with? Relate to spiritually? Find awe-inspiring?

- How often have you watched animals in motion? Have you ever attempted to find the essence of that movement within you?

- Is your astrological sign an animal? Which? What are the characteristics of that animal?

Nature

- What kinds of experiences have you had in nature?

- Are you partial to the desert, the mountains, the ocean? Are you an east coast or west coast person?

- Do you go camping or hiking?

- Do you garden?

- How has your family life influenced how you relate to nature?

- Talk about your favorite natural wonders of your country.

- Describe the landscape in which you grew up.

- What do conservation, sustainability and global climate change mean to you?

Sports

- What sports have you played? When? Where? How good were you?

- Do you prefer team sports or individual sports?

My Relationships to... (Cont.)

- Do you play ☐ basketball? ☐ baseball? ☐ hockey? ☐ soccer? ☐ tennis? ☐ lacrosse? ☐ golf? ☐ croquet? ☐ table tennis? ☐ volleyball? ☐ badminton? ☐ fencing? ☐ other _____
- Do you ☐ run? ☐ bicycle? ☐ swim? ☐ dive? ☐ sail? ☐ sky-dive? ☐ climb mountains? ☐ drive race cars? ☐ skateboard? ☑ hike? ☐ canoe? ☐ ski? ☐ kayak? ☐ bobsled? ☐ ride or race horses? ☐ box? ☐ wrestle? ☐ other _____
- Do you do Tai Chi, Tae Kwan Do or any other martial art?

My body

- Do you exercise ☐ regularly? ☑ infrequently? ☐ sporadically? ☐ never?
- Do you belong to a gym?

- How many diets have you been on? How much weight have you gained and lost over the years?

- How much do you weigh?

- Are you ☐ too thin? ☐ just right? ☑ too heavy?
- What is your favorite part of your body?

  eyes , mouth

- What part do you wish you could change?

- What about your hair?

- What about your complexion?

- Do you believe in abortion and a woman's right to decide, or in right to life?

  yes

- Have you had cancer or any radical surgery or medical treatment?

  breast cancer

- Are you prone to certain illnesses?

  no

- Are you healthy or do you have a chronic condition?

  healthy

Culture/Art

- What type of music are you partial to? Not partial to?

- What role does art play in your life?

- How knowledgeable are you about architecture?

- What types of books do you read?

- Do you go to concerts, theater, opera, ballet, dance concerts, art museums and galleries regularly?

- What would you like to try? ☐ to play a musical instrument
  ☐ go to an opera ☐ to study ballet
  ☐ to learn more about artists' lives and their work
  ☐ other _____

Money

- Trace your history with money. Where does your attitude toward money come from?

- How secretive are you with regard to money?

My Relationships to... (Cont.)

- Do you experience or have you experienced shame around money? Either having too much or too little?

- Have you ever been in a position where you didn't have enough money for basics?

- What is your annual income? Is it enough for you to live on?

- If not, how do you supplement your income?

- How much money do you have in your checking account?

- Do you support yourself? How much do you have to work to do this?

- Does your family support you or help you cover your expenses? How much do they provide?

- Can you afford to live alone?

- What do you spend your money on?

- Do you save regularly?

- Do you have a slush fund for a rainy day?

- How many credit cards do you have?

- Are you in debt? How deeply? If so, how did you incur your debt?

- Have you ever declared bankruptcy?

- Do you own your own home?

- Do you have more than one home?

- Do you own a car?

- Where do you go shopping?

- What is the most expensive possession you own?

- What financial responsibilities do you have?

- If you are in a relationship, who manages your financial matters?

- If you are in a relationship, do you have a joint bank account or do you have separate accounts?

- What do you know about the Stock Market? Do you have investments in property or stocks and bonds?

- What would you like to change about your financial arrangements?

- Do you travel?

- Do you gamble? If so, on what?

- What is your tolerance level for risk?

Dolly Levi. Money … money. It's like manure …it should be spread around encouraging young things to grow.
The Matchmaker –Thornton Wilder

My Essence

This may be a new way for you to think about yourself, or it may not make any sense to you at all.

Your essence is the intrinsic nature of your being. It is an indispensable part of you.

- Write about the aspects of yourself that are at your core.

Remember…

The four parts of your personality are:

1. What you know and others know about you.

2. What you know and no one else knows about you.

3. What you don't know but everyone else knows about you.

4. What you don't know and no one else knows about you.

What I Want out of Life

This **Me, Myself & I** leads you to thinking about what you want to achieve in this lifetime. This may be something that you have never considered. Steps that have led you to where you are at this moment may have been taken instinctively or unconsciously. You may have set a goal and then followed it exclusively. You may not have assessed what unconscious needs you have been satisfying or avoiding. There are no "right" answers. Listen to your heart and the small voice in your mind. Notice the anxiety or fear that comes up for you when you name and make your declarations. At any moment, your wants or aspirations might change. If you notice these shifts, honor them. This is not an exercise carved in stone. Let it be fluid and expansive as you grow and evolve.

> **Creon.** . . . My name, thank God, is only Creon. I stand here with both feet firm on the ground; with both hands in my pockets and I have decided that so long as *I* am king—being less ambitious than your father was—I shall merely devote myself to introducing a little order into this absurd kingdom—if that is possible.
>
> *Antigone* –adapted by Lewis Glantierre from the play by Jean Anouilh

Knowing what I want

- What do you want out of life?

- Write your own obituary. How do you want to be remembered?

- Write your own eulogy.

- You have to write a Statement of Purpose when you apply to a graduate program in Theater. Write your statement.

Dreams

- Do you daydream? What about?

- Do you stifle your dreams? If so, why?

- Imagine a dream come true. Use as much detail as possible in describing the result.

> Remember...
> There are no right or wrong answers.

Shifting sands

- Have any of your dreams or aspirations diminished or disappeared? Why?

- Have you replaced an old dream or unfulfilled dream with another that you still aspire to? If so, what is it?

My Skills and Work History

Preparing for the **Work** pages on **What "I" Do for a Living**, review your own career, profession and work experience. With this **Me, Myself & I** page, you have the opportunity to evaluate your skills and training and reflect on the various jobs you have had. You might be pleasantly surprised by your accomplishments and knowledge.

Employment

- What is your employment background?

- Have you ever worked for a large corporation, for the federal, state or city government, or have you been an independent contractor? If so, what did you do?

- What kind of training and skill did you need to hold the position?

- Are you working now? Do you like your job or do you do it grudgingly?

- Do you feel trapped in your job? What would you rather be doing?

- Have you always earned your living as an actor? If not, what jobs have you taken so that you can act?

Skills

- List all the jobs you've ever had.

- What materials, tools and techniques did you need for each job?

- With each job, evaluate your level of skill and expertise.

My hobbies

- Talk about your interests and hobbies.

- What is it about each one that attracts you? Could you teach any of these?

- How long have you pursued each? On a scale of one to ten, rank your ability in each.

Other accomplishments

Remember…
So much of your identity comes from your work.

List all the things you do really well and that give you pleasure when you do them.

My Schedule C

As an actor you are self-employed and can deduct certain business expenses on your Income Tax Return. List how much you have spent on these professional expenses this year:

Acupuncture
Acting classes
Alexander Technique class
Business entertainment
Chiropractor
Clothing/ wardrobe
Dance classes
Dry cleaning
Equipment
Facials
Food
Haircuts
Mailings
Manicures/pedicures
Massages
Medications

Personal trainer
Phone/internet
Photos and resumes
Pilates class
Postage
Private coaching
Publicity
Rent
Speech classes
The gym
Theater viewing
Transportation
Voice classes
Yoga
Other

Lillian. . . .Hello. I am Lillian Troy. I am Andrew's agent. The scum of the earth.
Felicia. Hi. Felicia Dantine. Real Estate.
I Hate Hamlet –Paul Rudnick

My Sense of Humor

Your sense of humor, or lack of one, is an important part of who you are. How you use humor reveals a great deal about you, as well.

- Consider what having a sense of humor means to you and how important it is to you. Is it connected to how you see the world? Is it related to your life disposition?

- Estimate your ability in perceiving or expressing humor. Do you have the ability to appreciate a joke?

- If you don't have a sense of humor, try cultivating one!

- Rent Some DVDs: rent DVDs of some stand-up comedians' one-person shows: Richard Pryor, Lenny Bruce, George Carlin, Victor Borge, Joan Rivers, Mel Brooks, Luci Arnez, Bill Cosby, Ellen DeGeneres, John Lequizamo, Whoopi Goldberg, Billy Crystal, Jon Stewart, Stephen Colbert and Bill Maher. Add to this list.

My own sense of humor

- Do you laugh at dirty jokes?

- Do you make fun of other people's weaknesses? Is your humor at the expense of others?

- Do you tell jokes?

- Do you play practical jokes?

- How literal are you?

- Do you have a sense of humor about yourself? Do make fun of yourself? Why?

- What makes you laugh?

Remember…

Laughter is massage for the intestines.

- Who makes you laugh?

- What topics are not funny to you? (i.e. dead baby jokes, rape)

- Describe your sense of humor. Is it dry? Wry? Sarcastic? Adolescent? Aggressive? Playful? Clever? Mean? Demeaning? Insensitive?

- Who is your favorite comedian/comedienne?

- How do you use humor?

- When do you default to humor?

- What do your friends say about your sense of humor?

- Whose sense of humor turns you off? Why?

Collect some jokes and tell them

Have a few of your friends tell you some jokes. If you can't remember them, write them in your notebook. Then practice them at home, and this week tell one every day.

My humor I.Q.

Check your favorites to see where your humor lies. Is it sophisticated or low-brow?

Anne Meara	Gracie Allen	Rich Little
Benny Hill	George Carlin	Tina Fey
Cheech & Chong	Jackie Mason	Sandra Bernhard
Chris Rock	Jerry Stiller	Stan Laurel
Danny Kaye	Joe Piscopo	Larry, the Cable Guy
Ellen DeGeneris	Bill Maher	The Three Stooges
Lucille Ball ✓	Lily Tomlin	Tracey Ullman
Fanny Brice	Mel Brooks ✓	Whoopi Goldberg
Carol Burnett	Phyllis Diller	Abbott and Costello
Flip Wilson	Prof. Irwin Corey	Steven Colbert ✓
George Burns	Red Buttons	Jon Stewart

My Favorite...

"Name My Favorite" is a fun exercise that may trigger an idea that will open up a connection you can use for the new "you". You never know what insight you may achieve by thinking about your own personal favorites.

My favorite:

Actor	Family member	Possession
After-shave lotion	Flower	Relative
Animal *dog*	Food	Restaurant
App	Game	Room in my house
Art form	Garment	Shampoo
Artist	Holiday *christmas* Soda	
Beer	Lipstick *red*	Song
Book	Magazine	Sport
Building	Memory	Store
Candy *chocolate*	Movie	Subject in school
Car	Music	TV program
City	Outfit	Vacation
Color *red*	Painting	Vegetable
Comedian	Pastime	Wine
Composer	Perfume	Writer
Country	Pet	Other _____
Curse word	Piece of jewelry	
Dance	Play	

Shocking Friends and Family

Consciously or unconsciously, we hold on to certain habits because we don't want to threaten or antagonize our friends and family. *This exercise is not an invitation to actually take the actions you think of.*

- If time and money were no object, what would you do that might shock people you know?

- What actions could you take that would really surprise people who know you?

- If you did any of the above actions, how would each individual you care about react?

- What would you love to do that might shock your friends and family?

- Think of an incident that encouraged you to follow, or that turned you away from, your natural inclination.

My Beliefs

These exercises are designed to give you time to look at your beliefs and points of view on various matters.

Sara. ...All he could talk about was how dirty and dangerous everything is.
Stop Kiss —
Diana Son

After you read the following statements, write your own. Your point of view can be in the form of a sweeping generalization. Make sure your statements reflect your belief. Take a stand and don't straddle the fence. For instance:

- A real friend is always honest with me. ✓

- If you are not Orthodox, you are not Jewish.

- Abortion is a crime.

- Crying is a sign of weakness.

- Anger is bad.

- Waiting tables is humiliating work.

- Stealing from big corporations is okay.

- People should control their emotions.

- Welfare is a right.

- If you say you are going to do something, you should do it. ✓

- No one has the right to treat another person badly. ✓

- When you love someone, you are never cruel to them. ✓

- This is a lousy world in which to bring up children.

- It is okay to spank a child.

- I have the right to say whatever I please, whenever I please.

- If you drink alcohol every day, you have a problem.

- Car salesmen are sharks.

- No civilian should have access to assault weapons. ✓

- Third-party ticket sellers should be outlawed.

My opinions

Make a list of things that matter to you. Write down the "shoulds," "should haves," "ought tos," "rights" and "wrongs" of your belief systems. They don't have to be deeply intellectual, or philosophical. You might question their importance. Do not judge your ideas prematurely. Little things matter, and if they matter to you, they mean something. You don't have to justify yourself to another human being. You simply have to know what matters to you. These next exercises are designed to give you time to look at your own ethical and moral standards.

Ethics, morals

- What are your beliefs about the environment? What position do you hold on Human Rights? Animal rights? Arts funding? Wildlife and wilderness preservation? Global climate change? Civil rights? The death penalty? Organized religion? Outsourcing? Gun control? Taxes? Entitlement programs? Gay marriage? Women's rights?

> **Barnes.** Be careful of words like that—"class distinction." Don't belong here. Lots of energy, you brilliant young men, but idiots. Discretion! Ever hear that word?
>
> *Waiting for Lefty*
> —Clifford Odets

- Name those things that you feel strongly about.

- What are your ethics?

- What are your morals?

- How do you feel about people who don't believe in the same things that you do?

- I think people who lie are _____.
- I think people who cheat are _____.
- People who are _____ drive me bananas!
- I feel uncomfortable around people who _____.

My Beliefs (Cont.)

Role models

- Whom do you admire?

- Why?

- What do you think they stand for?

- What is it that makes you respect them or not respect them?

Action and belief

- Are you able to live up to your own standards? How do you do that?

- Do you have a favorite cause? What do you do for that cause?

- Are you a self-appointed watchdog for a cause? What is your cause? (e.g. pothole watchdog who regularly calls 311 to report a pothole when you see one.)

- What power do social networking sites have in creating change? Which sites do you visit and support?

My Prejudices

As you read this list notice your first reactions to each item. Are you surprised by the first thoughts or feelings you have? Do you then try to "prettify" your first responses? Are they "politically correct"? Do you care?

Abortion *yes* ✓
Actors
Adolescents
African Americans
Aging *hard*
Alcoholics *sad*
Anorectic individuals *sad*
Arabs
Artists
Asians
Blind people *sad*
Birth Control ✓
Buddhists
Careless people *bad*
Catholics
Caucasians
Children
College tuition *too high*
Communists
Corporate America *bad*
Democrats
Designer clothing
Drug addicts *sad*
Drug dealers *bad terrible*
Firefighters *good*
Foreigners
Fundamentalists *bad terrible*
Fur coats *terrible*
Gamblers *sad*
Gas-guzzling vehicles
The Green Party
Handicapped persons *sad*
Hearing-impaired people *sad*
Heterosexuals
Hindus

Homophobes *bad terrible*
Homosexuals
Honest people
Jews
The Ku Klux Klan *bad terrible*
Monogamy
Moslems
Musicians
Newscasters
Old people
Open marriage *bad*
Pedophiles *terrible*
People who check iphones
People who have AIDS *sad*
People who are HIV positive *sad*
People who are overweight
People who are terminally ill *Sad*
People who are multilingual *lucky*
People who don't speak English
People who have 20 cats *sad*
People who live on the street
People who steal *bad*
People who litter *bad*
Phone menus
Phone solicitations *bad*
Policemen
Politicians
Pollution *bad*
Polygamy *bad*

Pornography *bad terrible*
President of the United States *current one psycopath*
Prima donnas *boring*
Private schools
Profoundly obese individuals *sad*
Protestants
Rapists *terrible*
Republicans *selfish*
Retarded individuals *sad*
Schizophrenics *sad*
Senior citizens
Skinheads *bad terrible*
Sloppy people *bad*
Smart people
Social networks
Spoiled children *bad*
Spoiled adults *bad*
Stupid people *Sad*
Superstar salaries *unfair*
TV and film stars
Tattletales *bad*
Teachers' salaries *unfair*
Technology
Teenagers who drink *bad*
The Media
Theater ticket prices
Transsexuals
Unfaithful spouses *bad*
Vegans
Vegetarians
Whistleblowers *good*
Young people
Other:_____

Difference and Eccentricity

Do you have an eccentric, "crazy" or mentally ill relative in your family? Have you bought into the family myth or reaction to that person or have you established your own relationship with that person? Have you educated yourself about that family member's illness or condition?

- Do you have shame connected to that person?

- Is that person your mom or your dad, your sister or your brother? What have you endured because of their condition?

- Have they been invited to the family social events or excluded?

- Have you had to separate yourself from that person because they were dangerous to you and other members of your family?

Hannah. It's too easy. As you say, it's one thing or the other. But no matter what it is, there's not one thing in this world or the next that we can do or hope or wish or pray that can change it one iota. Because, whatever it is, *is*. That's all. And all there is now is to be ready for it, strong enough for it, whatever it may be. That's all that matters because it's all that's possible.

All the Way Home
—Tad Mosel

A new view

Write about an event that altered or shifted how you looked at a situation or an individual.

Your pet peeves

What things really bug you? For instance: wet toilet seats, drivers who tailgate, TV commercials, public radio ads, texting in a theater, telemarketers, hype, ink cartridge packaging, bank charges.

Crazy-makers

Who are the people who make you crazy? Are they famous or people you know?

- List the things they do that make you crazy.

- Write each person a letter. Tell them why they push your buttons.

- *Tear the letter up once you have written it. Do not send it!*

- Now write about what you get out of these relationships—we all get something out of hanging around the people we choose to be with, even when we complain about the things they do and get hurt by them repeatedly. Often it is a vicious cycle.

Unchallenged Beliefs that Limit

Thinking in the box: put all of your ideas about appropriate behavior and personal image at home, in public, at work or in school in the box.

Remember…

Allow a space for what is when the one thing you don't want to have happened, happens.

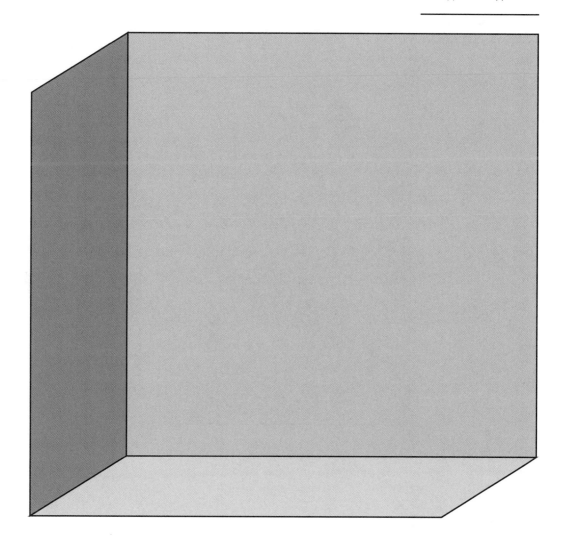

Expanding My Beliefs

Describe what may currently seem to you outlandish beliefs that might encourage and support what you consider inappropriate behavior. Enter these outside the box. Date your entries.

Return to this page occasionally to see if there have been any shifts in your beliefs or if you remain even more steadfast.

Remember...

Think: "I could do ...,
what will happen if ..."

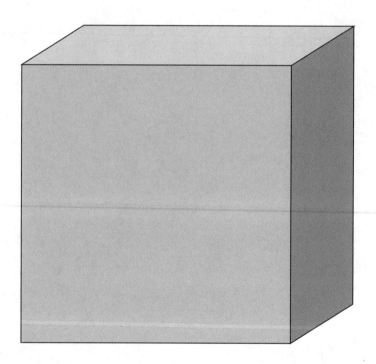

My Wardrobe

The following exercises will bring greater awareness of things you take for granted. Remember—there is nothing you have to do with the information.

How my clothes affect me

- What is your favorite garment? Write its story.

- What do you wear when you want to feel sexy? What is it about the garment that makes you feel that way?

- What color do you wear when you are going to be in a challenging situation?

- What color looks fabulous on you?

  red

- What do you wear when you want to feel professional?

- What do you wear if you want to feel secure, self-assured?

- What styles suit you best?

- What do you wear to make yourself feel older? Younger?

- What about shoes?

- What accessories do you gravitate toward?

  earrings

- Do scents you wear affect you? How?

- My favorite color is _____. I think _____ really suits me.

- I feel good when I wear anything _____.

- I feel awful when I wear anything _____.

- _____ is my favorite garment because _____.

- I got it _____.

> **Remember…**
> Your class, background, situation, and income determine your taste and the quality of your clothing. The time of day, season, year and occasion further affect what you wear.

My Wardrobe (Cont.)

A personal assessment

- What is the predominant color in your wardrobe?

- Where do you buy your clothes?

- Have you ever gone to a resale, vintage, or consignment shop?

- Talk about your hair. Do you wear it long or short? Why do you wear it the way you do? Where do you get your hair cut? How much do you pay for a haircut? How often do you cut your hair? How often do you change your hairstyle? Do you color your hair? Do you think your hairstyle becomes you? Do you think it makes you look older? Younger? More sophisticated?

- How do you dress for weather?

- What about your underwear?

- How much money do you spend on your clothes every year?

- What kind of jewelry do you wear?

- What style are you known for? Do you always wear clothes that are timeless or do you follow the seasonal trends even if they are unflattering to you?

- Write about makeup. Do you like to wear makeup? Do you buy a certain brand of makeup? Do you wear it every day? On special occasions? Have you ever taken a course in the proper application of makeup? What shades of base, powder, eye shadow and lipstick suit you?

My closet and my drawers

- How orderly is your closet?

- How are your clothes arranged?

- How many sizes are in your closet?

- What about your drawers?

- Do you have garments that you haven't worn in a year? Two years? More?

- Do you own any "classic" clothes that never go out of style?

- Do you have a dress or suit that you are holding on to for a special event?

Chick. Did you remember to pick up those pantyhose for me?
Lenny. They're in the sack.
Chick. Well, thank goodness, at least I'm not gonna have to go into town wearing holes in my stockings.

Crimes of the Heart
—Beth Henley

Perception

First impressions are immediate and often hard to correct. We all jump to conclusions about people based on how they are dressed and the condition of their hair and hands. Do this exercise with a friend. Choose different garments that you own and articulate the impression you hope each creates about you.

- How do you hope each garment affects those around you when you wear it, and how do you think you are perceived when you wear it?

- How do you feel when you wear each garment?

- What does your friend say?

- Do you care what others think about how you dress?

Dressing Up

These exercises can be fun to do with a friend.

Dress for an event

You have been invited to a Formal Opening Night at the Metropolitan Opera, followed by a midnight supper at your host's penthouse apartment on Fifth Avenue. Go through your wardrobe and put together an outfit that you could wear.

Shopping

- Where do you usually shop for your clothes?

- Name the upscale stores in your city.

- Where would you never shop? Why not?

- If you don't usually shop at them, have you ever gone into an upscale department store or boutique and tried on the clothes to see and feel the difference? Why not go to one this weekend?

- Can you tell the difference between a really exclusive well-made garment and one that is ready-to-wear? Describe the difference.

- Who are your favorite designers?

- Think about fabric. Are you sensitive to texture, softness, suppleness and sheen?

A fun outing

Imagine that you are going to the Oscar Awards ceremony or to the Tony Awards.

Go to a high-end, fashionable boutique or the shop of an original designer. Try on gowns or tuxedos as if you were getting ready to go to the event and the fabulous parties after. Would you have your makeup done by a professional? Would you go to a special salon to have your hair and nails done? Outfit yourself completely and itemize the cost: Gown or tuxedo, shoes, purse, makeup, jewelry, underwear, hair, makeup, nails and perfume.

Hair, Hands and Makeup

Hair and hairstyle

You have a unique history with your hair. You could probably talk about your relationship to your hair for a few hours.

Categorize your hair:

☐ straight ☐ curly ☐ kinky ☐ oily ☑ dry

☐ thin ☐ super fine ☑ coarse ☑ bleached ☐ dyed

☐ tipped ☐ streaked ☑ highlighted ☐ dreadlocks ☐ bald

☐ stringy ☐ unkempt ☐ wild ☑ long ☐ short

☐ shoulder length ☐ shaved ☐ uneven ☐ unmanageable

☐ other _____.

Who cuts your hair? Are you happy with your cut? What happens to you when you go to a new person for a haircut?

Megan / Margaret at ToDo
Yes — I don't

Your hands and nails

- What is your relationship to your hands? What do you do to take care of them?

> **Beebee.** I wish you'd have your hair cut. All I can see is hair!
>
> **Nettie Jo.** Most people like it long. Mother could sit on hers.
>
> *The Days and Nights of Beebee Fenstermaker*
> —William Snyder

- What is the condition of your hands? How would you describe your skin, nails, cuticles?

- How much do you use your hands in your work?

- Would you say that your hands are expressive, clumsy or graceful?

- Do you get manicures? Do you bite your nails?

  NO / NO

My Fashion Expertise

Test your knowledge

How many of the following words do you know? Look up the ones you don't know. Once you have identified the following, imagine yourself wearing them.

Bias cut	Fontange	Peplum
Bustle	Gay deceivers	Petticoat breeches
Cassock	Haute couture	Reticule
Chiton	Jabot	Ruff
Codpiece	Jodhpurs	Smoking jacket
Crinolines	Muff	Tuxedo
Falling band	Panniers	Waistcoat
Fillet	Peplos	

Your fashion I.Q.

True or False:

- Black makes you look thin. T

- Horizontal stripes make you look tall. F

- Everyone can wear olive green. F

- Only blondes should wear bright colors. F

- The Windsor knot in men's ties is considered more fashionable than the Four-in-hand.

- Men should always wear white socks. F

- One can never be too thin or too rich. F

- Redheads can't wear pink. F

- Levis are passé. F

- Plaids and floral prints should never be worn together. F

- Fashion is today but style is forever. T

A quiz on fabric

How many of the following do you know? Which fabrics do you have in your wardrobe?

Fibers: Silk, Wool, Cotton, Flax, Hemp, Bamboo.

Synthetics: Acetate, Rayon, Nylon, Polyester, Microfiber

Types of fabric: Tweed, Denim, Twill, Quilted, Organdy, Voile, Shantung, Tulle, Eyelet, Faille, Charmeuse, Pin-striped, Velvet, Satin, Linen, Jersey, Knit, Worsted, Burlap, Velour, Fleece, Monk's cloth, Lace, Felt, Madras, Gauze, Taffeta, Cashmere.

Leather and fur: Suede, Cowhide, Snakeskin, Alligator, Mink, Fox, Sable, Beaver, Chinchilla, Rabbit.

Ways to color or pattern fabric: Dye, Batik, Tie-dye, Silk-screen print, Hand-paint, Machine print, Weave, Embroider, Crewel, Crochet, Appliqué, Beading, Sequins.

The Work

"My" Background

PLAY: _____

ROLE: _____

DATE: _____

Always remember to respect and serve the play. Everything has significance and is there for a purpose.

- What information has the playwright provided with regard to "your" background?

Madge. It *was* true, a long time ago, just after the War. When I still thought we could suddenly make everything better for everybody. Socialism! Peace! Universal brotherhood! All that.

Time and the
Conways
—J.B. Priestley

- What information does the playwright give you regarding events that have taken place before the play begins?

- What information has the playwright omitted? Remember that the playwright's omissions are significant and do not give you permission to add "clever" background elements willy-nilly.

- Raise questions about "your" past, without forcing answers, to invent a background. They may be clever and sound good, but will still be meaningless until probed in rehearsal.

"My" Family; "My" Ancestors

PLAY: _____

ROLE: _____

DATE: _____

If the playwright mentions family members, past family events involving family members or relatives who don't appear in the play, this becomes an important work page.

On the other hand, it could be a waste of time if you spend the exercise inventing things about "your" family that don't really serve you. When you feel the need to ponder some of these questions you can always return to this page. Keep in mind that an unanswered question may be more valuable than an off-the-cuff answer. Avoid writing just for the sake of answering a question. Your answers have to have meaning for you and lead you to specific visceral connections.

- What is "your" relationship to "your" mother, father, siblings, and grandparents? Are there "as ifs" that you can draw on from your own life?

- What is "your" lineage?

- Where did "your" grandparents and great-grandparents come from?

- Did "you" know them? Do you remember them? Are you or were you proud of them? Embarrassed? etc.

Mother. Those gloves! I've been washing dishes for forty years and I never wore gloves! But my lady's hands! My lady's hands!

Young Woman. Sometimes you talk to me like you're jealous, Ma.

Mother. Jealous?

Young Woman. It's my hands got me a husband.

Machinal —Sophie Treadwell

What "I" Say about Myself/What Others Say about "Me"

PLAY: _____

ROLE: _____

DATE: _____

As you go through your play, take note of what "you" say about yourself and what the other characters in the play say about you.

Remember that the statements you write may or may not be accurate or true, but will certainly give you information about how the other characters see "you".

- What do "I" say about myself?

Nora. I won't look in on the children. I know they're in better hands than mine. The way I am now, I'm no use to them.

A Doll's House

—Henrik Ibsen

- What do other characters say about "me"?

Miss Tesman. And it was you who carried off Hedda Gabler. The beautiful Hedda Gabler! Imagine! She, who always had so many admirers!

Hedda Gabler

—Henrik Ibsen

Who Am "I"?

The Work

PLAY: _____

ROLE: _____

DATE: _____

As you did when you were writing about yourself in the **Me, Myself & I** exercise **Who Am I?,** list words and phrases that you think describe the new "you".

- Write about "your" personality, personal traits and qualities. Be sure that the script actually supports what you write.

- As you rehearse and work on your scene or your play, add your insights and speculations to your list.

This exercise helps you focus. You don't have to, nor should you, remember or hold on to what you write. Don't try to be or "act out" any of the things you write.

By finding at least 50 items, you avoid oversimplifying the character with one or two traits. For instance, Laura in *The Glass Menagerie* by Tennessee Williams is more than shy. Creating a human being rather than a two-dimensional character means that you must find the contradictory facets within the person.

Remember...

When the character begins to move through you, you may change your perfume, eat a tuna fish sandwich every day or use after-shave lotion.

Me, the Actor and "Me," the Character

PLAY: _____

ROLE: _____

DATE: _____

This exercise should stimulate more understanding of the new "you." Look at the things you have or don't have in common with the new "you." Fill in the sections about yourself first. Be as subjective as you can. Only be judgmental if it fits your personality. When working on the new "you," read the play often. You will discover even more in rehearsal. This is not to be an intellectual analysis of the new "you".

Return to the chart frequently to change things that you write. Experiment with your notations by circling similarities or marking them with a highlighter. Follow your train of thought… jot down the first things that come to mind. Add or delete entries as you discover something new, and date your entries.

ME	"ME" _____ (Your character's name)
Personality	Personality
Tastes	Tastes
Background	Background
Class	Class
Education	Education
Interests	Interests
Needs, conscious and unconscious	Needs, conscious and unconscious
Sense of humor	Sense of humor

What "I" Want out of Life—"My" Life Drive

PLAY: _____

ROLE: _____

DATE: _____

A person's *life drive* emanates from a deep place within one's being. It is a force that determines what you want out of life and how you go after what you want. It leads, guides or drives you through your life. You may not be conscious of the energy moving you through your life.

After you have "tilled and cultivated the soil" in rehearsal, begin to formulate the driving forces that you think push, drive, guide or determine what the new "you" wants out of life.

When you articulate "your" life drive, it can be expressed in a sentence, a word, a phrase or a paragraph. It does not have to be any particular length. Your life drive connects you to the "through line" or spine of the play – your journey through the play.

Use this page to help you search for what "you" want out of life. List things that you feel are driving you through the play. Compare this with your responses on the **Me, Myself & I** page

What "I" Want out of Life.

For example:

- My need to be accepted and understood.
- My need to hold on to my children.
- My family's well-being.
- My need for my father's love.
- My need to be the best _____ in the world.
- My need to spread the word.
- My need for revenge.   _____
- My desire to save the planet.

Remember...

We work in the dark—we do what we can—we give
what we have. Our doubt is our passion and our
passion is our task. The rest is the madness of art.

—Henry James

The Work

What "I" Do For A Living

PLAY: _____

ROLE: _____

DATE: _____

Research is called for here: serious investigation, hands-on if possible, but not dangerous. Consider the following:

- What skills are needed for "your" job? Do you have them?

- What level of education is required for "your" job? Do you qualify?

- What is "your" annual salary?

- What is the appropriate attire for "your" job?

- How did "you" get your current job?

- Do "you" work for a small company, for yourself, or for a huge corporation?

- What is the corporate culture where "you" work?

- Where do "you" work? Do you work in a store, a restaurant, a hospital, a clinic or an office? Do you have your own office? If so, what size, layout, furnishings, etc.?

- What are "your" hours?

- Do "you" have a title?

- What is "your" job description?

- What is "your" work ethic?

- How did "you" come to, or what led you to choose your profession?

- Are "you" happy with your job? Your place of employment? Your boss?

- Would "you" change your job if you could? What job would you rather have?

- Do "you" like your work or do you do it grudgingly?

- Do "you" feel trapped in your job? What would you rather be doing?

Rubin. I'm doin' the best I can, Cora. Can't ya understand that? I'm doin' the best I can.

The Dark at the Top of the Stairs

—William Inge

"My" Sense of Humor

PLAY: _____

ROLE: _____

DATE: _____

Some people have no sense of humor about themselves. Some people do. Some people tell adolescent jokes. Some people love dirty jokes. Some people find humor in ethnic slurs. Some people love playing practical jokes. Some don't have any sense of humor at all or take everything they hear very literally. Some people laugh because they are nervous, scared or uncomfortable.

- What is "your" new sense of humor, sense of the ridiculous, sense of fun?

- What information does the playwright provide regarding "your" sense of humor?

- Do "you" have a sense of humor?

- Do "you" tell jokes? What kind?

- Are "you" good at telling them?

- Do "you" laugh at yourself?

- What makes "you" laugh?

- How do "you" use humor?

Jeff. Come on, Dad. It's going to be hard enough for her coping with you, without your poufter son hanging around.

The Sum of Us

–David Stevens

"My" Favorites

PLAY: _____

ROLE: _____

DATE: _____

"Your" favorites may differ from your own. If the new "you" reads different books, listens to different music, etc., you now have an opportunity to try new things! You never know what insight you may achieve by experimenting with "your" new personal favorites.

"MY" favorite:

Actor	Family member	Play
After-shave lotion	Flower	Possession
Animal	Food	Relative
Art form	Game	Restaurant
Artist	Garment	Room in your house
Beer	Holiday	Shampoo
Book	Magazine	Song
Building	Memory	Sport
Candy	Movies	Store
Car	Music	Subject in school
City	Outfit	TV program
Color	Painting	Team
Composer	Pastime	Vacation
Country	Perfume	Wine
Curse word	Pet	Writer
Dance	Piece of jewelry	Other _____

Melchior. My favorite spot's under the oak. If you lean your head back against the trunk and stare through the branches up at the sky, it hypnotises you.
Spring Awakening
—Frank Wedekind

Research is Exciting!

The Work

PLAY: _____

ROLE: _____

DATE: _____

Go to whatever lengths you can to give yourself the kind of garments you need to believe in your new job, circumstances, status, class.

The following exercises will guide you as you put together the clothes "you" will wear in your scene. Even without buying or renting the actual types of garments "you" would have had at the time in which your play is set, your research and the kinds of garments you can put together from your own wardrobe or thrift stores will add a sensory connection to the new "you." These exercises provide some ideas to test.

- Collage pictures of clothing that "you" like or that you think reflects "your" taste: dresses, suits, shirts, coats, shoes, undergarments, hats, gloves, hairstyles of the time. Add accessories: eyeglasses, handbags, fans, stockings, etc.

- Think of fabrics and colors that attract "you," repel "you," etc.

- Always take into account the year, the month, the day of the week and the time of day. Is it Fall? Winter? Spring? Summer? Night or day?

- Do research online and at the library to learn more about the types of garments worn during the period of your play. While you are at it, look at hairstyles and makeup of the time as well.

- List all the clothes you feel "you" should/must have for your scene. Try to borrow an official uniform if you need one, or find garments at the Salvation Army, Goodwill or church thrift stores.

> **Ricky.** . . . I bought a new shirt for the weekend, believe that? Look at it, it's torn, it's got crud all over it . . . all for this lousy weekend.
>
> *Hooters*
> —Ted Dally.

The Work

Planning What to Wear: Female Roles

PLAY: _____

ROLE: _____

DATE: _____

Female Roles: Use this page to brainstorm about the garments you need for your scene.

- "I" want a _____ coat, a _____ handbag, _____ shoes and a _____ scarf for my scene.

- I wish "I" had _____ for the scene.

- I want the garments "I" am wearing in the scene to be
_____.

- "I" always wear _____ when I want to feel _____.

- "I" am most comfortable when I wear _____ because
_____.

- _____ is a horrible color for "me" because _____.

- "I" think _____ makes me look _____.

- "I'm" going to wear _____ to the next rehearsal.

- If I were in production for this play, I would want
_____.

- "I" should do something with my hair. I am going to
_____.

- "I" think my makeup should be _____.

- Since the scene takes place at _____ am/pm on a _____, and since it is ☐ early ☐ late ☐ fall ☐ winter ☐ spring ☐ summer, "I" could be wearing _____.

- I think "my" clothes should fit ☐ really well ☐ poorly ☐ skin-tight ☐ very loosely ☐ other: _____

- List the clothes "you" are going to wear in your scene. Why have "you" chosen each garment and accessory?

Brenda. How's my wig?

Collette. What wig?

Brenda. The wig on my head.

Collette. It's you.

Brenda. I look like Daisy Duck.

Four Dogs and a Bone

—John Patrick Shanley

Planning What to Wear: Male Roles

PLAY: _____

ROLE: _____

DATE: _____

Male Roles: Use this page to help you brainstorm about the garments you need for your scene.

- "I" need a _____ coat, a pair of _____, a _____ shirt, _____ socks, _____ shoes and a _____ for my scene. Other: _____.

- I wish "I" had _____ for my scene. I'm going to try to find one.

- The garments "I" am wearing _____.

- "I" always wear _____ when I want to feel _____.

- "I" am most comfortable when I wear _____ because _____.

- _____ is a horrible color for "me" because _____.

- "I" think _____ makes "me" look _____.

- "I" have always had trouble finding _____.

- "I'm" going to wear _____ to the next rehearsal.

- If I were in a production of this play, I would want _____.

- Since the scene takes place at _____ am/pm on a _____, and since it is ☐ early ☐ late ☐ fall ☐ winter ☐ spring ☐ summer, "I" could be wearing _____.

- I think "my" clothes should fit ☐ really well ☐ poorly ☐ skin-tight ☐ very loosely ☐ other: _____

- List the clothes "you" are going to wear in your scene. Why have "you" chosen each garment and accessory?

"My" Physicality

PLAY: _____

ROLE: _____

DATE: _____

Be very mindful! You might think that you are working hard because you are doing all the exercises in this book. They are a way of focusing your attention. They can stimulate your imagination but *they do not substitute for rehearsal*. They help you prepare and lead to insights that manifest when you are on your feet, physically and psychologically engaged.

Following the **Me, Myself & I** exercise **My Physicality**, list actions and phrases that you think describe the way "you" move. Write about "your" physicality under different circumstances. This may include physical habits, traits and qualities. As you rehearse and work on your scene or your play, add your insights and your speculations to your list. This can be tricky. You don't want to become intellectually analytical or begin to direct yourself into moving so that you artificially make adjustments that fulfil your image of the new "you." However, you must have a degree of awareness of your body in order to experiment with how you might move differently as you develop the new "you".

Experiment with clothing for your scene. How does each garment affect how you move?

Movement is never arbitrary. It is determined by many things – what you are wearing, whom you are with, what you are doing, what you want, etc.

Here are some things you might do to explore your new physical life:

- Take a shower or bath as the new "you."
- Get ready for bed as the new "you."
- Eat dinner as the new "you."
- Dance as the new "you."
- Sing as the new "you."
- Play cards as the new "you".
- Get ready for a party as the new "you".

Remember…

HOMEwork is just that.

"My" Point of View

PLAY: _____

ROLE: _____

DATE: _____

Go through your script carefully, line by line. Itemize the points of view that you glean from the text.

- Does "your" point of view change or shift during the course of the play? How? Why?

- Do "you" come to see things differently? What has changed?

> **Elizabeth**. Why do you call the basement a sanctuary?
>
> **Tom**. Why do you call the sanctuary a basement. It's all in your point of view. Take my advice. Change your point of view.
>
> *Better Living* —George F. Walker

- Do any of "your" feelings change? When does this happen? Why does it happen?

What "I" Say and Feel: More Points of View

PLAY: _____

ROLE: _____

DATE: _____

With the new "you" in mind, write about the way you feel about the situations in the play. Write what "you" say about the other characters in the play, as well as how "you" feel about the other characters and situations you encounter in the play.

Rosannah. No. Not from my point of view. From my point of view I am making no contact with this chair whatsoever. From my point of view I am still flying …

Brilliant Traces

—Cindy Lou Johnson

What the Other Characters Say about "Me"

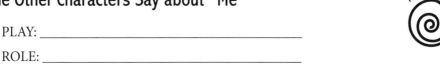

PLAY: _____

ROLE: _____

DATE: _____

Go through your script and, character by character, write out everything each one says about "you". Do you agree with their points of view? What do you think they mean? What do you learn about your relationship with them? What do you learn about yourself?

Marie. . . .Doc is nice to me. It's just in a few little things he does, like fixing my breakfast, but he's nice to everyone.

Turk. He ever make a pass?

Marie. No. He'd never get fresh.

Turk. He'd better not.

Marie. . . .Doc's such a nice, quiet man; if he gets any fun out of being nice to me, why not?

Come Back, Little Sheba –William Inge

Afterword

Well, here we are, the final words of the workbook.

You have been working with all the chapters. You have made discoveries. You have found your own questions. You have paid more attention and reached greater awareness. You have more possibility in your life. You have become more disciplined, you have practiced more, probed more deeply, risked more than you thought you could.

And now your final step: *forget everything.*

Begin as if for the first time—with innocence and curiosity.

When you are on the floor, you must let your homework go. When you hold on to it, you crumble. Your objective, unfortunately, becomes remembering your homework, rather than genuinely living through the circumstances of the play.

In the end you must commit to living in the *now*. The present isn't a still-life; it isn't a fixed image. The immediate present in a play will never be exactly the same. How could it be? You are a different person today than you were yesterday. And audiences are always different at each performance.

A performance is not etched in stone. It can be adjusted or changed—and it should be, within the rehearsed parameters of a production, when you feel your work is not fully realized, or you sense that it is getting stale.

Remember:

- "There is no single approach that has access to all reality."–Saul Kotzubei

- Mindfulness is paying attention, purposefully, to the present moment.

- "You are not prepared to act until everything hurts."–Andre Droznin

- "An inner life moves the outer life. You access it through imagination and eventually it becomes presence." –Larry Sacharow

- You begin to learn the power you have to transform yourself, to attain different sizes and weights and densities.

- "Death to an actor is worrying what everyone else is thinking." – Kristin Linklater

- Minds wander. That's what minds do, so there is no need to judge.

- When you are truly involved and functioning within your set of given circumstances, you will experience a mind/body synergy. The more involved you are in your circumstances, the more you let your partner affect you, the more the scene will *do you* rather than you do the scene. In the end, you will remember more about what your partner did than what you did.

- Control: Do you talk yourself out of doing? Do you hold back because you are thinking too much, rationalizing, or cannot "understand" what is happening when you release your control? Control is an illusion; it is a constricting vise that stifles and conceals.

- "You have to get away from your lazy… everyone has their lazy. Do you want to do the work? No. You do it anyway." –Ilse Pfeifer

- "You owe it to us to bring your sound to the room. You are generous when you do." –Ilse Pfeifer

- "Go out there and fuck up your first line. When you do that, you are telling your body to work, not to present your work. The rehearsal hall is the space where you work, and you teach your body that on the most profound level." –Seanna McKenna's advice to a young actress at her first rehearsal.

- "Players don't have to worry about the rules. They learn them and then forget them. Leave the rules to the umps and coaches so that the players are free to play the game." –Victor Slezak

- Tools are not rules, except when it comes to Stage Violence.

- "Putting on a play is like a blood sport. The audience is the bull."– John Guare

I hope that some of my stories encourage you to follow your dream and to train as an actor—whether or not you ever work as one. Here is a painful truth: most people who study acting will never act. But if truly committed and immersed in your training, there will be incomparable benefits that will impact your life forever.

While serving the great plays, large and small, past and present—thanks to the persons who people these plays—you learn what it means to be a human being. You expand your perspective and broaden your knowledge, you increase sensory awareness and aliveness, discipline, focus and compassion. If nothing else, you enrich the way you live in the world.

Theater and the plays you work on are larger than yourself. You channel and release your passion through your creativity. In service of something that is larger than you, you hold the paradoxes inherent in your life, your craft and your art.

Reading new scripts keeps you alive. Holding a script in your hand feels good. Standing on stage will always feel right. Hearing laughter, a communal silence or sudden gasps will feed you. Finding your light and loving it will make you feel whole. Give it away.

Welcome home.

Clowns sings. ...A great while ago the world begun

With hey, ho, the wind and the rain,

But that's all one, our play is done,

And we'll strive to please you every day.

Twelfth Night —William Shakespeare

Appendix A

Places and Locations

The following list covers some of the settings that you could encounter whenever you begin work on a new scene or play. Raise your awareness to the fact that no matter where you are, your surroundings are always specific and detailed.

Private/Living
House: Living room, Nursery,
  Kitchen, Bedroom, Study,
Bathroom
Apartment
Loft
Hotel room
Motel room
Cabin
Hut
Tent
Castle
Dormitory
Inn
Tenement
Abandoned building

Public/Communal
Indoor
Restaurant
Bar
Waiting room
Bus station
Train station
Court room
Hospital room
Doctor's office

Teacher's office
Art gallery
Museum
Store/Mall
Church/Synagogue
Jail cell
Subway tunnel

Outdoor
Street corner
Park
Woods
Mountaintop
Beach
Baseball field
Bus stop
Patio
Porch
Backyard
Terrace
Fire escape
Battlefield
Garden
Lake
Stone quarry
Prison yard
Army encampment

Dugout/Trench
City square
On the ocean

Work Related
Office
School/Classroom
Art studio
Restaurant kitchen
Hospital
Court room
Ranch
Farm
Barn
Stable
Circus

Theater
Stage
Dressing room
Store
Coal mine
Doctor's examining room/office

Transportation
Automobile
Bus
Plane
Train
Ship deck
Subway
Horseback

Appendix B

Occupations and Professions

Pay close attention when you encounter people in the following walks of life. Notice how they dress and the objects they use in their line of work. How do they do their job? What skills have they mastered?

Actor	Doctor
Agent	Electrician
Announcer	Emperor
Artist	Escort
Athlete	Farmer
Banker	Father
Blogger	Firefighter
Bus driver	Freedom fighter
Businessman	Garbage collector
C.E.O.	Gardener
Car salesman	Government official
Caretaker	National healer
Cashier	Hotel manager
Caterer	Housewife
Cheerleader	Janitor
Chef	Judge
Choreographer	Landlord
Cleaning lady	Lawyer
Clerk	Maid
Coal miner	Marine
Computer programmer	Masseuse
Contractor	Mechanic
Councillor	Merchant Marine
Cowboy	Military personnel
Dancer	Minister
Detective	Monarch
Disk jockey	Mother

Musician	Reporter
Nanny	Revolutionary
Nun	Sailor
Nurse	Salesperson
Painter	Secretary
Pilot	Singer
Pimp	Soldier
Plumber	Stockbroker
Policeman	Street cleaner
Politician	Stripper
President	Student
Priest	Taxi driver
Prince	Teacher
Professor	Truck driver
Prostitute	Tutor
Rabbi	Veterinarian
Real estate broker	Waiter

"You" may not be able to find or hold a job because you are:

- An alcoholic

- A compulsive gambler

- You may not describe yourself in these terms. Would you recognize, admit that you have a problem with drinking? Are you defensive? Are you in denial? Do you rationalize?

- Chronically ill

- Mentally or emotionally incapable

- Clinically depressed

- Physically handicapped

- Affected by societal restrictions

- Or: because times are bad, you have been laid off.

- Or: because you worked for a large corporation that made sweeping lay-offs to hold the bottom line, you have been "downsized".

- You may not need to work because you suddenly won the lottery or because you are independently wealthy.

- You are married and don't need to work.

- You may do charity or volunteer work.

- You may be your spouse's silent partner.

Appendix C

Types of Clothing

Outer garments
Coats, capes, hats, gloves, boots, scarves, muffs, and mittens

Work clothes
Coveralls, overalls, jumpsuits, caps, boots, 3-piece suit, button-down shirts, and ties, uniforms, helmets, vests, belts

Evening clothes, formal attire
Evening gowns, long gloves, fans, stoles, shoes, tuxedos, dress shirts, ties, cummerbunds, vests, belts, suspenders, cufflinks, overcoats, capes, scarves

Underwear, lingerie
Corsets, slips, teddies, garter belts, stockings, bras, T-shirts, tank tops, boxer shorts, long-johns, etc.

Travelling garments
Jackets, overcoats, dusters, goggles, boots, gloves, hats,

Lounging garments
Smoking jackets, dressing gowns, silk pajamas, caftans

Everyday clothes
Housedresses, jeans, sweaters, dresses, suits, and slacks

Sportswear
Jeans, shirts, shorts, sweats, uniforms, gym clothes, etc.

Sleepwear
Pajamas, robes, slippers, T-shirts, long johns, nightgowns, peignoir

Accessories
Shoes, hats, gloves, scarves, ties, jewelry, watches, stockings, socks, eyeglasses, handbags or purses, wallets, briefcases, goggles, etc.

Certain clothing is required by work, ethnicity or religion. If you play a role requiring a uniform of some sort, learning about the specific origins and uses of the garments will increase your faith when you wear them:

Clergy
Specialized professional garments or uniforms
Military uniforms
Ethnic garb
Garments dictated by religious beliefs

Appendix D

Naming Your Relationships

The following list of relationships and life roles gives you a means of becoming more mindful of all the relationships you take for granted.

If the relationship exists in your life, you have a person's name attached to the words in the list. You have a story full of specific personal images and memories (inner objects) connected those people.

Familial

Mother, father, son, daughter, brother, sister, aunt, uncle, cousin, grandparent, grandchild, godparent, husband, wife, mother-in-law, father-in-law, sister or brother-in-law, partner, stepmother, half-sister, adopted child, birth mother, donor parent, etc.

Personal

Friend, childhood friend, classmate, confidante, lover, fiancée, neighbor, roommate, Facebook friend, etc.

Professional

A person in a position of authority
Supervisor, teacher, professor, boss, police officer, doctor, lawyer, director, CEO, office manager, president, chairman, parole officer, principal, producer, stage manager , coach

A person who works with a person in authority
Trainee, student, secretary, employee, patient, client, maid, servant, waiter, etc.

Service personnel

Hostess, maitre d', concierge, waiter, hairdresser, salesperson, taxi driver, bus driver, cleaning lady, chauffeur, cashier, doorman, parking garage attendant, mailman, telephone operator, bank teller, nanny, au pair, gardener, electrician, plumber, contractor.

(These people may be strangers but your relationship may be more familiar if you see the same person on a regular basis.)

Social

People you meet at parties, conventions, meetings, bars, discos, clubs, cruises, churches, synagogues, online chat rooms, Facebook.

Acquaintances

People whom you don't consider good friends but whom you know.

People you Twitter, hear or read about or watch on TV

People you visualize as soon as you hear or read about them: celebrities, movie stars, politicians, world leaders, authors, artists, criminals, newscasters, game and talk show hosts.

Endnotes

1   Online Dictionary. Version 2.2.1 ©2005-2011 Apple Inc.

2   Excerpt from *Ideas* by R H Thomson, 4/9/10.

3   *A Hatful of Rain*, by Michael V. Gazzo. Samuel French, Inc. 1984. p. 32.

4   *Full Catastrophe Living*, Jon Kabat-Zinn. Delacorte Press. 1990.

5   *A Challenge for the Actor*, by Uta Hagen, p.101. I hope you give yourself the opportunity to explore and practice all of the exercises found in this world-renowned text on acting.

6   This story has a less frivolous side bar: Professor Hirsch was later a victim of the McCarthy era, a scandalous time in American History. Forced out of his job at the University of Miami, he moved to Boston where he taught at Boston University and became the drama editor for the *Boston Herald*.

7   *Dinner With Friends* by Donald Margulies. Dramatists Play Service Inc. 2000.

8   *Ludlow Fair*, by Lanford Wilson. *21 Short Plays*. A Smith and Kraus Book. 1993.

9   *Brilliant Traces*, by Cindy Lou Johnson. Dramatists Play Service Inc. 1989.

10 *Presence of the Actor*, Joseph Chaikin. Theatre Communications Group, New York, NY, 1972,1991.

11 *A Challenge for the Actor*, Uta Hagen. 1991 Charles Scribner's Sons. p. 60

12 *A Challenge for the Actor*. p.60

13 *Respect for Acting*, Uta Hagen. Wiley Publishing, Inc., 1973. pp 134-138

Acknowledgments

What you will find between these pages is the culmination of a lifetime of learning and experience. The wisdom herein is not original to me, but is knowledge culled from a rich life full of many teachers of all kinds. With deepest respect, admiration and affection, I offer my inspirations and some of my sources. The wisdom, of which there is so much, and much of which is ancient, belongs to them:

Uta Hagen, in and out of the classroom, onstage and in her writing: *Respect for Acting, A Challenge for the Actor, Love of Cooking,* and *Sources: A Memoir.*

Herbert Berghof, on and off stage, and in the classroom—as well as for being the person who taught me my harshest life lesson.

Alice Spivak, a truly great teacher and artist, who gave me more than I can ever repay.

Since 1965, the HB Studio. Since 1968, every student who has trusted me.

The Hagen Institute faculty, whose skill, dedication and integrity inspire me and from whom I constantly learn: Martha Bernard, Michael Blake, Mark Blum, Jim Boerlin, Arthur French, Carol Goodheart, Marion McCorry, Robin Christian-McNair, Edward Morehouse, Rochelle Oliver, Ilse Pfeifer, Erik Singer, Victor Slezak, and Trudy Steibl.

Edith Meeks, Executive Director, HB Studio, for her enthusiastic encouragement and support of my work, and the pleasure I have received from witnessing her own journey and her wisdom, leadership, humanity, exceptional brilliance, selflessness, and courage.

Rosie Goldensohn, for challenging me so brilliantly and bringing the book from 32 chapters down to six.

Catrin Lloyd-Bollard for her luminous editing, writing, good cheer and patience taking me all the way to the end.

Richard Mawe, The Hagen Estate, Letitia Ferrer, Theresa Teuscher, and Barbara Hogenson.

For reading parts of the book along the way and sharing their questions and suggestions culled from their own artistry: Lolita Davidovitch, Karen Zeitz, Esq., Scott Miller, Reneé Petrofes, Shaun Wilson, Mary Ellen Lukas, Nora McLellan,

Robert McQueen, Trudy Steibl, Jim Boerlin, Paul Bartholomew, Mick Preston, Hilary Gleekman Greenberg, M.D., Natalie Coulter and Ian Watson.

Laura Gardner, who has soared beyond my teaching into her own, for reading and offering valued significant clarifications concerning the work, and for connecting me with Ron Pullins and Focus Publishing.

Janine Pearson, Head of Coaches, The Stratford Festival of Canada, who lives a life of faith, trust, service, presence, generosity, common sense, compassion, honesty, intelligence, humility, delight and humanity.

Ron Pullins and his creative team for their enthusiasm and meticulous rendering of my book.

Chris Peterson for photographing **Rebirth**.

My friends: Beatrice O'Donnell, Jenny Van Horne Greenberg, Marge McGovern, Anne Skinner and Vicki Hart—brilliant women who encourage, spin positive and share.

Holly Harper, who guided me into the world of Mac computers and formatted my early work.

Robert Valin, who so generously encouraged me from the beginning and shared his ideas about formatting.

Susan Spector and her cottage in East Quoque, where I had my first weekend alone to begin writing.

Sylvia Furlong, the drama teacher who came to Miami Senior High School my sophomore year and set the theater's non-negotiable standards and ideals that guide my work.

Christopher Newton, Jerry Doiron, Neil Munro, Carol Galloway and the Shaw Festival, Niagara-on-the-Lake.

Arthur Bartow, for letting me know what I needed to do.

Nancy Reardon and Tom Flynn.

The gift of Canada and every Canadian actor who participated in my exhilarating workshops for more than seventeen years, thanks to:

> Kurt Reis and the Centre for Actors' Study in Toronto.
> Frances Flanagan, Vancouver, BC, the initiator.
> Marion and Louis Eisman, Vancouver, BC.
> Kathryn Shaw, Studio 58, Langara College, Vancouver, BC.
> Perry Schneiderman, The National Theatre School of Canada.
> Sherry Bie, The National Theatre School of Canada.
> Heather Lea MacCallum, Calgary.
> Terry Cherniak, Winnepeg.
> Niki Lipman, Halifax.

My European sojourns:

Merce Managuerra and the actors in Barcelona, The Institut del Teatre.
Bettina Ottenstein and the Actors Union in Copenhagen.
The Actor's Centre in London.

The writing that has influenced me:

Julia Cameron: *The Artists Way*
Jon Kabat-Zinn: *Wherever You Go, There You Are*
Jon Kabat-Zinn: *Full Catastrophe Living*
Thich Nhat Hanh: *Peace is Every Step*
Charlotte Joko Beck: *Nothing Special*

$$\begin{array}{r} \overset{1}{2}7\overset{2}{0} \\ \hline 5\ 4\ 0 \end{array}$$

Bibliography

Adler, Stella and Barry Paris. *Stella Adler on Ibsen, Strindberg and Chekhov*. Reprint edition. New York: Vintage, 2000.

Ball, William. *A Sense of Direction*. Hollywood: Drama Publishers, 1984.

Bartow, Arthur, ed. *Training of the American Actor*. New York: Theatre Communications Group, 2006.

Berry, Cecily. *Text in Action*. New York: Random House, 2011.

Brook, Peter. *There Are No Secrets – Thoughts on Acting and Theatre*. New York: Bloomsbury Methuen Drama, 1995.

Burstyn, Ellen. *Lessons On Becoming Myself*. New York: Riverhead Trade, 2007

Cabat-Zinn, Jon. *Wherever You Go There You Are*. Tenth edition. New York: Hyperion, 2005.

Cameron, Julia. *The Artist's Way*. New York: Jeremy P. Tarcher/Perigee Books, 1992.

Chaikin, Joseph. *The Presence of the Actor*. New York: Theatre Communications Group, 1991.

Clurman, Harold. *On Directing*. New York: Fireside, 1997.

Clurman, Harold. *The Fervent Years*. First edition. New York: Harcourt Brace Jovanovich, 1975.

Cole, Toby and Helen Krich Chinoy, eds. *Actors on Acting*. Fourth edition. New York: Three Rivers Press, 1995.

Faber, Adele and Elaine Mazlish, *How to Talk so Kids will Listen and Listen so Kids will Talk*, Avon Books, New York, NY. 1999.

Gallwey, Timothy W. *The Inner Game of Tennis*. New York: Random House Trade Paperback, 2008.

Gelb, Michael. *Body Learning: An Introduction to Alexander Technique*. New York: Henry Holt, 2004.

Graham, Martha. *Blood Memory*. New York: Washington Square Press, 1992.

Hagen, Uta. *A Challenge for the Actor*. New York: Charles Scribner's Sons, 1991.

Hagen, Uta. *Respect for Acting.* New York: Macmillan Publishing Co, 1973.

Hagen, Uta. *Sources: A Memoir.* New York: Performing Arts Journals, 1987.

Hanh, Thich Nhat. *Peace is Every Step.* New York: Bantam Books, 1992.

Herrigel, Eugen. *Zen and the Art of Archery.* Trans. R. F. C. Hull. New York: Vintage Books, 1999.

Jones, Robert Edmund. *The Dramatic Imagination.* Second revised edition. New York: Routledge, 2004.

Kabat-Zinn, Jon. *Full Catastrophe Living.* New York, NY. Delacorte Press, 1990.

Knight, Dudley. *Speaking with Skill.* New York: Bloomsbury Methuen Drama, 2012.

Nachmanovitch, Stephen. *Free Play.* Reprint edition. New York: Tarcher, 1991.

Rilke, Rainer Maria. *Letters to a Young Poet.* Seaside, OR: Watchmaker Publishing, 2012.

Rodenberg, Patsy. *The Right to Speak.* Reissue Edition. New York: Routledge, 1993.

Ruiz, Don Miguel. *The Four Agreements: A Practical Guide to Personal Freedom.* San Rafael, CA. Amber-Allen Publishing, 1997.

Sher, Antony. *Year of the King.* Pompton Plains, NJ: First Limelight, 1992.

Smith, Wendy. *Real Life Drama.* Reprint edition. New York: Vintage, 2013.

Stanislavksy, Constantin. *Stanislavsky's Legacy: A Collection of Comments on a Variety of Aspects of an Actor's Art and Life.* Ed. and trans. Elizaebeth Reynolds Hapgood. New York: Routledge, 1968.

Stanislavsky, Constantin. *My Life in Art.* Trans. Jean Benedetti. New York: Routledge, 2008.

The Dalai Lama. *Healing Anger.* Ithaca, NY: Snow Lion Publications, 1991.